THE SELF-SYSTEM

Developmental Changes Between and Within Self-Concepts

THE SELF-SYSTEM

Developmental Changes Between and Within Self-Concepts

Annerieke Oosterwegel
Louis Oppenheimer
University of Amsterdam

LAWRENCE ERLBAUM ASSOCIATES, PUBLISHERS
1993   Hillsdale, New Jersey   Hove and London

Lawrence Erlbaum Associates, Inc., Publishers
365 Broadway
Hillsdale, New Jersey 07642

Library of Congress Cataloging-in-Publication Data

Oosterwegel, A.
    The self-system : developmental changes between and within self-
concepts / A. Oosterwegel, Louis Oppenheimer.
      p. cm.
    Includes bibliographical references and indexes.
    ISBN 0-8058-1216-4
    1. Self-perception in children — Longitudinal studies. 2. Self-
perception in children — Social aspects. I. Oppenheimer, Louis.
II. Title.
BF723.S28067 1993
155.4′182 — dc20

92-19809
CIP

Books published by Lawrence Erlbaum Associates are printed on acid-free paper, and their
bindings are chosen for strength and durability.

Printed in the United States of America

10 9 8 7 6 5 4 3 2 1

Contents

Preface   ix

Introduction   xi

    Plan of the Book   xiii

1   A THEORETICAL OVERVIEW AND
RESULTING MODEL ON THE SELF-SYSTEM   1

    The Self as Knower Versus the Self as Known   1
    The Content of a Self-Concept: Self-Descriptions   4
    Concepts Within the Self-System   6
    The Influence of the Social Environment   9
    The Active Person   12
    Structural Characteristics   18
    An Integrative Model on the Organization of
       the Self-System   33

2   METHOD   41

    Choice of Variables   42
    Choice of Instrument   43
    The Repertory Grid   44
    Design   46
    Subjects   47
    Procedure   48
    Preliminary Analyses   52
    Conclusion   53

3   RELIABILITY AND RELATED DATA   **55**

    Reliability of the Grid-Scores   55
    The Effect of Drop-Outs   57
    Something about the "Others"   58
    The Circles as Balls: The Abstractness and Clearness
        of the Descriptive Dimensions   59
    Conclusions   65

4   DIFFERENTIATION BETWEEN
INTRAINDIVIDUAL SELF-CONCEPTS   **69**

    Differentiation Studies   70
    Results   73
    Conclusions   82

5   DIFFERENTIATION BETWEEN
INTERINDIVIDUAL SELF-CONCEPTS   **87**

    The Self in Environments   87
    Results   89
    Conclusions   97

6   DISCREPANCIES BETWEEN
INTRAINDIVIDUAL SELF-CONCEPTS   **101**

    Research on Discrepancies   101
    Method   104
    Results   105
    Conclusions   118

7   DISCREPANCIES AND
EMOTIONAL FUNCTIONING   **121**

    Self-Concepts and Emotions   121
    Method   123
    Results   124
    Conclusions   131

8 CONCLUSIONS: THE MODEL AND THE DATA   **135**

The Model   135
The Model Through the Lenses of the Data:
    Confirmation and Need for Further Differentiation   137
Cognitive Versus Social Explanations of the Findings   151
Indications for Future Research from the Present Data   156
Elaborations for Future Research from the
    Recent Literature   161
Conclusion   163

References   167

Author Index   179

Subject Index   183

Preface

This book describes a longitudinal study on the development of the self-system, a study that was initially formulated as a longitudinal examination of the contents of the self-concept over an age period from 6 to 18 years. In the many discussions about the phenomenological self – the "Me" – and the structures and dynamics thought to characterize the "I" and to inform the "Me," we have often wondered whether it would be possible to study aspects of the dynamics of the self-system by transcending the study of the "I" by means of the contents of the self-concept only. Such a question is directly related to issues concerning assessment and measurement, as is the case in any longitudinal research. To study the self-system over the proposed wide age range, an instrument was required that would offer *identical* responses with different age groups and simultaneously would incorporate cognitive and social developmental progressions with the assessed participants in its procedure.

Whether we succeeded in attaining either or both goals (i.e., studying dynamics of the self-system and developing an appropriate assessment procedure) is for the reader to judge.

The study that is described in this book was completely conducted by the first author and is based on her PhD thesis (Oosterwegel, 1992; readers who are interested in more detailed information about the data and the analyses are invited to consult the latter PhD thesis or to contact the authors). The study itself, approved as a PhD research project, was conducted from 1986 to 1990 at the Department of Developmental Psychology of the University of Amsterdam. The second author of this book had the privilege and good luck to be the supervisor of this PhD thesis.

ACKNOWLEDGMENTS

To do a study like the present one, especially to do so within the available time of 4 years, would have been difficult without the help and support of many people. We would like to acknowledge their assistance here. In particular we would like to thank Jacqueline Legerstee, Marc Noom, Sigrid van de Poel, Linda Vodegel Matzen, Nel Warnars, and Marjon de Zwart, for their assistance in the data collection, Conor Dolan and Wouter Wijker, who were always available when computer programs for the analyses of the data had to be developed, and Luba Horich who corrected the English of the manuscript.

We are in particular grateful for the many questions, comments, and suggestions from Michael Chandler (University of British Columbia) and Bill Damon (Brown University), who from a great distance were always prepared to discuss aspects of this study. A first critical reading of the manuscript was done by Henriëtte van den Heuvel (University of Amsterdam) who offered many suggestions for its improvement. Such improvements also resulted from the critical reading of the manuscript by the members of the dissertation committee: Cees van Lieshout (University of Nijmegen), Koos van der Werff (University of Groningen), Maurits van der Molen, Joop van der Pligt, and Jo Sergeant (University of Amsterdam). Finally, we are indebted to a number of anonymous reviewers who commented on preceding papers as well as the present manuscript.

Despite this help and support, the project could not have been realized without the cooperation of the children, their parents, and the schools who participated in this study. The children spent many hours telling about themselves and answering hard questions. Their parents, too, invested considerable time and energy. They all knew their children well but found themselves now confronted with the difficult task to actually describe their children.

We also want to mention the directors and teachers of 'de Hoeksteen', 'de Jac.P.Thijsse Scholengemeenschap', 'de Juliana van Stolbergschool', 'het Murmellius Gymnasium', 'de Sokkerwei', 'het St. Maartenscollege', 'de Tweede Daltonschool', and 'de Vondelschool'. By means of their schools and educational institutions the children were approached, and at their schools and during normal school hours the interviews were conducted. They consented to the simple request to participate in the present study, and, subsequently, found themselves saddled with an interviewer who stayed for weeks or even months. We are indebted to all of them.

Louis Oppenheimer   *Annerieke Oosterwegel*
                                                        Amsterdam

Introduction

This book reports on the organization of the self-system in childhood and adolescence. It reports the results of a time-sequential study dealing with developmental changes within and between self-concepts within the self-system and the relation between these changes and personal functioning. The purpose of the present introduction is to briefly offer an outline that enables the reader to situate the chapters to follow within the overall framework of this book.

Besides self-system and self-concept, a wide range of concepts, such as self-conception (Van der Werff, 1985), self-schema (Markus, 1977), self-theory (Epstein, 1973), and self-understanding (Damon & Hart, 1982), is used to refer to the organization of knowledge about the self. Although all these concepts refer to knowledge about the self, each emphasizes a different particular aspect of such self-knowledge.

The study of self-knowledge is important for the self-evident reasons that people not only attend to and process information about themselves, but they also act on the basis of the resulting (cognitive) representations of themselves. Self-knowledge is not organized in a static structure but in an active, dynamic structure that continuously interpretes and organizes self-relevant actions and experiences and, consequently, mediates and regulates behavior and affect (Markus & Wurf, 1987). Because of these characteristics of self-knowledge, its study is assumed to be crucial to our understanding of human behavior. In this book, the term self-system will be used to refer to the structural organization of self-knowledge. The term self-concept will be used when a sample of self-descriptions is dealt with, that is, a sample of statements about the self that refer to a particular aspect within the self-system.

The reason for the use of this multitude of concepts to describe knowledge about the self is that the presence of such a knowledge system dealing with the self is theoretical and represents an assumption still in need of ongoing evaluation. That is, it is a psychological construct proposed by social scientists in an attempt to understand, predict, and control human behavior. It is because of the evolving nature of this hypothetical construct that different theoretical meanings and purposes have been assigned to it. The acceptance of such a construct, as well as the significance ascribed to it in the hystory of psychology, has not only been repeatedly influenced by the prevailing *Zeitgeist*, but also by the nature of societal norms and values that differ in their emphasis on the individual(istic) self. After all, individuals both constitute society and are its products (e.g., Meyer, 1986). Thus, the contemporary interest in and study of self-knowledge is the product of the prevailing *Zeitgeist* in our Western society.

As was noted above, but as also can be seen from a historical point of view, the study of the self-concept reflects many different theoretical approaches (Oppenheimer & Oosterwegel, in press). For instance, James (1890/1950) regarded the self as an entity consisting of "fluctuating material," that is, "the same object being sometimes treated as a part of me, at other times as simply mine, and then again as if I had nothing to do with it at all . . . In its widest possible sense . . . a man's Self is the sum total of all that he CAN call his" (p. 291). This concept of self was divided by James into three parts involving (a) its "constituents," (b) "the feelings and emotions they arouse," and (c) "the actions to which they prompt" (p. 292).

For Baldwin (1897/1973) an individual's thinking could be conceived as a continuous dimension, that is, "what the person thinks as himself is a pole or terminus at one end of an opposition in the sense of personality generally, and . . . the other pole or terminus is the thought he has of the other person, the 'alter'" (p. 9). The self (i.e., the person as a self) is a product of a dialectical relationship between the individual and the environment that permits the individual to incorporate elements that were earlier those of others.

According to Mead (1934/1972), the self, "as that which can be an object to itself, is essentially a social structure, and it arises in social experience" (p. 140). The person gets to know himself only through others, that is, he cannot experience himself directly as such, "but only indirectly, from the particular standpoints of other individual members of the same social group, or from the generalized standpoint of the social group as a whole to which he belongs" (p. 138).

These diverse theoretical approaches conceive of the self and the self-concept in three essentially distinct ways. It is either perceived: (a) as a core construct within the person that is partly dependent on (i.e., the self-as-known) and partly independent of the social environment (i.e., the self-as-knower; James, 1890/1950); or (b) as a kind of accommodative scheme or *structure d'ensemble* (i.e., a relational totality), that is a product of a dialectic between the person and his environment, and in which the self-as-knower and the self-as-known are inseparable parts of one and the same dimension (Baldwin, 1897/1973); or (c) as a social construct, that is, the product of 'socialization' through appropriating the attitudes of others in the social environment towards oneself (i.e., by way of role-taking processes; Mead, 1934/1972).

What these approaches have in common, though, is that they all consider the self from a comprehensive, multidimensional perspective. Consequently, the study of the self-concept as a multidimensional construct and the course by which the self becomes understood can be approached for quite different purposes and from a wide and diverse range of perspectives. During the 1960s and 1970s, however, a reduction took place from the above multidimensional conception of the self to the empirical study of one "global" or "unidimensional" self-concept. In these studies, the general evaluation of the self (i.e., the self-esteem) was emphasized. Although at a later stage self-descriptions (i.e., statements about the self) related to this unidimensional self-concept were also attended to, human behavior could be only partly explained by such a global and unidimensional self-concept. The work of Wylie (1961/1974, 1961/1979) gives an excellent overview of these studies and their shortcomings during this period. According to Wylie, the results of these studies did not match the enormous amount of effort that was put into the study of the global self-concept.

During the last decade, a renewed interest can be observed in the study of self-knowledge (e.g., Markus & Wurf, 1987). Probably reinforced by the increasing emphasis on individuality and the concept of a "free will" (e.g., Luhmann, 1986; Meyer, 1986) and guided by Wylie's (1961/1974, 1961/1979) conclusions, a more differentiated conception of self-knowledge has been proposed. In this conception, self-knowledge is perceived as a "multidimensional" and dynamic system in which several context-related and domain-related self-concepts can be distinguished (e.g., Markus & Wurf, 1987).

The study that is reported in this book is based on this more recent and renewed interest in a "multidimensional and dynamic self-system." An attempt was made to integrate the recent literature on self-knowledge from a process oriented and structural developmental perspective and to study developmental changes in this self-system. The extent to which this study is a product and part of the prevailing *Zeitgeist* will become evident from the large number of publications on the self-system that has appeared in the literature since the start of the present study. As a consequence, this book reflects a growing understanding of the self-system based on the empirical data obtained in the present study, as well as the continous stream of new information available in the literature.

PLAN OF THE BOOK

In chapter 1, various aspects of the self-system are discussed, based on the available literature. Among these aspects are the assessment of the self-as-knower through the self-as-known; some aspects of the content of the self-concepts within the self-system; the relationship between the real self-concept and possible selves, such as the ideal self-concept (i.e., the evaluative and motivational function of possible selves); the mutual influence of both the environment and the individual on the development of the self-system; and the structural characteristics that reflect and mediate the organization of the self-system. Where possible, the development in each aspect is emphasized. Chapter 1 ends with a model that results from the discussion of the above aspects that focusses on the structural characteristics. These characteristics are thought to be present in the relationships between the self-concepts. Further, these self-concepts are thought to develop in the interaction between the person and the environment by a process of differentiation and integration, resulting in alternately increasing and decreasing balance (i.e., distances) between the self-concepts. A more extensive summary of the model is found at the beginning of chapter 8.

In chapter 2, the choices for the self-concepts and structural characteristics to be studied and the method to assess these are argued. Subsequently, the design, the sample, and the procedure are described. In total, 14 self-concepts and the relationships among these concepts are measured. These concepts are the real self-concept from children's own perspective and the perspective of the father, the mother, and a male and female friend as perceived by these children (five concepts), the ideal self-concept from each of these perspectives (five concepts), and the actual real and ideal concepts of the parents (four concepts). The self-concepts and the relationships among them are studied by means of a Repertory Grid procedure, allowing for an idiosyncratic, age-adequate, and personally relevant content of the self-concepts. The Repertory Grid is administered over 3 years according to a time-sequential design to 204 children from age 6 to 18 and their parents (the original number at the start of the study).

In chapter 3, the data dealing with the reliability and appropriateness of the Repertory Grid procedure are presented. Although the reliability of the data increases with the younger ages, they are found to be sufficiently reliable for all age-groups. In addition, in this chapter some characteristics of the specific others included in the study (i.e., the degree to which each parent and peer is liked and known) and of the content of the measured self-concepts (i.e., the abstractness and clearness of the self-descriptions within each self-concept) are examined. The children are found to like and to know each of the others at an above average level, to become increasingly aware with age of the relativity of likeability and familiarity, and to be somewhat less close to the opposite-gender friend as compared to the remainder of the others. Further, it is concluded that with increasing age the self-descriptions used become more abstract, but that it is not this degree of abstractness, but the content of the self-descriptions that influences the relationships between the self-concepts. Finally, it is found that the self-descriptions used were about equally clear for all ages. On the basis of these data, it is concluded that the Repertory Grid procedure offers a reliable and valid way to assess the self-concepts of children and adolescents, and that the procedure is closely related to the emotional world of the children.

In chapter 4, the development of differentiation between the intraindividual self-concepts (i.e., the real and ideal self-concept from one's own perspective, the perspective of both parents, and of both peers) is addressed. In particular, the question of the existence itself of the differentiation between those concepts, the relative degree of differentiation between the self-concepts, and eventual age-related effects are examined. It is found that differentiation between each pair of concepts is evident from age 6 onwards, but that the stability of the differentiation between the real and ideal self-concepts, as well as the ideal own and perceived self-concepts precedes the development of the stability for the differentiation between the real own and perceived self-concepts. In addition, the degree of differentiation between one's own and perceived self-concepts (reflecting distinctness) is less than – or at the utmost equal to – the degree of differentiation between the real and ideal self-concepts. Furthermore, children identify more with the perceived self-concepts of their parents than with those of their peers. Finally, a significant developmental trend is found for the differentiation between the real and ideal self-concepts, but not for the differentiation between one's own and perceived self-concepts of others. During childhood, an increase in differentiation between the perceived real and ideal self-concepts of both parents and peers is present. In adolescence, this degree of differentiation remains stable and large for the parents but decreases again for the peers.

In chapter 5, the relationships between the interindividual self-concepts are analyzed. In this chapter, the fit between the children's intraindividual self-concepts with those in the environment (i.e., the actual ideas and expectancies of significant others about the children) is considered. The child's own real and ideal self-concepts and the perceived real and ideal self-concept of the parents are compared to the actual ideas and expectations (ideals) of the parents about their children. In addition, the relative difference between intra- and interindividual self-concepts, and the development of the difference between the actual real and ideal concepts of the parents about their children are analyzed. In general, it is found that the fit between the children's self-concepts and the actual concepts of their parents increases until approximately the age of 11 years, followed by a stabilization. Differences between intraindividual self-concepts are smaller than between these self-concepts and the concepts of their parents (i.e., the comparison between inter-individual self-concepts). In contrast to what children believe (chapter 4), no age-related changes can be demonstrated in the difference between the real and ideal concept of the parents about their child. These results are consistent with the predictions based on the development of perspective taking and the motives for self-consistency and self-enhancement.

The major issue in chapter 6 concerns itself with the development of discrepancies between and within one's own real and ideal self-concept and the perceived real and ideal self-concepts of the parents and the peers. Though differentiation scores present the unqualified distance or differentiation between self-concepts, the discrepancy scores involve conflicts between two self-concepts (i.e., between self-concept discrepancies) or conflicts between self-relevant self-descriptions within one self-concept (within self-concept discrepancies). The results indicate that discrepancies *between* the perceived real and ideal self-concepts of the parents increase during childhood, and that the discrepancies *within* all concepts increase during adolescence. No age-related changes for the discrepancies between one's own and the perceived self-concepts, one's own real and ideal self-concepts, and the perceived real and ideal self-concepts of the peers are evident. The results are discussed in terms of social cognitive development.

In chapter 7, the discrepancy measures obtained in chapter 6 are related to the scores on a Dutch questionnaire for emotional (in)stability (ABV-K). It appears that discrepancies between one's own real and ideal self-concepts and between the perceived real and ideal self-concepts of the parents are positively related to negative affect, whereas discrepancies within the self-concepts are negatively related to negative affect but positively related to positive affect. No relationship between the discrepancies between and within the perceived self-concepts of the peers and affective functioning can be demonstrated. It is argued that the effect for discrepancies within self-concepts results from the possibilities for self-enhancement that are included in an inconsistent self-concept. Children who receive negative feedback on one pole of the discrepancy may shift their attention and priority to the other pole, where they are evaluated more positively.

In the final chapter, chapter 8, the results from the reported study are discussed within a larger framework and in relation to the developmental model for the self-system as presented in the first chapter. In this discussion, a picture emerges of self-system development as a process of differentiation and integration resulting from the dynamic interaction between the developing children and their social environment (i.e., their parents and peers). Although cognitive developmental abilities are considered to be a prerequisite to the development of the organization of the self-system, the present data suggest that the social development of the child is decisive. Also, it is concluded that further differentiation of the construct self-system into even more dimensions is required. Following this discussion, several recommendations for future research are given. The chapter concludes with a specified description of the model.

Finally, although the purpose of this study was to integrate hitherto separate and different components or aspects of self-knowledge into one encompassing, multidimensional self-system, the findings show that this book can only be a first step in the construction of an even more differentiated and complex self-system.

1 A Theoretical Overview and Resulting Model on the Self-System

In the present chapter, the self-concept is described as a multidimensional and dynamic self-system that refers to both the product of self-conception as well as the active process of perception and organization of information about the self. The purpose of this chapter is to present an integrative model of such a self-system. Prior to this, consideration will be given to those aspects of the self-system that are relevant to the model as they appear in the existing literature. In the model, as well as in the relevant overview of the literature, the structural, functional and developmental aspects of the self-system are emphasized.

THE SELF AS KNOWER
VERSUS THE SELF AS KNOWN

Although during the 1960s and 1970s the self-concept was often considered a static and global construct, the contemporary view of the self-concept is that it is a dynamic and multidimensional construct. This change in the perception of the self-concept corresponds to the understanding of the "Self" by early theorists such as James (1890/1950) and Mead (1934/1972, cf. Gordon & Gergen, 1968; also Markus & Wurf, 1987). Hitherto only the "Me" was emphasized, that is, "an empirical aggregate of things objectively known" (James, 1890/1950, p. 400; i.e., the self as known to the individual or agent, or the social environment). The perception of the self-concept as an active and dynamic structure, however, required the introduction of the "I" as an integral part of the self-concept. The "I" involves the agent as thinker or that which knows the self as objectively known (James, 1890/1950). It is the organizing and structuring self, that part of the self that processes, interprets, and organizes knowledge about the self.

Simultaneously with the renewed interest in the "I," the problem whether the "I" can be empirically studied reemerged. Whereas according to James (1910/1968) the empirical study of the "I" was not possible, Mead (1934/1972) assumed that it could be done, though only through the "Me", that is, by way of static self-representations given by the subject.

Studying the "I" implies studying the intrapersonal activities and processes, the way the self-concept is formed and how organization is established. Because the formation and organization of the self-concept are the result of often implicit and unconscious processes, these processes themselves are difficult to assess. Consequently, although it is often claimed that the "I" is studied, in reality the "Me" has been assessed; that is, often the manifestations, reflections, or temporary states (i.e., their contents or the "Me") of the "I" are assessed from which the "I"-processes are deduced. In other words, because the "I" is defined as the knower and the "Me" as what is known, the direct study of the "I" is thought to be impossible by definition. Hence, all knowledge about the "Self" (i.e., here denoted as self-system) is part of the "Me." The "I" is inseparable from contexts and contents.

Only two recent attempts to study the contents of the "I" from a developmental point of view have been found (i.e., the models of Damon & Hart, 1982, 1988, and Harter, 1983). Damon and Hart presented a model for "self-understanding" that involves the two dimensions of the self-the "Me" and the "I." The model permits the exploration of the individual's understanding of the self as knower, that is, the individual's understanding of the "I." Following James (1890/1950), four "I"-characteristics were presented: continuity, distinctness, volition, and self-reflectivity (Damon & Hart, 1982). Only three remained in a latter publication: agency, continuity, and distinctness (Damon & Hart, 1988). Children's understanding of these components was studied through self-descriptions and was thought to develop gradually from the concrete in infancy to the more abstract in adolescence. Continuity was expected to shift from the conception of an unchanging physical body to the conception of continuous psychological and physical processes through which the nature of self evolves. Distinctness was thought to shift from a conception based on bodily or material attributes to a conception derived from the subjectivity and privacy of the self's experiences. Volition or agency was postulated to develop from the idea that one body part "tells" another to do something, to active and self-initiated modifications of conscious experiences. Finally, self-reflection was thought to shift from an awareness of body features, typical activities, and action capabilities to the recognition of conscious and unconscious psychological processes (Damon & Hart, 1982, p. 860). In discussing the latter component of this model, Damon and Hart (1988) noted that because this dimension is "inaccessible to us because of methodological difficulties" (p. 70), it was omitted from the model. However, the study of the former components, that is, continuity, distinctness, and volition, was also limited because of the methodology. The active "I"-components were not only derived from, but also defined in terms of the content of the self-concept or the "Me" (i.e., by means of self-descriptions). As Damon and Hart (1988) emphasized, their model involves "progressions in conceptions of the self-as-subject and not in the self-as-subject per se" (p. 69).

In her review of the literature on the development of the self-concept (i.e., self-system), Harter (1983) described several theories dealing with the processing of self-relevant information in adults. Based on these theories, she presented a model for the development of the "Me" and the "I" in which structural changes (i.e., changes in the organization of the self-system) are the result of a process of differentiation and integration. The model includes four developmental stages that involve simple descriptions, trait labels, single abstractions, and higher order abstractions, in this prescribed order. Each stage is divided into two levels. At the first level, higher-order integrations of items from the preceding stage take place. At the second level, these integrations become differentiated again and require new and higher order integrations in the first level of the succeeding stage. As with Damon and Hart (1982, 1988), these structural changes were derived from the content of self-descriptions. The organizational changes with regard to the "I," assessed by the "Me-tool" (i.e., self-descriptions), reflected how the content dimensions of self-descriptions are organized (Harter, 1983, p. 305).

Hence, in both of these contemporary approaches to the study of the "I" (i.e., either through Damon and Hart's study of the development of self-understanding or Harter's study of the self-system), support is given to Mead's (1934/1972) assumption that the "I" can only be studied through the "Me." That is, in both models, the study of self-descriptions forms the basis for an examination of the development of children's ideas about "I"-components of the self-system. In short, changes in the organization of Me-characteristics in relation to "I"-components are studied rather than structural characteristics of the "I" itself. In short, both Harter and Damon and Hart considered these problems to be methodological constraints with respect to the study of the "I."

However, there is an alternative way to study the "I" - though, again by means of the "Me" - by emphasizing its structure and structural organization. It may well be that "I"-concepts such as agency, continuity, and distinctness (Damon & Hart, 1988) are related to (subjective) experiences based on the interrelations among different structural components of the self-system. For instance, Shavelson, Hubner, and Stanton (1976) described the self-system as a hierarchically organized structure thought to consist of different self-concepts that are organized along a continuum from situation specific to abstract (see also Marsh, 1989). Based on James' (1890/1950) assumption that "a man has as many social selves as there are individuals who recognize him" (p. 294), Markus and Wurf (1987) postulated "working self-concepts," assuming that the overall self-concept consists of a number of self-representations that are not simultaneously conscious. The working self-concept is that part of the self-concept or those characteristics of the self that become salient in a particular situation.

In accordance with the approach of Shavelson et al. (1976) and Markus and Wurf (1987), the model for the self-system that will be presented in this chapter is structure oriented, that is, the emphasis is on the organization of self-knowledge as reflected in the relationships between several parts of the self-system. This model is presented following a description of the relevant aspects of the self-system as they appear in the literature on the self-concept. These aspects involve the content of the self-system, the several subconcepts within the self-system, the influence of the environment, the active role of the individual, and the characteristics that reflect the organization of the self-system. Accordingly, the emphasis is on the function and especially the development of each aspect.

THE CONTENT OF A SELF-CONCEPT: SELF-DESCRIPTIONS

In the first part of this chapter it was noted that the self always exists within contexts and that the self-system is inseparable from contexts and contents. The way people describe themselves and the characteristics they use constitute the body of the self-system or a self-concept. Despite the large number of studies dealing with the question of how people describe themselves, only a few general notions are discussed here, that is, the situation specificity, the personal relevance, and the level of abstractness of self-descriptions.

The study of the self-concept by means of self-descriptions has resulted in an accumulation and stock-taking of characteristics and items used to describe the self. These items or descriptions can be hierarchically grouped into several descriptive categories belonging to context-related self-concepts such as the academic, social, physical, and emotional self-concept. The descriptive categories of each of these context-related self-concepts can again be ordered along a continuum consisting of general descriptions at one pole (i.e., valid for all different context-related self-concepts) and situation-specific descriptions at the other pole (i.e., characteristics only applicable to one particular context-related self-concept). General self-descriptions are more stable than situation-specific descriptions (Shavelson et al., 1976).

Self-descriptions also differ in their importance. Some descriptions possess a high personal relevance and function as central or core characteristics of the individual, whereas other descriptions are less personally relevant and more peripheral (Markus & Wurf, 1987). This differentiation between central (or core) and peripheral characteristics is, among others, reflected by Markus and Wurf's (1987) distinction between the "working" self-concept in a particular situation and the various nonactive self-concepts. Not all self-representations (i.e., self-concepts) are simultaneously functional. Which self-representations are active at a particular moment depends on the individual's experiences in a particular context. In the active self-concept, that is, the self-concept that is activated in a particular context (i.e., the working self-concept), the self-relevant core characteristics are relatively stable. Depending on the circumstances, peripheral characteristics can also be observed (Markus & Wurf, 1987).

Irrespective of their personal relevance, the characteristics used to describe the self have been found to follow a developmental course identical to those used to describe other people. Numerous studies have indicated that the understanding of other people, assessed by means of other-descriptions, follows a developmental shift from concrete to abstract (e.g., Livesley & Bromley, 1973; Oppenheimer & De Groot, 1981; Peevers & Secord, 1973; Scarlett, Press, & Crockett, 1971). In their developmental model for self-understanding, Damon and Hart (1982, 1986, 1988) also assumed such a developmental progression. Based on their review of the literature, they expected self-descriptions in early childhood, late childhood, early adolescence, and late adolescence to show progressive shifts in content, respectively from physical, to activity-related, to social, to psychological. This developmental shift was studied by Oppenheimer, Warnars-Kleverlaan, and Molenaar (1990) with children between the ages of 7-12 years. The latter authors reported that simultaneously with a shift from physical, to activity-related, psychological, and social descriptions, an increase in the variety of descriptive contents could also be observed. Oppenheimer et al. (1990) further concluded that Damon and Hart's (1982) category of social self-descriptions is too global and should be divided into psychological (i.e., trait) and social (i.e., relational) categories of self-descriptions. Damon and Hart's category of psychological self-descriptions was then redefined as "self-reflective" self-descriptions. According to the model of Harter (1983), the developmental progression from concrete to abstract self-understanding fits a stage-like developmental course through a process of differentiation and integration (see earlier).

In short, the characteristics to describe the self (i.e., self-descriptions) can be more or less abstract, more or less relevant, and more or less situation specific. In addition, a relative increase in the number of abstract self-descriptions is observed, whereas the way in which children describe themselves becomes more varied and context-dependent.

CONCEPTS WITHIN THE SELF-SYSTEM

Real Versus Possible Selves

In addition to the issue of context dependence outlined earlier, a further dimension of self classification is possible. This alternative categorization scheme involves the postulation of "domains" (Higgins, 1987), which James (1890/1950) characterized as the "immediate and actual, and the remote and potential" selves (p. 315). That is, within the self-system a further distinction can be made between different types of self-concepts or domains of the self-system, such as the real, ideal, and ought-to-be self-concepts. In contrast to the real or actual self-concept, the ideal and ought-to-be concepts were referred to as "possible selves" by Markus and Nurius (1986). The real self-concept presents the way people actually perceive themselves and is that aspect of the self assessed by Damon and Hart (1982, 1988) when they studied the development of self-understanding, and presented by Harter (1983) in her studies of the self-system. Possible or potential selves refer to how people think about their potentials and future, and they describe what the person would like to be or should become. Possible selves, by contrast, are cognitive representations of a person's goals, aspirations, and fears and serve a motivational function, because people strive to achieve their positive or desirable selves and to avoid their negative or undesirable possible selves (Markus & Nurius, 1986; see also Hewitt & Genest, 1990). These possible selves also serve an evaluative function, because people perceive their real self-concept in relation to their possible selves. The potentials that the possible selves present give meaning to the real self-concept (Markus & Nurius, 1986; see also Ogilvie, 1987) and are important in the process of self-regulation (Markus & Wurf, 1987). Although the ideal self-concept involves ideas about how people would like to be or become (Rogers, 1951), the ought-to-be self refers to what they believe they should be or become (Higgins, 1987), with the latter self-concept involving moral or cultural norms. Additional possible selves such as the self one could become, the hoped-for self, and dreaded selves have also been distinguished (Markus & Nurius, 1986; Ogilvie, 1987).

Like different context-related real self-concepts, the possible selves will also be salient at different moments and in different contexts. The possible selves are less obvious to other people than the active real self-representations. According to Markus and Nurius (1986), this partly accounts for the lack of agreement between a person's self-evaluation and their evaluation by others (cf. Shrauger & Schoeneman, 1979), that is, it is often unclear to others which possible self the individual is utilizing to evaluate the self. Because possible selves are more private and (therefore) less anchored in social experience than the real self-concept, they can be more sensitive to incentives from and changes in the environment. However, for the same reason, a possible self can function beyond reality and either maintain or distort a person's self-evaluations (Markus & Nurius, 1986). An individual can construct a possible self in such a way that it almost matches the real self so that the real self is evaluated in an extremely positive light, or an individual can aim at such high goals that they never can be met. Such unrealistically low or high goals in the possible selves will be less rectified by the environment than real self-concepts because of the more private, uncontrollable character of the former.

The Development of Differentiation
Between Real and Possible Selves

According to Markus and Nurius (1986), possible selves develop from previous social comparisons or from past selves. "Development can be seen as a process of acquiring and then receiving or resisting certain possible selves" (p. 955). Based on Werner's (1957) orthogenic principle by which higher levels of development are perceived to imply a greater degree of differentiation, Zigler and colleagues (Katz & Zigler, 1967; Katz, Zigler, & Zalk, 1975; Phillips & Zigler, 1980; Rosales & Zigler, 1989; Zigler, Balla, & Watson, 1972) studied the presence of age-related changes in the relationship between the real and the ideal self-concept. They hypothesized an increase in differentiation between the real and ideal self-concepts as children become older. In these studies different groups participated, consisting of children from Grades 5 to 11 with a high and a low IQ, from high and low socioeconomic backgrounds, institutionalized and non institutionalized, adjusted and maladjusted, and Black and White children, as well as boys and girls. An additional study was done with children from Grades 2 to 5. The results of these studies show a larger difference between the real and ideal self-concepts in the older and more mature children than in the younger children. Cognitive developmental factors, such as intelligence, orientation on thought versus action, and role-taking ability, contributed significantly to this differentiation between the real and ideal self-concepts. Whereas these cognitive variables were thought to be causally related to the differentiation between these self-concepts, children's social experiences were found to exert a moderating influence on this relationship (for an extensive review of these studies, see Glick & Zigler, 1985).

According to Mead (1934/1972), social experience plays an important role in self-understanding. A person gets to know himself only through others; that is, he cannot experience himself directly as such "but only indirectly from the particular standpoints of other individual members of the same social group, or from the generalized stand-point of the social group as a whole to which he belongs" (p. 138). In agreement with this assumption, Leahy and colleagues (Leahy & Huard, 1976; Leahy & Shirk, 1985) assumed that the differentiation between self-concepts was related to role-taking abilities. To study this relationship, 63 children, aged 10, 11, and 12 years, were administered the Katz and Zigler's (1967) self-concept questionnaire and Chandler's (1973) cartoon series, which assess children's role-taking abilities. Leahy and colleagues reported that nonegocentric children showed larger differences between the real and ideal self-concept than egocentric children. Although no changes could be observed in the real self-concept as a function of progressively better role-taking abilities, such changes were evident in the ideal self-concept. That is, the variance between the real and ideal self-concepts was accredited to age-related changes in the ideal self-concept, which in turn were related to developmental changes in the role-taking ability.

Strachan and Jones (1982) reported that the difference between the real and ideal self-concept was larger in middle adolescence than in early and late adolescence. Although the difference between the real and ideal self-concept increased from early to middle adolescence, the difference decreased again from middle to late adolescence. The latter finding might indicate that the differentiation of self-concepts was followed by an integration. Additional empirical evidence suggests that this integration of different elements of the self-system into a consistent structure also depends on cognitive abilities. For instance, Livesley and Bromley (1973) reported that although children between the ages of 8 and 12 years are aware that people may possess very contradictory characteristics, they are not able to deal with or integrate these contradictions, whereas adolescents are. Between the age of 14 and 16 years, the use of nonintegrated, single psychological statements disappears, whereas between the ages of 10 and 16 years the proportion of organizing and integrating principles increases (Barenboim, 1977). According to Selman(1980), children between the ages of 10 and 15 years have acquired nonreciprocal role-taking abilities (Level 3). Consequently, they are aware that conflicting motives, thoughts, or feelings can exist within the same person. However, only when mutual or reciprocal role-taking is acquired (i.e., approximately from the age of 12 years; Level 4) will children attempt to integrate the various facets into an "integrative core" (p.135). A similar progress in the abilities to differentiate, integrate, and abstract characteristics between the ages of 10 and 20 years, with the main improvements between the ages of 15 and 20 years, was reported by Bernstein (1980). These findings suggest that even if differentiation between self-concepts is present during middle childhood, the different self-concepts as well as the characteristics within each self-concept will not be integrated. They will exist as separate elements of knowledge. From early adolescence, however, integrative abilities can be expected to emerge and will increase until late adolescence (cf. Damon & Hart, 1982, 1988; Harter, 1986).

In conclusion, it appears that these developmental progressions support the assumptions that the real self-concept and the possible selves emerge from one global and undifferentiated (real) self-concept (Werner, 1957), exist as separate and nonintegrated entities in middle childhood and early adolescence, and become related and integrated in middle and late adolescence. This developmental progression for the self-system is said to be due to growing cognitive abilities, such as differentiation, integration, and role-taking.

THE INFLUENCE
OF THE SOCIAL ENVIRONMENT

Like the individual, the self-concept does not function in a vacuum but is part of one's social environment (e.g., Damon, 1983; Erikson, 1968/1971). This fact is often interpreted in terms of symbolic interactionism as proposed by Mead (1934/1972) and Cooley (1902/1968; e.g., Harter, 1983; Rosenberg, 1979; Shrauger & Schoeneman, 1979). According to the theories of Mead and Cooley, knowledge about the self is derived from knowledge about others. Cooley (1902/1968) introduced the term "looking glass self," referring to the idea that the self-concepts of people represent their inferences about how others perceive them. For Mead, people come to a notion of self by taking the role of the "generalized other" instead of individual others. Although empirical evidence has been obtained that supports the latter assumption, the perceived attitudes of significant others toward the self were found to relate even more strongly to a person's self-concept than the perceived attitude of the "generalized other" (cf. Rosenberg, 1979).

Rosenberg studied which persons can be validly classified as significant others. Not all persons who might reasonably be considered significant to an individual are experienced as (equally) significant to all. The findings of different studies (cf. Rosenberg, 1979) reveal that in order to assess the significance and the influence of particular others in the social environment, at least three types of characteristics should be taken into account. These characteristics relate to the other person, the individual himself, and the particular situation (for a similar overview see Shrauger & Schoeneman, 1979).

Characteristics of the Other Person

A person is perceived as significant by an individual if this other person is thought to have favorable opinions about him or her and if these opinions are highly credible. High credibility, in turn, is affected by the degree to which the other person is liked, the level of expected expertise of the other, and the degree of consensus between several others, as well as the role of the other. When the role is considered, the mother is most likely to be perceived as highly significant for children, followed by the father, brothers and sisters, teachers, friends, and classmates, in this order (Rosenberg, 1979). If the self-concept and its formation are affected by the attitudes of (significant) others, this influence will be differentially related to the other in respect to whom this effect is assessed.

Pekrun (1990) studied the relative influence of parents, teachers, and peers on the self-concept of academic ability and general self-esteem of children from Grades 5 to 8. Although support offered by parents, teachers, and peers were all correlated with the self-concept of ability, the support of teachers correlated highest. General self-esteem was primarily influenced by family support and acceptance by the parents. No relevant interactions between the three context categories were found. Pekrun concluded that the influences seem to be additive and that the family appears to play a central role in the development of the self--concept (i.e., self-esteem) in early and middle adolescence. Factors related to the school primarily affect the development of the more domain-specific, school-related self-concepts (i.e., self-concept of abilities). These findings, however, also suggest that context-relevant others are more likely to influence the active context-related part of the self-system directly (i.e., the working self-concept), although others who have less relevance in that specific context affect primarily general self-esteem (cf. Shrauger & Schoeneman, 1979).

Characteristics of the Individual

The order of significance for others as described by Rosenberg (1979) and Pekrun (1990) may be detailed when the age and gender of the subject are taken into account. In general, previously significant others will become less significant as a child grows older (McGuire & McGuire, 1982; Pekrun, 1990). The results from McGuire and McGuire's study showed that with progressing age significance shifted from family members and friends to teachers, friends, fellow students, and nonfamily. Beside these age-related changes, gender-differences were also evident. Girls mentioned other people and family members more frequently than did boys, and although girls differentiated between children and adults, boys referred to people in general. Boys, on the other hand, mentioned negatively valenced significant others (enemies) more often and romantic friends less often than did girls. Girls and boys were more oriented toward the same-gender parent than toward the opposite-gender parent; that is, boys more often referred to their father and girls more often to their mother as a significant other (McGuire & McGuire, 1982).

The characteristics of the self-concept (i.e., contents), which are revealed in various contexts (i.e., related to the working self-concept; Markus & Wurf, 1987), are also dependent on the age of the individual. Smollar and Youniss (1985) interviewed participants (i.e., age ranges 10-11, 14-15, 18-19, and 22-23 years) about their self-concept in the company of a close friend, their father, and their mother. With preadolescents, prosocial aspects of self were most often revealed in the close-friend context, followed by the mother context, and least in the father context. In the father context, the prosocial items were supplemented by feelings of capability, seriousness, and anxiety. Contrary to both parent contexts, spontaneity was the major feature for middle adolescents in a peer context. The self was perceived more often in terms of anger, defensiveness, and withdrawal in both parent contexts. In middle adolescence, a larger distinction was evident between the private self and the public self, and between the different contexts used. With the older subjects, a smaller differentiation between contexts was evident: Contentment, intimacy, sensitivity, and spontaneity were mentioned more often as important characteristics of the self.

Characteristics of the Situation

McGuire, McGuire, and Cheever's (1986) findings show (consistently across age, gender, and response modality) that the self in the family context is perceived as more passive than in the school context (that is, more static terms to describe overt actions, physical actions, cognitions, and affirmations were used). In the school context, the self was more often described in terms of becoming, covert reactions, social interactions, affects, and reflexive negations.

More detailed information about the influence of situational or contextual variables on the development of the self-concept can be derived from a study by Rosenholtz and Simpson (1984). Rosenholtz and Simpson reviewed the literature dealing with the ways in which children develop conceptions of their own and their peers' intellectual abilities. On the basis of this review, Rosenholtz and Simpson were not able to find support for the assumption that younger children (especially before the second grade) overestimate their abilities (for more detailed information, see Rosenholtz & Simpson, 1984). In this theory, which is more situational than developmental, three factors are emphasized that are thought to influence the formation of a person's self-concept of ability: the amount of information, the degree to which the information is consistent, and the degree to which the information is easily interpreted and integrated. What these authors called the dimensional characteristics of the environment play an especially important role in their theory. An environment is considered one-dimensional if pupils and their performances are evaluated along a single criterion. Multidimensionality involves an evaluation of pupils and their performances along several criteria. It is clear that a one-dimensional environment offers clear criteria for such evaluations. Consensus about someone's capabilities will be high and the person will receive clear and differentiated feedback about his capabilities. The person's ideas about his own capabilities are then guided in a certain direction. If the environment is multidimensional, the feedback is less clear and, hence, less differentiated, because then the evaluation can be interpreted by several criteria. Consensus is more likely to be low and the person will be confronted with a larger variety of criteria to choose from in attempts at self-enhancement. Although a one-dimensional environment (i.e., a high consensus) will result in a clear self-conception of ability, a multidimensional environment (i.e., a low consensus) will offer greater opportunities to maintain a favorable (i.e., positive) self-concept of abilities.

In summary, the influence of the environment on a self-concept is differentially related to others who are considered significant others. The greatest influence is expected to be exerted by real significant others whose significance changes as children grow older. The nature of the opinions of significant others (i.e., favorability versus infavorability), the credibility of the significant other, and the relevance of the other in a particular context, as well as the age and gender of the person and the dimensionality of the situation, affect the influence of the environment on the self-concept. When various social contexts and related significant others play a relevant role for the person, these influences on the self-concept appear to be additive.

THE ACTIVE PERSON

The Active Role of the Individual

Although Cooley (1902/1968) and Mead (1934/1972) strongly emphasized the role of the environment in the development of the self, others, like James

(1890/1950) and Baldwin (1897/1973), pointed to the active role of the individuals themselves in this process. For James, the self-concept was an autonomous cognitive construct relatively insensitive to social constraints. For Baldwin, the self was a product of reciprocal interactions between the organism (i.e., the individual) and the environment. Only in Baldwin's theory was attention given to explicitly developmental processes. According to Baldwin, children's notions of self arise by imitation of others and the projection of their own experiences toward others. Children need the environment to obtain examples for behavior and to develop some standards about how they should or ought to behave. Hence, the environment influences the development of the self-concept of children. In Baldwin's theory, children learn by imitating more experienced others, by practicing the newly acquired skills on others, and by projecting their own thoughts and motivations on others. The more children learn, the better the projections will fit. Children do not become entirely defined by others, though, because they are active individuals who exert influence on the development of their self-concept themselves. Not only the children's genetic or innate characteristics, but also their prior experiences determine which examples will be imitated and what is learned from them. The same event in an environment can then be perceived and processed differently by different children and result in different projections toward (the same) others.

The ideas of Baldwin (1897/1973) correspond to the emphasis in contemporary theories on the active role of the individual in the process of self-conception. Individuals are perceived as actors with a will of their own (e.g., Gecas & Schwalbe, 1983). Often, the active role of individuals becomes manifest in cognitive biases. For example, people tend to rewrite their personal histories to justify their acts (e.g., Conway & Ross, 1984) or to experience continuity in their self-cognitions (Ball & Chandler, 1990). More explicitly elaborated phenomena were described by Greenwald (1980). He introduced cognitive biases, such as egocentricity, beneffectance, and cognitive conservatism, as normal, healthy mechanisms that preserve the organization of knowledge. Egocentricity refers here to self-reference in perception and memory (see also Kuiper & Rogers, 1979; Lapsley & Quintana, 1985; Lewicki, 1984; Markus, 1977; Markus & Sentis, 1982) and an exaggeration of the role of the self in interactions; beneffectance is described as the tendency to take credit for success, but to deny responsibility for failure; and cognitive conservatism involves the tendency to preserve existing knowledge structures by means of object or category conservation, the confirmation bias, and the rewriting of memory.

Sometimes contradictory self-regulating motives, such as the motive for self-enhancement and the motive for self-consistency (e.g., Markus & Wurf,

1987), are ascribed to individuals in the theories that emphasize the active role of the individual. Self-enhancement involves the urge to bring the individual's own real self-concept in congruence with the individual's positive possible selves. For instance, in their theory on symbolic self-completion, Wicklund and Gollwitzer (Wicklund & Gollwitzer, 1982, in Gollwitzer & Wicklund, 1985; Wagner, Wicklund, & Shaigan, 1990) stated that people attempt to attain selves to which they are highly committed by means of symbols. The manifest symbols of an individual function as an indicator of the environment that he is heading for or that the individual has reached a particular characteristic. Similarly, Baumeister (1982) suggested that "much human behavior can be understood as being the result of the individual's attempts to *communicate* information rather than to seek it" (p. 22). According to Baumeister's theory on self-presentation, people actively use their behavior to communicate information about themselves towards others – either to make a favorable impression (i.e., "pleasing the audience") or to convince others that one resembles one's own ideal self.

Similarly, according to Tesser's self-evaluation model (Tesser & Campbell, 1983; Tesser, Millar, & Moore, 1988), people strive to maintain or enhance their self-evaluation. Two processes play a role in such attempts: the process of reflection and the process of comparison. People will enhance or maintain their positive self-evaluation by reflecting in the glory of a close other person. However, by comparing oneself with a glorious other, the person's positive self-evaluation may be endangered. The closer the other person and the better the other person's performance, the more an individual can gain by reflecting in the other person's success. As the other person's performance becomes more relevant to the individual's own self-definition the more likely the process of comparison will be triggered. This process of comparison is avoided if the other's performance is less relevant to the individual's own self-definition or if the other's performance differs so much from one's own performance that it may be considered to belong to a different "class." Threats to an individual's self-evaluation, therefore, can be reduced by reducing one's closeness to the better performer, increasing the perceived difference between the performances, or decreasing the relevance of the performance to the individual's self-definition.

The motive for self-consistency involves people's preference to be in congruence with their own real self-concepts. Self-consistency serves the experience of continuity. Several self-serving biases can be listed that are used by people to attempt to perpetuate their self-concept (e.g., Kulik, Sledge, & Mahler, 1986; Swann, 1987). Examples of more elaborate theories on self-consistency are those of Swann (e.g., 1983, 1987) on self-verification and Backman (1988) on interpersonal congruency. Self-verification (Swann, 1983,

1987) refers to people's preference for self-confirmatory feedback and their efforts to acquire such feedback. Persons obtain information about themselves by feedback from others and from their own behavior in a particular context. Although the feedback from the social environment stabilizes the individuals' self-concepts (Swann & Predmore, 1985), the individuals themselves may actively influence this feedback by creating idiosyncratically skewed social environments. People may communicate signs and symbols that are characteristic of their particular identity. People may avoid certain people and situations but seek out others. They may behave toward others in a way that stresses particular features of their self-concept, for example, by behaving authoritatively to stress their dominance. In addition, if people do receive feedback that is inconsistent with their self-concept, they can take steps to avoid it by looking away, for example, or forgetting, or attributing its causes to external factors (cf. Swann & Hill, 1982; Swann & Read, 1981).

In Backman's (1988) theory on interpersonal congruency it is assumed that people prefer and strive for congruency between their self-representations, their interpretations of behavior that is relevant to these self-presentations, and the relevant behaviors and perceptions of the environment. Three forms of congruency are distinguished by Backman: congruency by implication, by validation, and by comparison. Congruency by implication involves the perception that others ascribe characteristics to the individual that are also part of the individuals' self-concept. Congruency by validation occurs when others behave towards the individual in accordance with the individual's own self-concept. Congruency by comparison takes place when comparisons with others result in the individuals' conclusion that others possess characteristics that are consistent with the individual's self-concepts. Hence, congruency is achieved by several intra- and interpersonal processes, such as cognitive reconstruction, selective attention, selective evaluation, response evocation and self-presentation, and selective and biased comparison.

Current research is no longer directed towards the confirmation of the individual's active roles in either self-enhancement or self-consistency but in the relationship between both motives. Initially, it was found that individuals with high self-esteem tend to show self-enhancement, although individuals with low self-esteem tend to protect their selves and to strive for self-consistency. In accordance with these findings, Schlenker, Weigold, and Hallam (1990) reported that behavior motivated by self-enhancement was moderated by the individuals' perception of the cost–benefit ratio (beneficiallity) and the credibility of the behavior. That is, people avoid self-enhancing behaviors that can easily be invalidated by others. According to Brown, Collins, and Schmidt (1988), people with low self-esteem also show self-enhancing behavior but, in contrast to people with high self-esteem, this behavior is shown in an indirect way. Swann, Pelham, and Krull (1989) stressed the recognition of the self-concept as a context-related multidimensional construct. These authors demonstrated that although people prefer self-enhancing feedback for their positive self-representations, they use self-consistent feedback for their negative self-representations. Furthermore, Swann and his colleagues (Swann, Griffin, Predmore, & Gaines, 1987; Swann, Hixon, Stein-Seroussi, & Gilbert, 1990) suggested a differentiation between the motive for self-enhancement and self-consistency on the basis of cognition and affect. They concluded that self-verification might need a more extensive cognitive processing of information than self-enhancement. Swann et al. (1987) found that consistent feedback was primarily related to cognitive responses, whereas enhancing feedback was primarily related to affective responses. Both motives were relatively independent, with affective responses occurring somewhat quicker than cognitive responses (Swann et al., 1987; cf. also Zajonc, 1980). When the cognitive loading was increased, people with low and high self-esteem reacted to enhance the self. Without such a cognitive load people with low self-esteem were more self-verificative (Swann et al., 1990).

In conclusion, besides the influence of the environment on the process of self-conception, also the effects of an "active, regulating role of the individual" are apparent. That is, the process of self-conception is assumed to develop by means of a reciprocal interaction, in which both the person and the environment change as a result of their interaction (Lerner & Tubman, 1989).

The Development of the "Active Role of the Individual"

Little is known about the development of the "active role of the individual" (cf. Markus & Nurius, 1984; Ruble & Flett, 1988; Smith & Smoll, 1990) and of the relative importance of the environment and the "active role of the individual" in childhood (e.g., Lapsley & Quintana, 1985). Backman (1988) assumed that children are more influenced by others than adolescents and adults, because child-adult relationships are asymmetrical and based on an unequal balance of power, and because children are less able to reflect on their own behavior (cf. Selman, 1980). Others (e.g., Damon & Hart, 1982; Harter, 1986; Markus & Nurius, 1984; Peevers, 1984; Ruble & Flett, 1988; Stipek & Tannatt, 1984) reported that children's self-judgements are absolute rather than relative to others and that it is only during middle childhood that children become attentive to social comparisons. That is, until middle childhood the influence of the environment seems to be direct rather than exerted through the processes of comparison. In middle childhood, self-regulation becomes increasingly a matter of coregulation, directed by the society and the self (Markus & Nurius, 1984), by which the child incorporates social standards into its own self-guides.

It might be concluded from research on the ability to actively delay rewards, that self-regulative processes are present at age 4 (Shoda, Mischel, & Peake, 1990; also Maccoby & Martin, 1983). Among the self-regulation processes, self-enhancement rather than self-consistency seems to prevail in childhood (cf. Smith & Smoll, 1990). It is often reported that children systematically overestimate their abilities in comparison to their actual performance and to the ratings of their peers, with the degree of overestimation gradually declining during elementary school (e.g., Stipek & Tannatt, 1984). In addition, between the ages of 7 to 11 years, children with a low self-esteem appear to prefer self-enhancing information over self-consistent information. For example, children with low as well as high self-esteem preferred baseball coaches who were encouraging, advising, and reinforcing to punitive and relationship-oriented coaches. However, children with low self-esteem showed these preferences more than did the children with high self-esteem (Smith & Smoll, 1990), and preferred social comparison information (i.e., multidimensional information; Rosenholtz & Simpson, 1984) above absolute or self-consistent information about their abilities (Ruble & Flett, 1988).

In contrast to these findings for younger children, research by Harter (1986) indicated that sixth grade children reacted to self-enhancing or self-consistent information in a way similar to adults. Children with a high self-esteem performed well and demonstrated self-enhancement by decreasing the importance of domains in which they were less competent. In contrast, children with a low self-esteem did not decrease the importance of domains in which they performed less well. Because children with a low self-esteem were also less competent, Harter assumed correspondence with a low level of beneficiality and credibility of self-enhancing behavior in such cases. Similar conclusions resulted from Harter's (1986) research on the tendency of children to inflate their sense of competence and to bias their sense of control over successes and failures. Although children with a high self-esteem tended to rate their competencies slightly higher than did their teachers, children with a low self-esteem tended to score themselves lower. In addition, although children between the third and ninth grade, with both low and high self-esteem, initially accepted equal personal responsibility for both academic success *and* failure, the acceptance of responsibility for their failures in contrast to their successes decreased gradually as they grew older. These findings are in agreement with Greenwald's (1980) results on beneffectance (see also Harter, 1985).

In sum, whereas young adolescents seem to react in a way that is comparable to the reactions of adults, younger children are assumed to be under more direct influence of the environment and seem to let self-enhancing information prevail over self-consistent information. This prevalence of self-enhancement is not surprising. The relatively concrete, situation-specific, and unstable self-knowledge of children (e.g., Damon & Hart, 1982; Harter, 1986) gives little reason to support a search for self-consistency. If their self-descriptions themself bear a somewhat *ad hoc* character, then any attempt toward consistency would be a waste of energy. Furthermore, self-enhancement was found to be a more affective than a cognitive motive for self-regulation (Swann et al., 1987; Swann et al., 1990) and children tend to react more affectively than cognitively (Feldman & Ruble, 1988; Stipek & Tannatt, 1984). That is, children explained their preference for a particular person or partner in terms of likeability and friendship rather than instrumentality. Thus, although the empirical evidence is thin, it seems reasonable to conclude that whereas children from early to middle childhood demonstrate self-regulation, this regulation is more directed toward self-enhancement than self-consistency.

STRUCTURAL CHARACTERISTICS

It is generally assumed that the self-system functions to structure self-relevant information (e.g., Markus & Wurf, 1987). The quality of the self-system structure is thought to influence personal functioning and emotions. If these assumptions are true, it is important to consider the structural characteristics of the self-system and their function, both in processing information and in regulating affective responses. However, because more theory than data is available with which to construct such a pattern of structural characteristics, various authors have featured different, but only partially overlapping characteristics.

The two most well-known structural characteristics of the self-system, derived from James's (1910/1968) theory, are distinctness and continuity. Other characteristics that relate to the self-system as a self-theory were introduced by Epstein (1973). For the self-system to function adequately as a theory about the self, it needs to be expansive (i.e., flexible and open to new experiences rather than restricted and rigid). In addition, the self-system should be parsimonious (i.e., well integrated and efficiently organized), empirically valid, internally consistent (i.e., without conscious contradictions), testable, and useful. According to Fitts (1981), a desirable self-system is positive, realistic or valid, clear and well differentiated, and internally consistent. The most extensive list of "meta-dimensions" or characteristics of the self-system was offered by Super (cited in Bailey, 1970). Bailey (1970) analyzed the factor structure of these dimensions (i.e., except the dimension stability) and compressed the dimensions into five general dimensions (i.e., factors). These dimensions are harmony versus discord, growth and elaboration versus constriction, social integration and self-differentiation versus social isolation and self-diffusion, cognitive simplicity versus complexity, and concrete realism versus abstract realism (i.e., the extent to which self is described in concrete or abstract terms).

Although little empirical research is available on these characteristics and their interrelationships, several of these characteristics have been studied separately. Among those that have been studied, a distinction can be made between characteristics that reflect the actual organization of the self-system (i.e., the temporary state of organization), characteristics that reflect the active process of structuralization and organization themselves, and characteristics of the descriptions that are used to characterize the self (i.e., characteristics of self-descriptions) that facilitate or otherwise influence the structure or organization of the self-system. In the following paragraphs several of these characteristics are described. This involves a general description of each characteristic and, where possible, the development of that characteristic. In addition, the relationship between the characteristics and affect are considered.

Temporary State of Organization

Complexity. One of the first structural characteristics of the self-system to be studied was the complexity of the self-system. One of the most important differences between the self-system and other cognitive systems is that the self-system is more frequently activated (e.g., Millar & Tesser, 1986; Pratt, Pancer, Hunsberger, & Manchester, 1990; Prentice, 1990). Because of this greater familiarity, the self-system is also relatively large and complex, with relatively clear connections between the subparts (Markus & Sentis, 1982). Cognitive complexity refers to "the capacity to construe social behavior in a multidimensional way" (Bieri, 1966/1975, p.185), and, thus, to the amount of differentiation within the system (Adams-Webber, 1970; Bieri, 1966/1975). The more dimensions that are differentiated (i.e., the greater the cognitive complexity), the greater is the variety of events that can be perceived and interpreted. With a more complex cognitive system, perception becomes more precise (Adams-Webber, 1970; Bieri, 1966/1975).

The idea that a cognitive system becomes more complex because of experience is apparent in theories on cognitive development (e.g., Werner, 1957). Consistent with such notions, the self-concept has been found to become more differentiated and elaborated with increasing age (e.g., Glick & Zigler, 1985; Montemayor & Eisen, 1977). Bailey (1970), for example, found a factor loading of .82 for age on complexity indicating an almost direct relationship between progressing age and complexity.

The complexity of the self-system has been found to relate to shifts in affect (Linville, 1985; see also DeChenne, 1980) and to impact of stress (Linville, 1987). Linville (1985, 1987) defined complexity as a function of the number of self-descriptions and the degree of relatedness between these self-descriptions. The higher the number of self-descriptions and the lower the relatedness, the higher the complexity. The lower the number of self-descriptions, and the higher their relatedness, the lower the complexity. Utilizing these definitions of complexity, Linville (1985,1987) reported that undergraduates with high levels of self-complexity were found to experience less negative shifts in affect, both in degree as well as in number. In addition, measures of depression, perceived stress, and physical symptoms revealed that, in contrast to low complexity, high complexity buffered against stress. Linville gave two complementary explanations for her findings. Firstly, among highly related self-descriptions of the self-system negative, affective consequences of an event for one's self-description were said to be more easily generalized to the related self-descriptions; among less related self-descriptions the consequences of an affective shift were assumed to be limited to a single self-description. Secondly, general affect is said to be a function of the particular affect that is associated with a self-description of the self. That is, the more that the self-descriptions are differentiated, the more potential affective compensation is available.

There is reason to assume, however, that it is primarily the association between the self-descriptions that accounts for differences between people with high and low self-complexity. Linville (1985, 1987), for instance, reported that the statistics that combined number and degree of relatedness revealed much stronger results than a simple count of the self-descriptions, for which no significant effects were evident. In addition, Millar and Tesser (1986) studied changes in attitudes towards individuals and groups as operationalizations of changes in attitudes within high- and low-complex cognitive systems, respectively. These authors found that the occurrence of attitude polarization under conditions of either high or low cognitive complexity was a function of commitment and thought. More polarization (i.e., a shift towards an extreme) occurred if subjects thought about their attitudes and were highly committed to them. Both commitment and thought increased the correlations among attitudes within the cognitive system about an individual or group. Hence, polarization between attitudes seems to be primarily a consequence of high correlations between these attitudes. Because these findings occurred in cognitive systems about groups as well as individuals, they might also be evident for the cognitive system about a special individual, that is, the self.

Clearness. The role of relatedness in the complexity construct demands a consideration of the clearness of a self-system. Clearness explicitly refers to the degree to which self-descriptions are explicitly defined and differentiated; it can be considered the opposite of diffuseness (cf. Hauser, 1972). Similar to complexity, then, clearness involves the relationships between self-descriptions. In contrast to complexity, clearness does not involve the extension of the self-system. For instance, for clearness to be present between the self-concept and the ideal self-concept, the person must know in what terms he describes himself and his ideals. He must know what he means by the descriptions in these concepts and where, as well as how, they differ from each other.

A clear self-concept implies certainty. Certainty in self-attributes is expected to generate positive affect and self-confidence, because certainty promotes a sense of control over the future (Baumgardner, 1990). Clearness as well as certainty have been operationalized by short reaction times, extreme and stable ratings, and a high confidence in the ratings. People with low self-esteem, as opposed to people with high self-esteem, are reported to be less certain about their self-ratings (Baumgardner, 1990; Campbell, 1990) and showed a slower reaction time to self-descriptions but not to other-descriptions (Baumgardner, 1990; Campbell, 1990), and in addition, they rated themselves less extreme and showed less stable ratings over time. People with high self-esteem showed higher correlations between their self-concept and situation-specific behavior and reported memories of this behavior that were more biased towards their self-concept than people with low self-esteem (Campbell). If people were provided with information about their self-concept that was considered to be certain, their positive affect towards themselves and their egotism increased (Baumgardner). Although it is not clear which is the causal part in this relationship between self-esteem and certainty of the self-concept, both Baumgardner and Campbell assumed that both directions are possible and that the relationship is reciprocal.

Markus (1977) found that "schematics" (i.e., people with a schema, operationalized as scoring at the extremes of a self-descriptive dimension) were more resistant to counterschematic information as compared to "a-schematics." Chaiken and Baldwin (1981) measured the degree to which attitudes were well defined by the affect related to the attitudes instead of by extreme ratings. Similar to Markus (1977), Caiken and Baldwin found that subjects with well-defined attitudes are less influenced by experimental manipulation than subjects with poorly defined attitudes. They also found a higher intercorrelation between subaspects of the well-defined attitudes as compared to poorly defined attitudes. Although Linville (1985, 1987) interpreted such high relatedness negatively, Chaiken and Baldwin took this finding as a sign of better integration.

Fitts (1981) argued that with regard to clearness, both extremes of the continuum affect health negatively. At one extreme the self-system tends to be fuzzy, uncertain, and undifferentiated; at the other extreme it tends to be overly differentiated, certain, fixed, and rigid. Troubled and disturbed people tend to be situated at both extremes. Campbell (1990) found no empirical evidence for such a u-curved relationship between self-esteem and certainty, in which people with a very low as well as people with a high self-esteem show high degrees of certainty, whereas people with a moderately low self-esteem report uncertainty. However, because her subjects came from a normal, healthy population, people with a truly low self-esteem were probably not represented in her study.

Internal Consistency. Clearness can occur not only between self-descriptions but also between self-concepts. Two types of clearness can be distinguished between the self-concepts. These types refer to the degree of differentiation between real self-concepts and possible selves, on the one hand, and the degree of differentiation between self-concepts from one's own perspective and from the perceived perspective of others, on the other hand. The latter type is referred to as distinctness. In addition, a distinction can be made between mere differentiation and discrepancies between self-concepts. Differentiation between self-concepts involves the awareness that the self-concepts differ in some aspects and to a certain degree. Discrepancies between self-concepts, by contrast, appear when such a differentiation results in the awareness that these self-concepts are incompatible or contradictory. The absence of consciously experienced discrepancies is referred to as *internal consistency.* For instance, the statement "I am what I want to be and what other people think me to be" is an example of an internally consistent self-concept. If discrepancies are present among the different self-concepts, an inconsistent structure results.

As was indicated above, internal consistency is inversely related to the presence of discrepancies between the real and possible selves as well as discrepancies between the self as perceived by self and others. However, the two types of discrepancy are derived from different subdisciplines within psychology and can be found in the literature on personal strivings and uniqueness, respectively; in addition, both types function in distinct ways. Consequently, only the discrepancies between the real and possible selves will be considered here. Discrepancies between personal and attributed self-concepts will be considered below under the heading "Distinctness."

A prerequisite to self-discrepancies to occur is the ability to differentiate between real and possible self-concepts. Differentiation involves the distance between self-concepts, that is, the extent to which clear distinctions between these self-concepts are made. Both Zigler and Leahy and their colleagues found that differences between children's real and ideal self-concept were related to age and level of cognitive maturity (Glick & Zigler, 1985; Leahy & Shirk, 1985). The older or more mature the children, the larger the distance between their real and ideal self-concepts. It can be argued, however, that children do not experience such distances as (conflicting) "discrepancies" until adolescence when integrative abilities attempt and sometimes fail to reconcile real discrepant distances (cf. Harter, 1986).

Lack of internal consistency in general is considered to have serious consequences. Fitts (1981) mentioned "conflict associated with turmoil, confusion and anxiety as to who and what persons really are" (p. 268). According to Epstein (1973), inconsistency is a potential source of stress and disorganization. It could even make the structure collapse. Traditionally, discrepancies between the real self and possible selves, the ideal self in particular, were thought to negatively affect feelings of subjective well-being (e.g., Ogilvie, 1987).

Undoubtly, the self-discrepancy theory of Higgins (1987) is of the highest relevance to the study of discrepancies within the self-concept. Self-discrepancy theory predicts that different types of chronic discrepancies between the real self-concept and possible selves result in different types of negative emotion. Although the type of emotion is dependent on the type of discrepancy, the intensity of the emotion is dependent on the availability and accessibility of the discrepancy. The larger a discrepancy (availability), the more recently and frequently it has been activated, and the more it is applicable to the situation (accessibility), the more intense the emotion will be. Higgins and colleagues actually studied the consequences of discrepancies between real and ideal, and between real and ought-to-be self-concepts. They reported that discrepancies between real and ideal self-concepts were related to dejection-related depression and that discrepancies between the real and ought-to-be concepts were related to agitation-related emotions (Higgins, 1987; Higgins, Bond, Klein, & Strauman, 1986; Higgins, Klein, & Strauman, 1985). In addition, the relationships appeared to be causal (Higgins et al., 1986). Furthermore, Strauman (1989) found that discrepancies between real and ideal, and between real and ought-to-be self-concepts differentiated between depressives (who perceived most dejection) and social phobics (who perceived most agitation).

Thus, Higgins and colleagues showed that discrepancies between the real and possible self-concepts have a distinct psychological relevance. However, as was discussed previously, discrepancies may also serve a motivational function for personal growth. Both Epstein (1973) and Van der Werff (1985) stressed the possibility that such inconsistencies, as opposed to having only negative consequences, may also have positive effects, with collapses as well as inconsistencies prompting reorganization (see flexibility; cf. also Harter, 1983; Markus & Wurf, 1987).

Distinctness. In contrast to the presence of inconsistencies or discrepancies between real and possible self-concepts, or discrepancies, the inconsistency between one's own ideas about the self and the perceived ideas of others about oneself has a more positive flavor. The recognition that people can see themselves differently from how others perceive them results in a feeling of distinctness. Distinctness refers to the degree to which a person is aware of possessing a unique personality of his own, as opposed to being similar to others. The experience of uniqueness in relation to others is a core aspect of the self-concept (Broughton, 1981; Markus & Kunda, 1986; Snyder & Fromkin, 1980; see also Erikson, 1950/1969; James, 1890/1950). People have been shown to strive towards a balance between feelings of uniqueness and similarity to others. Although people prefer to belong to some group and to be, to a certain degree, similar to others, there is always the urge to be unique (Snyder & Fromkin, 1980).

The emergence of a sense of distinctness or uniqueness starts to develop as early as infancy by means of self-other differentiation (Snyder & Fromkin, 1980) and develops more fully after the child becomes aware that others not only are different but also think differently (Selman, 1980). Children tend to describe their distinctness in increasingly more abstract terms, that is, in correspondence with the descriptions for the self-concept, in terms of first physical characteristics, followed by activities and preferences, psychological characteristics, and finally subjective and private characteristics of the self's experience (Bannister & Agnew, 1977; Damon & Hart, 1982; Kwiatkowska, 1990). The developmental course for a sense of distinctness in childhood and onward seems also to be influenced by social or situational variables. In a study with Polish preschool and elementary school children (ages 6 and 8 years), Kwiatkowska (1990) found that similarities between themselves and others are rarely mentioned in either group. The younger group, however, mentioned only differences more often, although the older group more often mentioned both similarities and differences simultaneously. Kwiatkowska concluded that the elementary school children who were already aware of their own distinctness emphasize their similarity to others more than the preschool children. She interpreted this conclusion in the light of the school system that attempts to minimize individual differences. According to Snyder and Fromkin (1980), the family context, the neighbourhood, the school, therapeutical settings, as well as the political context all work to both stimulate and prevent distinctness.

The importance of a sense of uniqueness has been shown in children as well as in adults. Even though they rate themselves mostly in reference to a (peer) group, people value terms related to uniqueness as higher than terms related to similarity to others (Markus & Kunda, 1986). Srull and Gaelick (1983) found that people judged others to be more similar to themselves than they judged themselves to be similar to others. People who were deprived of the sense of uniqueness attempted to correct this by means of behavior (e.g., choosing a rare experience, perceptual anticonformity, attitude change) or cognitive biases (Fromkin, 1970; Snyder & Fromkin, 1980). Broughton (1981) reported on adolescents who indicated that sharing the whole self with others without keeping something private means a loss of self, or as Broughton (1981, p. 22) put it, "A nonunique self is no self." For this reason, children attend to aspects of the self thay are distinctive because they are novel, unpredictable, and informative (McGuire & McGuire, 1988). In their studies using free self-descriptions, McGuire and McGuire reported that children from 7 to 18 years described themselves with characteristics that were rare in their usual social groups, that is, in terms that discriminated them from the major part of the group.

The importance of this sense of uniqueness or distinctness is nevertheless limited. First, the positive affect that is associated with distinctness is characterized by a u-curved development (Snyder & Fromkin, 1980). People prefer neither too little nor too much distinctness. Based on affective reactions, self-esteem, and personal space, a moderate degree of similarity (and thus distinctness) has been found to be most positive. Similarly, Campbell and Fehr (1990) reported that a large difference between one's own self-concept and the perceived conception of self by others was associated with lower self-esteem. Second, people differ in the degree to which they prefer distinctness. Although some people primarily focus on their own opinions about, and ideals for, themselves (i.e., private self-consciousness), others focus more on the expected or perceived opinions of others (i.e., public self-consciousness; Barnes, Mason, Leary, Laurent, Griebel, & Bergman, 1988; Pratt, Pancer, Hunsberger, & Manchester, 1990; Scheier & Carver, 1983; Snyder, 1979; Srull & Gaelick, 1983). Although people with a private consciousness also seem to focus on social opinion, they do this indirectly (Schlenker & Weigold, 1990). At a more concrete level, people with a private and social consciousness aim at different goals (Scheier & Carver, 1983). That is, whereas people with a social consciousness try to conform to social opinion and prefer a higher degree of similarity to their group, people with a private consciousness prefer a higher degree of distinctness and try to stay within their own standards.

Validity. The acceptance of similarity and distinctness as relevant constructs leads to questions pertaining to the degree to which (a) similarity or distinctness actually exists and (b) self-concepts of people accurately reflect reality. That is, to what degree are self-concepts *valid* representations of the self? Two types of validity can be distinguished. First, the degree to which perceptions of the person are in agreement with the perceptions of others and, second, the degree to which the perceptions of a person are in agreement with that person's actual behavior. The first form of validity involves the agreement between the interindividual self-concepts. That is, the agreement between the person's own self-concepts and the perception of the same self by others. This type of validity is referred to as the *fit* between the self-concepts of the person and the concepts of his social environment. The second type of validity refers to the consistency between the self-concept and actual behavior or to the *predictability of behavior* from the self-concept.

For both fit and the predictability of behavior, low to moderate measures have been found. Typically, correlations are around .30 (e.g., Shrauger & Schoeneman, 1979). Several explanations are offered for these low scores reflecting two types of validity. Some of these turn on supposed faults in the experimental procedure, such as the low reliability of the measurements (Wicklund, 1982; Wicklund & Gollwitzer, 1983) or the specificity of the measured attitude or self-concept characteristic (Lyon & MacDonald, 1990; Wicklund, 1982; Wicklund & Gollwitzer, 1983). By these lights the actual validity of the self-concepts is assumed to be high, and the low correlations obtained are written off to procedural shortcomings. Other explanations assume an actual lack of validity that is inherent in the individual. Despite valid measurements, little congruence between the self-concepts and the actual concepts or behavior is evident.

Experimental validity increases if specific information is asked for (Lyon & MacDonald, 1990; Wicklund, 1982; Wicklund & Gollwitzer, 1983). The more specifically defined the attitude or characteristics, the better the fit and predictability of behavior. In addition, it has been argued that probing the maximal possible manifestation of a trait might give more valid results than studying the characteristic level of a trait (Wicklund, 1982; Wicklund & Gollwitzer, 1983). Another explanation is framed in terms of situational constraints that can cause a ceiling effect for behavior, prohibiting the intended behavior from occurring. Competing motives and normative prescriptions could also prevent the person from acting in accordance with the measured characteristic or attitude (Wicklund, 1982; Wicklund & Gollwitzer, 1983). The predictability of behavior from an elicited concept increases if the person is made conscious of his former behavior (Wicklund, 1982; Wicklund & Gollwitzer, 1983; Zanna, Olson, & Fazio, 1981), and it depends on the extent to which relevant information is available (Osberg & Shrauger, 1986).

Explanations that assume actual invalidity of the self-concepts typically refer to contextual and personal factors. Contextual explanations emphasize the self-descriptions that are perceived, the others who are involved, and the situation in which the validity occurs. From this perspective, validity is seen to be characteristic specific. For instance, Moskowitz (1990) found correlations between self-ratings and observer ratings or a behavior count for the characteristic of dominance but not for friendliness. More generally, validity has been found to depend on the frequency of occurrence for a behavior (Osberg & Shrauger 1986), the lack of variance in the behavior over situations, the extremity of the characteristic (Benesch & Page, 1989), the importance or meaningfulness of the characteristic and the related behavior (Benesch & Page, 1989; Osberg & Shrauger 1986), the distinctness of the characteristic, and the person's confidence in this characteristic or attitude (Osberg & Shrauger). In addition, fit has been found to depend on the cognitive complexity of the other person doing the ratings and of the familiarity of the target individual with that person. The cognitive complexity of the other person interferes with the fit between the concepts. This interference disappears once the other person becomes more familiar (Neimeyer, Neimeyer, & Landfield, 1983).

Finally, the validity of a self-description might depend on the characteristics of the person, such as his degree of introspectiveness, defensiveness, and impulsivity (Osberg & Shrauger, 1986), or the psychological state of the person (Wicklund, 1982). Self-reports can be influenced by emotions or by motives to either behave consistent with the self-concept or not (Wicklund, 1982). In addition, self-reports can be consistent with either the real self-concept, or the ideal self-concept (Wicklund (1982). Self-focussed attention, self-consciousness, or self-reflection can increase the validity of self-reports (Wicklund, 1982; see also Osberg & Shrauger, 1986). Osberg and Shrauger found that people who showed a high public self-consciousness, that is, who focused on the opinion of others, had less valid self-concepts than people who showed a low public self-consciousness. Wicklund (1982; Wicklund & Gollwitzer, 1983) demonstrated how the motive for self-completion can interfere with the validity of self-descriptions. If respondents reported on characteristics of the self to which they were not committed, a correlation of approximately .30 was found between self-report and behavior. If, however, participants reported on characteristics to which they were committed because these functioned as symbols for an incomplete self-definition, then the motive for self-completion interfered with the validity of the self-concept. People with incomplete self-definitions tended to disregard the perspective of others and showed a lower tendency towards self-reflection.

The self-concepts of children are even less valid than the self-concepts of adults. The validity of their self-concepts, however, increases with age. Children between 5 and 10 years have been shown to become increasingly more accurate in their self-descriptions when compared to teacher ratings and objective scores (Benenson & Dweck, 1986; Butler, 1990; Eshel & Klein, 1981; Stipek & Tannatt, 1984). Three factors can be distinguished that account for this age effect: perspective taking, social comparison, and the complexity of the self-concept. The ability to take perspective develops during childhood. Wicklund and Gollwitzer (1983) described several studies in which the relevance of perspective taking for the validity between the self-concept and behavior is demonstrated. The perspective-taking ability permits the child to adapt a self-report to the perspective of the other person, thereby increasing the ability of the other person to predict the behavior of the reporting person correctly. Perspective taking plays an even more direct role in the fit between perceived self-concepts and the actual concepts of another person. After all, it is by means of perspective taking that the perceived self-concept is formed. Furthermore, besides inferring the self-concept from behavior and objective standards, it can be inferred from social comparisons. There is little social comparison, however, used in childhood (e.g., Ruble & Flett, 1988; Stipek & Tannatt, 1984). Five-year-old children use social comparisons incorrectly and, as a consquence, lack access to an important source of information about their own functioning (e.g., Butler, 1990). Finally, it has been argued (see earlier) that the complexity of the self-concept increases the capacity to process information and to do so correctly. Because the complexity of the self-concept develops with age, the ability to process information and to do so correctly will also increase with age.

The search for factors that might improve the validity of self-descriptions indicates that theorists assume that there is high agreement between self-concepts, actual opinions of others, and behavior. Any simple version of this assumption needs to be questioned, however. The repeated finding of an only moderate correspondence between one's self-concepts as perceived by self and others and the actual concepts of others and behavior might well reflect a real phenomenon. Apart from the other factors mentioned, evidence may eventually show that people often function by the grace of invalid self-concepts. Although this argument only holds if the *belief* in validity stands firmly, the motives for self-enhancement and self-consistency may actually require a certain degree of invalidity. Empirically supported theories like the self-completion theory and the self-verification theory postulate such inaccuracy to arise as a consequence of various cognitive biases and defensiveness. Of course, one would expect that if no commonalities are present in the perspectives of a person and his social environment, communication will be impossible. Further, the attainment of a valid self-concept also generates some healthy consequences. There is no more need for deception or defensiveness and, consequently, less energy is required to keep the self-concept consistent (cf. Epstein, 1973) and the social environment predictable and under control. To some extent, however, a moderate, as opposed to perfect, degree of validity may not only be natural but even desirable to permit a person to feel complete, enhanced, verified, and consistent (cf. Greenwald, 1980).

The Process of Organization

Besides the characteristics that refer to the organization of the self-system as a temporary product, two characteristics can be mentioned that reflect the process of organization itself. These characteristics – flexibility and stability – are to some degree counterforces to each other.

Flexibility. The flexibility of the self-system permits the reorganization of self-conceptual elements in the light of new experiences (Epstein, 1973) and accounts for the growth of the self-system. It prevents collapses of the self-system structure, determines the degree to which internal inconsistency can be endured before the structure will collapse, and is important in the recovery of internal consistency. The organization of the self-system, as defined by the structural characteristics, and the flexibility of the system are reciprocally related. Although flexibility accounts for the (re)organization of the self-system, it is also in turn affected by it. The flexibility of the self-system is thought to be related to the degree that the self-system is well structured and to its complexity in particular. A complex system is more flexible than a less complex system. Even a small amount of new information can have a relatively big impact on a less complex system, in contrast to the impact of the same amount of information on a highly complex system. In addition, a highly complex system is better suited to process (i.e., to distinguish and integrate) complex information such as contradictory feedback or discrepancies (Bieri, 1966/1975; see also Sande, Goethals, & Radloff, 1988) than a less complex system. Furthermore, such a system is more flexible when positive, affective information is obtained than when it has to deal with negative affective information (DeChenne, 1980). In turn, Murray, Sujan, Hirt, and Sujan (1990) reported that a positive mood resulted in greater cognitive flexibility in categorization tasks.

Although little research is available on flexibility as a concept or process, it is comparable to ego resiliency (Block & Block, 1980). Whereas ego resiliency involves the control of impulses, flexibility involves the structural process of experiences. Ego resiliency points to "the linkages of the ego structure that keep the personality system within tenable bounds or permit the finding again of psychologically tenable adaptational modes" (Block & Block, 1980, p. 42). The concept of ego resiliency is derived from Lewin's boundary property referred to as "elasticity" (cited in Block & Block, 1980). The degree of ego resiliency is related to the adaptive organizing function of the ego. A high degree of ego resiliency implies a very large adaptive capacity; the person is able to process many changes. A low degree of ego resiliency relates to little adaptive capacity and an inability to process changes; it implies "a tendency to persevere or to become disorganized when encountering changed circumstances or when under stress, and a difficulty in recouping after traumatic experiences" (Block & Block, 1980, p. 48).

Because the complexity of a self-system is expected to develop with increasing age, the same can be expected of its flexibility. Like ego resiliency, flexibility has a positive flavor. Lack of flexibility precludes the emergence of new subsystems. In order to remain able to predict the outside world, the person may withdraw into a continually narrowing and constricting system. Once information breaks through, the damage will be all the worse (Adams-Webber, 1970). In contrast, high degrees of flexibility – or, in this case, openness to experience – has been found to be related to creativity. Creativity, in turn, was found in people who were better adjusted, more energetic, more sociable, and more achievement oriented (McCrae, 1987). However, flexibility in itself is not an unlimited positive variable. High flexibility also implies a very loose organization of a system, which precludes the possibility of ordered thought and prediction. Once the system is too flexible, changes or reorganizations in the system cannot be anticipated adequately. As a consequence, information that requires such a reorganization of the system may prove to be as disruptive as was the case with an unflexible system (Adams-Webber, 1970).

Stability/Continuity. Although flexibility can be considered as a progressive characteristic, stability can be considered as a conservative characteristic. *Stability* refers to the degree to which a feeling of *continuity* is reflected in the self-concept; for instance, by the use of identical self-descriptions at different times and across different situations. A sense of continuity involves the degree to which people feel that they have been and always will be the same person, despite new behavioral patterns in new circumstances. The need for continuity gives a direction to the organization of new experiences and for behavior. It is conducive to consistency between past and future and allows distinctness to develop (and vice versa). According to Markus and Wurf (1987), this is one way to regulate affect. A sense of continuity facilitates predictions in the social environment and results in positive affect that is related to a feeling of control. The motive for self-consistency and the energy that people are prepared to exert in order to acquire a sense of continuity were discussed previously.

Empirical findings with respect to the stability of the self-system over time and situations are contradictory. For instance, it has been argued that stability is influenced by the characteristics that are measured (e.g., Dusek & Flaherty, 1981), by the personal relevance of the characteristics (e.g., Markus & Kunda, 1986), and by the method of measurement (e.g., Damon & Hart, 1986). The sense of continuity itself has been found to develop with age and to shift from a continuity described by lack of change in one's physical body to continuity resulting from psychological and physical processes through which the nature of self continues to evolve (Damon & Hart, 1982; see also Oppenheimer, Mur, Koeman, & Chandler, 1983). Spontaneous mentioning of continuity has been found in children as young as 6 years old (Peevers, 1984). The awareness of continuity with reference to the past occurs more frequently at an earlier age (Oppenheimer et al., 1983; Peevers, 1984) than with reference to the future. Once asked about their continuity directly, children of 6 and 8 years old did not differ in mentioning stability or change but 8-year-old children mentioned a combination of both and could argue their answers more often than the 6-year-old children (Kwiatkowska, 1990). The spontaneous answer of "no change" as an indication for continuity appeared most often at age 6 but decreased in frequency until age 17. Change in the self was the last indication for the understanding of the sense of continuity that appeared spontaneously, at age 13 (Peevers, 1984). Chandler and Boyes (1982) proposed a two-stage model for the development of a sense of continuity with three and two levels, respectively. The first stage involves content-centerd interpretations of continuity. This stage develops from continuity described by physical markers between the first and third grade, through continuity described by simple habits and generic attitudes and simple psychological traits described by behavior between the third and fifth grade, to continuity described by psychological characteristics. The second stage refers to the continuity process and the idea that all contents are open to change. At the first level of this stage continuity is seen from a deterministic perspective. At the second level the past is reconstructed to permit understanding of the present.

Characteristics of Self-Descriptions

In addition to the structural and structuring characteristics of a self-system discussed earlier, some characteristics of the self-descriptions that form the contents of the self-system can also influence the organization of that system or the impact of that organization on a person's functioning.

Positiveness. According to Fitts (1981), the self-system should be positive. Positiveness refers to the evaluative affective perspective on the self-system, that is, it can refer to the evaluation of the self-system as a whole or to the evaluation of specific items within the self-system. The first refers to the general self-esteem. General self-esteem has sometimes been defined as the sum of affective loadings on several self-concept items. This sum and general self-esteem, however, are not equivalent (Harter, 1982; Moretti & Higgins, 1990). Harter (1982) described the affective evaluative perspective on the self-system as a hierarchically organized structure, identical to the structure of the self-system. In this evaluative structure, the general self-esteem is considered as the most superordinated construct, the several context-specific domains are subordinated, and the individual items are again more subordinated constructs. Moretti and Higgins (1990) did not describe a model but demonstrated that self-descriptions are only related to general self-esteem if the self-descriptions are considered in the light of the ideal self. That is, affectively positive self-descriptions were not significantly related to a high self-esteem (as measured by the Rosenberg and Coopersmith Self-Esteem Scales), and affectively negative self-descriptions were not related to a low self-esteem, except if the former were not discrepant from, or the latter were discrepant from, the ideal self. If no relationship between a self-description and the ideal self was found, then there was also no apparent relationship with self-esteem.

That self-esteem and the affect related to a self-description are also related to the organization of the self-system was discussed earlier. Self-esteem has been found to be related to the clearness of the self-system and to the distinctness in the self-system. Further, Greenwald, Bellezza, and Banaji (1988) found that self-esteem (as measured by the Rosenberg Self-Esteem Scale and the Texas Social Behavior Inventory) is related to the number and type of self-descriptions that are mentioned in a self-report. High scores on self-esteem are related to larger numbers of self-descriptions than low scores on self-esteem. In addition, high scores on self-esteem correlate positively with affectively positive self-descriptions and negatively with affectively negative self-descriptions.

Abstractness. Bailey (1970) found that the level of abstractness of the self-descriptions also plays a role in the structure of the self-system. However, little is known about this variable. Concrete self-descriptions tend to be more valid than abstract self-descriptions (Lyon & MacDonald, 1990; Wicklund, 1982; Wicklund & Gollwitzer, 1983). Conversely, abstract self-descriptions are thought to be more stable than concrete self-descriptions (e.g., Markus & Wurf, 1987). In addition, it is possible that self-concepts consisting of concrete self-descriptions are more easily differentiated and more clear than self-concepts consisting of abstract self-descriptions. Because the level of concreteness or abstractness of self-descriptions is influenced by cognitive development (e.g., Damon & Hart, 1982), it may be that children have an easier task in organizing their self-system than, for instance, adults.

Personal Relevance. Finally, a characteristic of self-descriptions is introduced that was not mentioned by either James, Epstein, Fitts, or Bailey, but that nevertheless influences the impact of the organization of the self-system on personal functioning: the personal relevance of self-descriptions. The personal relevance of self-descriptions involves the extent to which self-descriptions are important to the individual. Highly personal relevant self-descriptions form the core concept within the self-system and are as such more stable than less relevant or peripheral self-descriptions (Markus & Wurf, 1987). In addition, the consequences of discrepancies, distinctness, and self-regulating and enhancing motives can be considered to be much stronger for self-descriptions that are of high importance to the person than for self-descriptions that are of minor personal relevance.

In sum, several characteristics of the self-system can be distinguished that reflect the organization of the self-system. Several characteristics of the self-descriptions within the self-system can also be distinguished that affect the former characteristics. The characteristics that reflect the temporary state and process of organization impact on its functioning as well as the affect that goes with it. Although these characteristics are clearly interrelated (see also Bailey, 1970), they also serve a distinct function.

AN INTEGRATIVE MODEL
ON THE ORGANIZATION OF THE SELF-SYSTEM

The Dynamic of the Self-System as a Result
of Individual Motives and Environmental Influences

From the literature cited above, the self-concept is seen as an increasingly complex, multidimensional system that develops in reciprocal interaction with the environment and influences and is influenced by an individual's functioning. On the one hand, the development of such a self-system is affected by the social environment, especially if this environment contains significant, favorable, and credible people who are relevant to the situation and who offer unambiguous information about the self. On the other hand, individuals themselves also play an active, regulating role in this development; they are motivated by the desire for self-enhancement and self-consistency. Because of these motives, people will strive to organize the self-system is such a way that it serves opportunities to grow, simultaneously offering positive affect through a sense of distinctness and continuity, clearness, and consistency between real and possible selves. Although incentives from, and changes in the environment may require a reorganization of the self-system, people will try to maintain the present state or to restructure the organization of the self-system in such a way that these motives are fulfilled. In doing so, several strategies such as self-presentation and self-serving cognitive biases are used. In addition, although the (social) context will evoke the salience of particular self-descriptions in, and characteristics of, the self-system, resulting in a particular working self-concept, the actual working self-concept is codetermined by the personal relevance that the individual ascribes to the self-descriptions and structural characteristics. In other words, highly personally relevant or core descriptions and characteristics will become salient and will be present more often than peripheral self-descriptions and structural characteristics. Descriptions and characteristics that are considered peripheral by the individual will be influenced more easily by the environment but will exert less influence on the functioning of the individual than core descriptions or characteristics.

Developmental Aspects of the Dynamic of the Self-System

Although the self-system in adulthood consists of several context-related real and possible self-concepts, perceived from one's own perspective as well as from the perspective of several other persons, it is thought to develop from one global self-concept. Due to social experience and developing cognitive skills – such as self–other differentiation and role-taking – children will not only acquire increasingly differentiated self-descriptions with progressing age, but they will also differentiate increasingly between real self-concepts and possible selves (e.g., the ideal self-concept and the ought-to-be self) and between their own perspective and the perspective of people in their environment. During this process, the self-descriptions will become increasingly more abstract and the self-system will become increasingly more complex. Although initially the

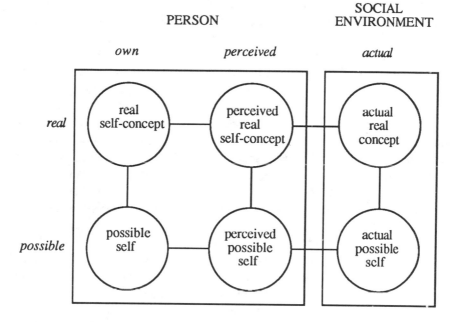

FIG. 1.1. A schematic representation of the self-system.

self-system may be largely regulated by direct influence from the environment, more and more self-regulation will be apparent. In the beginning, such self-regulation may be primarily motivated by self-enhancement. During childhood, however, as the self-system becomes more stable and a sense of continuity emerges, the motive for self-consistency will also become apparent. As the self-system becomes more clear and differentiated, more awareness is evident of possible distinctness between one's own self-concept and the ideas of others about the self, and awareness of contradictions between the real and possible selves. Such contradictions, though, are not expected to trouble children until adolescence, when they begin to perceive the need to integrate the several aspects of the self-system and become aware of possible contradictions within the several aspects of the self. During childhood the self-system will also become increasingly more valid because of an increase in complexity of the self-system and in role-taking abilities.

The Temporary Organization of the Self-System

Figure 1.1 depicts a schematic representation for the organization of the self-system. As Fig. 1.1 shows, several intraindividual real self-concepts and possible selves can be distinguished within the self-system. A distinction can be made between the self-concepts perceived from the individual's own perspective (i.e., how individuals describe their real and possible selves) and those perceived from the perspective of other persons (i.e., how individuals expect others to perceive them and what expectancies they have toward them). Within each of these self-concepts a large variety of self-descriptions is possible. These self-descriptions will be hierarchically organized and differ in level of abstractness, personal relevance, salience, clearness of definition, and positiveness. Apart from relationships between the intraindividual self-concepts, interindividual relationships between the intraindividual self-concepts and the actual concepts of other persons about the individual are considered. Such concepts are expected to be organized similarly to the intraindividual concepts.

The dynamic processes that constitute the organization of the self-system can be understood in terms of the ongoing processes of differentiation and integration that are reflected in the interrelationships between the different forms of the self-concepts. This dynamic, based on Werner's (1957) orthogenetic principle, has as its purposes the attainment and maintenance of balances or internal consistency between and among these concepts. That is, although differentiation is required, discrepancies tend to be avoided and distinctness tends to be maintained at a level that is comfortable to the individual. Disturbances of the internal consistency will lead to the experience of discomfort and a reorganization or restructuring of the self-concepts will often be required in order to restore the consistency. Inconsistency is caused by changes in the real or possible selves from one's own perspective or the perceived perspective of others due to personal or situational circumstances.

The degree of internal consistency in the organization of the self-system can be conceived as follows. Differentiation and integration between the intraindividual self-concepts are reflected in the degree of overlap, that is, the distances among the concepts. Thus, a large distance between the real self-concepts and possible selves will represent differentiation; a small distance, however, may indicate an absence of differentiation in early childhood, but suggest the presence of integration in adolescence. Similarly, a sense of distinctness will be represented by the distance between the self-concepts from the individual's own perspective and from the perceived perspectives of others; a small distance between one's own and perceived self-concepts will indicate little distinctness; a large distance between these self-concepts is evidence of a lot of distinctness. Although differentiation can be represented merely by the difference between two self-concepts, discrepancies additionally presume incompatibility between the self-concepts. Therefore, discrepancies between real self-concepts and possible selves or between one's own and perceived self-concepts will be reflected in distances between these self-concepts only if the self-descriptions within these self-concepts are contradictory. That is, discrepancies between the real and possible selves are apparent if a possible self includes self-descriptions that are opposite to or in contradiction with matching self-descriptions in the real self-concept. Discrepancies in the individual's sense of distinctness are evident if one's own self-concept includes self-descriptions that are contradictory to matching self-descriptions in the perceived self-concepts. Finally, the estimation of the validity or fit of the intraindividual concepts as compared to the perceptions of the environment is reflected in the distance between one's own and perceived real and possible selves and the actual real and possible concepts of others.

The Purpose of the Study and the Plan of Study

The purpose of this research was to study the development of the structural organization of the self-system in childhood and adolescence. This was done by considering the structural characteristics of the self-system in terms of the relationships among subjects' intra- and interindividual self-concepts. Although this approach indirectly deals with the study of the development of the "I," here again the "I" is studied through the "Me." Although information processing and self-regulating motives are assumed, the emphasis of the study is on the observable or phenotypical manifestations of such processes and motives as they appear in the organization of the self-system in a familiar setting and at different ages.

According to the model described earlier, the development of differentiation and integration between one's own and perceived real self-concepts and possible selves, discrepancies, and the validity of the self-concepts within the self-system is considered by means of an examination of the interrelationships among several intra- and interindividual self-concepts. In chapters 2 to 7, the empirical examination is described with respect to the development of these relationships in childhood and adolescence. For a more appropriate understanding of these chapters, some relevant conceptions that appeared in the present chapter are summarized in Table 1.1. In chapter 2 the design, the children that participated, and the procedure in the present study are discussed. Data with respect to the reliability of the procedure used in this study are presented in chapter 3. In chapters 4 to 7, various issues discussed in chapter 1 and relevant to the development of the structural characteristics of the self-system are detailed and studied. In chapter 4, the findings dealing with the development of differentiation between self-concepts within the self-system is presented. The development of the validity of the self-system is discussed in chapter 5. If a

TABLE 1.1

Definitions of some Basic Conceptions in the Present Volume

Basic Concept	Definition
Self-system	The conglomeration of self-knowledge as a whole, whose organization and functions were described in the present chapter (i.e., chapter 1)
Self-concept	A domain-related concept within the self-system, such as the real or the ideal self-concept, considered from either the individual's own perspective or the perceived perspective of others
Self-descriptions	Characteristics that are used to describe the self and that are thought to be related to a particular self-concept. Self-descriptions refer to the content of self-concepts
Distance or difference	The absolute measure of distance between self-concepts or self-descriptions without any specific interpretation of that relation
Differentiation	The difference between intraindividual self-concepts or self-descriptions expressed by distances and interpreted in terms of cognitive development
Discrepancy	The difference between intraindividual self-concepts or self-descriptions in terms of contradictions and expressed by distances which exceed particular criteria
Own self-concepts	Intraindividual self-concepts perceived from children's own perspective, that is, how children describe themselves or their ideals
Perceived self-concepts	Intraindividual self-concepts perceived from the perspective of others, that is, how children think that others perceive them or would like them to be
Actual concepts	The actual concepts, ideas, or expectancies of others about the children, that is, how others (e.g., the parents) really perceive (their) children and how they really would like the children to be

differentiation between self-concepts exceeds a particular criterion, it will have become a discrepancy. The development of such discrepancies within the self-system is presented in chapter 6. The assumption that a relationship exists between discrepancies within the self-system and affect is studied in chapter 7.

Although the research questions taken up in the separate chapters are derived in relation to the model presented in chapter 1, each chapter can be read as an independent research report. In chapter 8, an integration of the findings in the aforegoing chapters is presented. In this chapter, the model presented in chapter 1 becomes central and functions as the organizational principle for the self-system and the discussion of the findings. In the final chapter, also the implications of the study as a whole for the understanding of the development of the self-system will be discussed. Hence, whereas chapters 4 to 7 can be read as independent studies, chapters 1 and 8 offer the broader theoretical framework for and theoretical consequences of these studies, respectively.

2 Method

The purpose of the present study is to examine the dynamics of the self-system in childhood and adolescence according to its temporal, phenotypical structural organization. In chapter 1, several structural characteristics that reflect the organization of the self-system were described. These characteristics were complexity, clearness, internal consistency, and validity. Of these characteristics, *clearness* was considered to apply to self-descriptions within self-concepts as well as to the self-concepts themselves. *Clearness of self-descriptions* was thought to be present if the self-descriptions were well defined. *Clearness of self-concepts* was thought to be present if the self-concepts were clearly differentiated. Clear self-descriptions were expected to facilitate differentiation between the self-concepts. *Internal consistency* of the self-system was described as a special type of clearness that involves not only differentiation but also absence of incompatibilities or discrepancies within the self-system. With regard to consistency between concepts, two types of internal inconsistency were distinguished: discrepancies between real and possible selves; and discrepancies in terms of distinctness, that is, between one's own and one's self-concepts as perceived by others. *Validity* of the self-concepts involves the predictability of behavior and the fit or congruence between the intraindividual self-concepts and the actual concepts of others about the individual. In addition to these structural characteristics, the features of the self-descriptions such as abstractness, personal relevance, and positivity that influence the function of the structural characteristics were taken into account. A model was presented in which the structural characteristics, clearness (in terms of differentiation and integration), internal consistency, and fit were defined by different forms of interrelations between intra- and interindividual self-concepts. In the present chapter the way in which these characteristics are assessed in the self-system with children and adolescents at several ages and moments is discussed.

CHOICE OF VARIABLES

The self-system involves a structure and content that can hardly be measured in its totality because of its extended nature and because it is never entirely present in consciousness; that is, at each particular moment only the salient, working part is assessable (cf. Markus & Wurf, 1987). Consequently, only a limited number of self-concepts and a limited number of self-descriptions within each of these self-concepts will be studied. For this purpose, the complexity of the self-system was limited to an examination of its extensiveness, and only the relationships between the remaining self-concepts and their descriptions were examined (see Fig. 1.1, chapter 1). In total, 14 self-concepts were included in this study. These were: one's own real and ideal self-concept; one's real and ideal self-concepts as perceived by both parents and the best male and female friend; and the real ideas and expectancies (i.e., ideal concepts) of both parents about their children. The ideal self-concept was chosen in addition to the real self-concept because it is the most well-known possible self (see chapter 1). Parents and peers were selected as "others" because of their role as significant others and because of differences in cognitive complexity. Whereas the significance of the other persons has been credited with influence on the self-system of the child (e.g., McGuire & McGuire, 1982; Rosenberg, 1979), the cognitive complexity of the other person is said to affect the ease by which the ideas of others are inferred (e.g., Chandler & Boyes, 1982). The cognitive complexity of persons increases with age; that is, parents are considered to possess a higher cognitive complexity than peers. The difficulty to infer the ideas of a cognitive complex other is, again, moderated by the degree to which a person is known and liked by the subject. Studies dealing with person perception have shown that these variables (i.e., age, familiarity, and likeability of the target person) influence the perception of a person (e.g., Livesley & Bromley, 1973; Peevers & Secord, 1973; Scarlett et al., 1971; see also Shantz, 1983). According to Livesley and Bromley, the perception of a person is also affected by the gender of the target person, with boys being described in more psychological terms than girls. Because of these influences on the perception of a person, it is likely that the perceived concepts of others are also affected by these variables. The choice of parents and peers as significant others covers a systematic variation of age and gender and permits the control of these variables. Because these persons are expected to be familiar and liked, the latter variables are kept approximately constant (see chapter 3). The parents were approached to offer their actual real ideas about and their expectations toward their children because of their significance and because they were most acquainted with the children. For methodological reasons, described below, the number of self-descriptions within each of the intraindividual and environmental concepts was fixed at nine. To be of use, the instrument selected should offer insights into the relationships among the various self-concepts and reflect clearness, internal consistency, and validity (i.e., fit) of the self-system. In addition, it should take into account the personal relevance, level of abstractness, clearness, and evaluation of the self-descriptions within the self-concepts.

CHOICE OF INSTRUMENT

The most obvious way to assess self-concepts is by self-report (e.g., Burns, 1979). An extensive overview of the instruments that have been used to obtain such self-reports has been provided by Burns (1979). Within the range of possible instruments a distinction can be made between fixed questionnaires and open-ended techniques, such as free self-descriptions or the Repertory Grid technique (e.g., Burns, 1979; Jackson, 1987; McGuire & McGuire, 1988; Salmon, 1976). Self-concept questionnaires have the advantage of standardization and ease of comparability between participants and studies. In addition, they can be easily administered in groups and can be scored quickly and easily by the respondents as well as the experimenter. An important disadvantage of questionnaires, however, is their restricted range of applicability. This disadvantage is twofold. First, their fixed character limits questionnaires to a particular age-range. Appropriate questionnaires for adolescents may be too difficult for younger children. Conversely, questionnaires that are appropriate for younger children can be considered dull and childish to adolescents. Separate questionnaires for children and adolescents on the other hand may hamper the comparability between age-groups. Second, questionnaires are designed according to general norms or according to what the designer considers to be important descriptions in the self-concept of the subject. Such descriptions, however, may be of little personal relevance to the subject, thus producing meaningless results (e.g., Benesch & Page, 1989; McGuire & McGuire, 1988).

Free self-descriptions, either written or recorded, are appropriate for all age-groups, and are generally thought to result in personal relevant self-descriptions. However, the processing of free descriptive data not only requires a considerable effort, but, moreover, depends to a large extent on the subjective interpretations of the experimenter.

The Repertory Grid technique, a method designed by Kelly (1955/1963; for an excellent introduction see Fransella & Bannister, 1977), combines the advantages of the free description method with the scoreability of the questionnaires (Jackson, 1987; Salmon, 1976). A Repertory Grid procedure consists of the scoring of several objects (elements) on a number of descriptive dimensions (constructs). The applicability of each description to each object is noted in a matrix (Grid). In the original design of the Grid (Kelly), several roles of persons, such as the father, mother, spouse, a liked other, a disliked other, and so on, are scored according to several descriptive characteristics individually obtained from each person. These descriptive characteristics are obtained from the individual by means of triadic comparisons. That is, several combinations of three role-persons each are made and the subject is asked to indicate in which way two of these persons are similar but different from the third person. The particular way in which two persons are described to be similar but differ from a third person (along with its opposite) is used to define a descriptive continuum. The roles (elements) are listed along the horizontal axis of the matrix, the descriptions (constructs) as generated by each subject are listed along the left side, vertical axis of the matrix, the opposites of the descriptions along the right side, vertical axis, and the applicability of either the description or its opposite for each role-person is indicated in the corresponding cell of the matrix (e.g., Fransella & Bannister, 1977).

The Repertory Grid technique has been successfully used with 5-year-old children (Salmon, 1976), as well as with adults. Because it offers the possibility of having individuals themselves generate the dimensions to be employed in their own self-descriptions, the technique gives some guarantee that the information obtained not only reveals self-descriptions that are personally meaningful to each subject, but also appropriate for the descriptive abilities of each child. In addition, because the children themselves have to score the applicability of each description for each element (i.e., the relevant target person), the subjective interpretation of the self-descriptions by the experimenter is avoided. Therefore, a Repertory Grid procedure was used as the main instrument in this study. In addition to using the Repertory Grid procedure, some related questions were added that had to be rated on a Likert-scale (see below).

THE REPERTORY GRID

In the Repertory Grid technique, matrices (grids) of all sizes can be used. In the original design by Kelly (1955), 24 different elements (i.e., roles or entities that have to be described) are suggested (Fransella & Bannister, 1977). In addition, it is not uncommon to have 15 to 20 constructs (i.e., descriptive dimensions; Slater, 1977). However, a grid with, for example, 24 elements and 15 constructs requires that 24 objects are scored on 15 dimensions, resulting in 360 scores, making this a rather taxing task for the subjects. The use of a grid implies that the addition of one element or construct results in the addition of a considerable number of scores. For instance, the addition of one element to a 10 x 10 Grid matrix results in the addition of 10 extra scores for the applicability of the 10 descriptive dimensions on this element. A 10 x 10 matrix will evoke enough scores to determine relationships between the elements (Slater, 1977). In addition, Slater, as well as Easterby-Smith (1981), pointed to the need to keep the Grid (i.e., the scoring-matrix) small, advice that is especially applicable to the use of the Grid with children.

The present Grid consists of 10 elements: one's own real self-concept; the perceived real self-concept of both parents and a male and female peer; one's own ideal self-concept; and the perceived ideal self-concepts of both parents and a male and female peer. For statistical reasons, Slater recommended an *n* (collumns) x *n-1* (rows) Grid. When the target elements are described on fewer dimensions than there are elements, the result is that the distances between the elements become statistically interdependent, which is advantageous for correlational analyses. Although such analyses are not used in the present study (see later), they are often used in similar studies with the Repertory Grid, as well as in studies dealing with the relationships between self-concepts. Consequently, the present grid consists of a 10 x 9 matrix, with 10 elements (the self-concepts) and nine constructs (the descriptive dimensions).

For the reasons mentioned above (i.e., age-appropriateness and personal relevance) the constructs (self-descriptions) were obtained from individual children. This is usually done by means of comparing triads, that is, the subject is asked to indicate in which way two elements are similar but differ from a third. However, studies that have employed this method suggest that, because children demonstrated conceptual problems with triads, comparisons by means of dyads are preferable (Fransella & Bannister, 1977; Keen & Bell, 1981; Salmon, 1976). A pilot study involving six 6-year-old children confirmed this assumption. The children were able to mention differences or similarities between two persons but were confused when they were asked to do the same with three persons. Triads formed by *(perceived) self-concepts* of people can be expected to lead to even more problems. Consequently, it was decided to obtain the self-descriptions by comparing dyads consisting of two target persons. In order to stay as close as possible to the original method (i.e., the triads) a similarity and a difference were alternately asked for.

This procedure enabled the attainment of the first condition, requiring that the self-descriptions be personally relevant for the participant. A second and important feature for the Grid technique is that the constructs (i.e., descriptive dimensions) generated are perceived to be relevant to the target elements that are studied; that is, the constructs are applicable to (i.e., lay in the "range of convenience" of) the elements (Fransella & Bannister, 1977; Kelly, 1955/1963). When the self-descriptions are not relevant for the person, or when the descriptions do not relate to the elements that have to be scored, meaningless answers will result. Participants should be able to think meaningfully about the elements in terms of the descriptions. In the Grid that is used in this study each element presents a self-concept. Therefore, the self had to be involved in each dyadic comparison. In addition, when no meaningful relationship between the self-description and the element could be identified despite the inclusion of the self in each dyad, the participants were allowed to indicate this during the testing procedure.

Salmon (1976) suggested that to use the Grid with young children it should be as concrete as possible, by using for instance brightly colored stand-up dolls. The outspoken character of such dolls might, however, affect the answers of the children. Instead, plain, white, abstract paper dolls, whose design was patterned after signs in public buildings, were used to help the elementary school children in representing the elements (i.e., the self, parents, and peers). Because the dolls did not possess any cues with respect to the persons they represent, it was expected that they would elicit little if any bias in the answers of the children when mentioning similarities or differences between the persons. The children were asked to react to the dolls as if they were their parents, peers, and self, respectively. To emphasize this procedure, the actual names of the persons were written on the dolls and the children were allowed to supply the dolls with faces and characteristics of the persons using drawings and painting. Because it seemed inappropriate to present adolescents with these dolls, they were given instead small white cards on which they wrote the appropriate names. The dolls or cards were used to present the dyads as well as to address the (perceived) self-concepts of the self, parents, and peers during the completion of the Grid (see Fig. 2.1).

DESIGN

The development of the relationships between the several intraindividual concepts of the children and the actual ideas of their parents was assessed by a time-sequential model (Schaie, 1965) or longitudinal sequential model (Baltes, Reese, & Nesselroade, 1977). A time-sequential model was preferred to a cross-sectional or longitudinal model because it allows for control for cohort effects and effects of repeated testing (Baltes et al., 1977; Schaie, 1965). The time-sequential experimental design permitted the study of children and adolescents within the age range of 6 to 18 years (elementary school, age 6 to 12, and secondary school, age 12 to 18) over a period of 3 years. During this period children of six age-groups and the parents of these participants were assessed once each year for 3 years. The age-groups differed from each other by approximately 2 years.

SUBJECTS

In total 204 Dutch children participated in the first wave of the study, with 108 pairs of parents participating. The children were divided into six age-groups with mean ages of 6.7, 8.7, 10.8, 12.8, 14.7, and 16.3 years. In the second wave of the study, 167 children and 76 pairs of parents were still available for testing. Mean ages of the children were 7.9, 9.9, 12.0, 13.9, 15.7, and 17.4 years. Finally, by the time of the final testing, 149 children and 59 pairs of parents were available for inclusion. The last sample of children tested included 7 participants who accidently missed the second wave but rejoined the study in the third wave. Differences between participants who dropped out and continued participation are described at their relevant places in the subsequent chapters. The mean ages of the children in the third wave were 8.8, 10.7, 12.7, 14.7, 16.5, and 18.3 years. The number of children by age-group and gender, the mean ages by age-group, and the number of pairs of parents who participated for each wave are shown in Table 2.1.

Most of the children were approached through their schools. All schools were situated in middle to high socioeconomic status neighborhoods. Following the schools' consent for its students participation in the study, letters to the parents requesting permission and cooperation were distributed. Only children who returned a signed permission were included in the study. Drop-outs were sometimes due to practical circumstances such as moving, long illness, or inability to reach a child for a long period of time. Most often, however, it was the children who wished to terminate, because they lacked time or were no longer motivated to continue. Drop-out by the parents was largely due to the time-consuming nature of the task and was often initiated by the fathers. In addition, whereas in the first wave the parents were individually interviewed at their homes or at the schools of their children, in the second and third wave the questionnaires for the parents were sent and returned by mail. The latter procedure undoubtedly contributed to the unwillingness of some parents to continue their participation in the study.

TABLE 2.1

Number of Children by Gender, Number of Pairs of Parents who both Returned
All Questionnaires, and Mean Age of the Children for Wave 1, 2, and 3

		Wave 1		Wave 2		Wave 3	
		n children	n parents	n children	n parents	n children	n parents
Group 1	boys	16		13		11	
	girls	21		21		21	
	total	37	21	34	17	32	13
	mean age	6.7		7.9		8.8	
Group 2	boys	15		11		10	
	girls	29		26		25	
	total	44	20	37	16	35	13
	mean age	8.7		9.9		10.7	
Group 3	boys	20		11		16	
	girls	16		8		10	
	total	36	17	19	6	26	8
	mean age	10.8		12.0		12.7	
Group 4	boys	14		13		10	
	girls	13		12		10	
	total	27	16	25	15	20	13
	mean age	12.8		13.9		14.7	
Group 5	boys	14		12		10	
	girls	20		19		11	
	total	34	16	31	12	21	6
	mean age	14.7		15.7		16.5	
Group 6	boys	9		5		2	
	girls	16		16		13	
	total	25	18	21	10	15	6
	mean age	16.3		17.4		18.3	

PROCEDURE

Each child was individually interviewed by means of the above Repertory Grid
procedure. In total nine descriptive statements were solicited in this method.
The children were asked to name personally relevant similarities as well as
differences when comparing themselves with each of the four significant others
(i.e., both parents or caretakers and a male and female friend). If possible, they
also gave opposites of the given self-descriptions to permit the construction of
continua. The similarities and differences were noted on the left side and their
opposites on the right side of the grid. In order to get nine self-descriptions, one
extra comparison (either a similarity or a difference) was made with respect to
the peer of the same gender, because this peer was considered to be the easiest

target person. For instance, responses on the comparisons could be that the child and his friend are both good "soccer" players, whereas he and his father both play "chess."

The Repertory Grid itself consisted of descriptive statements in which the 9 self-descriptions (i.e., contents) obtained were related to the 10 intraindividual self-concepts (i.e., elements), that is: for the real self-concept (S) one element; for the perceived real self-concept of others (O) four elements (i.e., both parents, a friend of the same, and a friend of the other gender); for the ideal self-concept (S') one element, and for the perceived ideal self-concept of others (O') four elements again. This resulted in a total of 90 statements. For instance, the following statements were formulated with respect to the self-description "playing chess":

The real self-concept (S):	"You play chess well."
The ideal self-concept (S'):	"You would like to play chess well."
The perceived real concept of self by others (O):	"Your mother thinks that you play chess well," or "John thinks that you play chess well."
The perceived ideal concept of self by others (O'):	"Your mother would like you to play chess well," or "Mary would like you to play chess well."

The descriptive statements had to be rated or scored on a 5-point scale (i.e., from 1 to 5) in terms of their correctness. When children decided that a particular self-description was not applicable ("convenient") with respect to a particular self-concept element, they could score a zero. To establish the test–retest reliability of this procedure each child was asked to provide ratings of two of the self-concept elements twice. The retested self-concept elements were varied systematically among the children. Fig. 2.1 shows an example of the Repertory Grid as it was used in the present study. The self-descriptions were offered by a 9-year-old boy.

For each descriptive statement offered by their child the parents or caretakers were required to score the relevance of these descriptions to their child from their own perspective (RO: "Your child plays chess well") and their expectations of their child with respect to these descriptions (RO': "You would like your child to play chess well"). Whereas the scores on the elements in the Repertory Grid of the children allowed for the examination of the relationships between the intraindividual self-concepts, the additional scores of the parents on the same

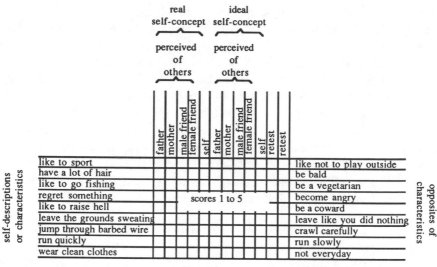

FIG. 2.1. An example of the Repertory Grid matrix used in the present study. The self-descriptions are those of a 9-year-old boy.

descriptions made it possible to assess the degree of fit between the intraindividual self-concepts of the child and the actual views of the parents.

In addition to the Repertory Grid procedure, some additional information was obtained to assess the characteristics of the self-descriptions and to control the familiarity and likeability of the other persons (i.e., the parents or caretakers and peers). First, the children were asked to define each self-descriptor more elaborately. These were the same descriptors they had used to indicate similarities and differences between themselves and the four others and that they had used to rate their self-concept. Although the opposite of each description already offered some impression about the meaning of the descriptions, these more extended explanations allowed the evaluation of how well defined or clear the self-descriptions were for the child. Second, the children were required to compare each of one's own descriptive statements as well as their opposites with all the other descriptive statements. Through this comparison it was possible to obtain the children's evaluations of the degree to which these statements were positively related or contradictory. This comparison was again made by means of a 5-point Likert-scale (i.e., from totally incompatible [1] to totally compatible [5]). The obtained compatibility scores were recorded in a 18 x 18 matrix. Further, the children had to score each descriptive statement and its opposite for its personal relevance (i.e., importance) by means of a 5-point Likert-scale. A score of 1 indicated that the self-description was perceived as marginally relevant; a score of 5 indicated that the self-description was very relevant. Finally, the children indicated how well they knew and how much they liked their father, mother, male friend, female friend and self. Again, the answers on these question were scored on a 5-point Likert-scale from not at all (1) to very well/much (5).

As distinct from the attempts outlined earlier to secure additional definitions of the self-descriptions and information regarding their personal relevance, no follow up questions were asked concerning the abstractness or positivity of the self-descriptions. The definitions were required to assess the clearness of the self-descriptions within the self-concepts and to indicate the credibility of the clearness between the self-concepts in terms of differentiation. That is, the obtained differentiation scores are more meaningful if the child is clear about the self-descriptions that are involved in such a differentiation. One method of assessing the degree of clearness in the self-descriptions is by means of qualitative analysis of the definitions. In general, the present procedure, based on the elicitation of idiosyncratic self-descriptions, facilitates securing personal relevant descriptions. Nevertheless, an extra check seemed desirable because the personal relevance of the self-descriptions was considered essential (for the application of this check, see chapter 6). In contrast, the positiveness of the self-descriptions was not explicitly considered an important characteristic, because the relationships between the self-concepts implicitly reveal information about the desirability, that is, personal positivity, of the self-descriptions (Moretti & Higgins, 1990). Experimenter ratings on positivity do not so much reflect children's individual evaluations of the self-descriptions as they indicate the social desirability of the descriptions. Personal positivity of a self-description, however, results from an evaluation from the perspective of the ideal self-concept. Finally, abstractness was not assessed directly because it could be obtained by means of a qualitative analysis of the elicited self-descriptions. To determine the clearness and abstractness of the self-descriptions by means of qualitative analyses is thought to be less hazardous than to determine the positivity of the self-descriptions. The qualitative analyses will be less biased by social desirability than subjective ratings of positiveness.

To study the relationship between discrepancies between and within self-concepts and emotional functioning (see chapter 1), following the Repertory Grid and its additional measures, the *Amsterdamse Biografische Vragenlijst voor Kinderen* (i.e., Amsterdam Biographical Questionnaire for Children [ABV-K]; Van Dijl & Wilde, 1982) was administered to all children in the last wave. The ABV-K is a Dutch questionnaire on emotional instability for children and adolescents from 9 to 17 years old. The questionnaire includes a scale for neuroticism expressed by psycho-neurotic complaints (N), a scale for neuroticism expressed by physical complaints (NS), an extraversion scale (E) related to social competence, and a scale for test-attitude (T). The ABV-K consists of 115 precoded items with the response possibilities "yes" and "no." This questionnaire was included to assess the influence of the organization of the self-system on the emotional functioning of the children.

PRELIMINARY ANALYSES

Based on the Repertory Grid detailed above, nine applicability ratings for each self-concept were present (i.e., one's own and perceived real and ideal self-concepts and the actual ideas of the parents), that is, one for each of the nine descriptions obtained by the dyadic comparisons. These ratings concern the applicability of each self-description to each self-concept. To compute the relationship, that is, distance, between two self-concepts, difference scores were calculated. In previous research dealing with the relationships between self-concepts within the self-system, correlations were most often used. A high positive correlation was interpreted as showing little differentiation between the self-concepts; a negative correlation as the presence of discrepancies between the self-concepts; and the absence of any correlation as the lack of any relationship. However, such correlations are only meaningful if the mean scores for each of the self-concepts are approximately identical and if the scores show enough variance (Benesch & Page, 1989; Van der Werff, 1985). That is, a high correlation can also occur if the self-concepts show an equal pattern of scores, although the actual scores differ in absolute magnitude. In turn, when the scores do not differ at all because all scores for both self-concepts are identical, the resulting lack of variance will prevent the computation of a reliable correlation score. Difference scores do not have these limits. On the contrary, they allow a direct insight into the distances between the self-concepts (Van der Werff).

To compute the difference scores, the absolute differences between the two self-concept elements involved in the comparison were calculated for each of the nine self-descriptions separately. The absolute differences were averaged across descriptions, resulting in a mean differentiation score. The differentiation scores were computed for 23 comparisons and reflect the clearness between the intraindividual and the fit between the interpersonal self-concepts:

$S \times S'$ the children's real ideas about themselves (S) versus their
          ideas about how they would like to be (S').

S x *O*   the children's real ideas about themselves (*S*) versus their ideas about how others think about them (*O*; i.e., with respect to their parents and their friends separately: four comparisons).

S x *RO*   the children's real ideas about themselves (*S*) versus their parents' real ideas about the child (*RO*, with respect to both parents separately: two comparisons).

S' x *O'*   the children's ideas about how they would like themselves to be (*S'*) versus the children's ideas about how others would like them to be (*O'*, with respect to their parents and their friends: four comparisons).

S' x *RO'*   the children's ideas about how they would like themselves to be (*S'*) versus the parents' ideas about how they would like their child to be (*RO'*, with respect to both parents: two comparisons).

O x *O'*   the children's ideas about how others think about them (*O*) versus their ideas about how others would like them to be (*O'*: four comparisons).

O x *RO*   the children's ideas about how others think about them (*O*) versus the parents or caretakers' real ideas about their child (*RO*: two comparisons).

O' x *RO'*   the children's ideas about how others would like them to be (*O'*) versus the parents' ideas about how they would like their child to be (*RO'*: two comparisons).

RO x *RO'*   the parents' real ideas about their child (*RO*) versus their ideas about how they would like their child to be (*RO'*: two comparisons).

A test–retest score was obtained by comparing the applicability score for the two retested self-concepts with their original. The raw scores for the ABV-K were transformed into percentile scores according to the norms of the ABV-K for age and gender.

CONCLUSION

In sum, the purpose of the present study was to examine the development of the relationships between intra and interindividual self-concepts in children and adolescents over an age-period of 6 to 18 years in a time-sequential design. Included were the participants' own real self-concept, their own ideal self-concept, the perceived real self-concepts of both parents and a male and female friend, the perceived ideal self-concepts of both parents and both peers, and the actual real and ideal concepts of the parents about their child. These concepts were assessed by means of a Repertory Grid procedure, which allowed the use of elicited, idiosyncratic self-descriptions within the self-concepts. The self-descriptions were controlled for personal relevance, clearness, and abstractness. The relationships between the concepts were computed through difference scores. In addition, the ABV-K, a Dutch questionnaire to measure emotional (in)stability, was administered in the third year of the study to assess the influence of the relationships between the self-concepts on the emotional functioning of children and adolescents.

3 Reliability and Related Data

In chapter 2, the Repertory Grid procedure was described by means of which the relations between children's own real and ideal self-concepts, their perceived real and ideal self-concepts of their parents and two peers, and the actual real and ideal concepts of the parents were assessed to indicate the clearness, internal consistency, and fit of the self-system. In this procedure, several additional control measurements were included. These control measurements were meant to indicate the degree of likeability and familiarity of the others from whom the perceived self-concepts were obtained, that is, the parents and peers, as well as the level of abstractness and clearness of the self-descriptions, and to examine the development of these variables. In this chapter, the results from the first wave of this study are presented. Prior to this presentation, the reliability of the data from the Repertory Grid itself, assessed by the test–retest scores, is considered for the whole study and for the participants who dropped out of the study separately.

RELIABILITY OF THE GRID-SCORES

The relationships between the several self-concepts employed in this study were operationalized as difference scores between the elements in the Repertory Grid, that is, the self-concepts. Such differences, however, may be coincidental if a respondent is uncertain or uncareful about an answer. Ideally, the results for two identical questions should result in no differences. Although the individual and careful administration of the Repertory Grid was supposed to minimize careless reponding, the retest scores were introduced in the procedure as a check for the reliability. Each child had to rescore two self-concepts on each of the descriptive dimensions. A difference score of zero between the scores from the first and second administration of the self-concept would indicate perfect reliability of the scores at the time of testing. A difference score higher than zero

TABLE 3.1

Mean Test -- Retest Scores with Standard Deviations by
Age-Group for the Three Assessment Waves

Age-group	Wave 1		Wave 2		Wave 3	
	mean	sd	mean	sd	mean	sd
Group 1	.479	.274	.446	.261	.332	.270
Group 2	.388	.264	.271	.218	.137	.156
Group 3	.300	.244	.225	.188	.165	.200
Group 4	.316	.273	.208	.192	.162	.181
Group 5	.199	.163	.224	.212	.206	.138
Group 6	.304	.211	.191	.148	.176	.125

would indicate a somewhat lower reliability. As can be inferred from Table 3.1, the latter was the case. The test–retest difference scores were analyzed for effectof age, and the reliability of the difference scores was calculated by Cohen's Kappa, correcting for chance (Cohen, 1960).

In order to asses age-effects in the reliability of the grid-scores, the absolute differences between the retest scores and the matching test scores were calculated and averaged for each child. An ANOVA, with repeated measurements, age and wave as factors, and the differences as dependent measure showed a main effect for age-group [$F_{(5,126)} = 7.38$, $p < .0001$] as well as for wave [$F_{(2,126)} = 16.90$, $p < .0001$]. The differences between the test and retest scores (henceforth test–retest scores) decreased with age, especially between the ages of 6 and 10 years. In addition, the test–retest scores became smaller in each subsequent wave (see Table 3.1). In Fig. 3.1 the mean test–retest score by age-group for each wave are schematically presented.

Cohen's Kappa (1960) between the test and retest scores was calculated to asses reliability. This was done by age-group and wave due to the effects mentioned above. Cohen's Kappa ranged from .62 to .79 in Wave 1, from .65 to .78 in Wave 2 and from .66 to .83 in Wave 3, indicating sufficient to satisfactory reliability (Cohen, 1960).

Consequently, it can be concluded that, although the test–retest scores did not equal zero and the reliability of the Grid-scores increased during childhood, an adequate reliability for the Repertory Grid, as used in this study, is present for all the age groups studied.

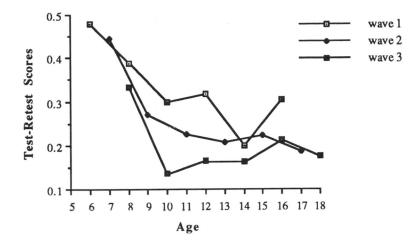

FIG. 3.1. Mean test-retest scores by age-group for the three assessment waves.

THE EFFECT OF DROP-OUTS

Thirty-seven participants dropped out between the first and second assessment, with an additional 18 dropping out between the second and third assessment. Any loss of participants may affect the outcomes of the study and bias the sample, which could reduce the generalizability of the findings. Separate ANOVAs, with the test–retest scores as the dependent measure and the drop-outs and remaining subjects as factors revealed a significant effect for drop-out in both wave transitions [$F_{(1,187)} = 7.50$, $p < .01$ and $F_{(1,163)} = 4.37$, $p < .05$, respectively]. The children who dropped out scored significantly lower on the test–retest measurement; that is, they appeared to be more certain and serious about their answers as compared to the children who continued their participation in the study. If this assumption is valid then the differentiation scores for these children should also be higher than for the children who continued their participation in the study (see chapter 4). Consequently, it is, with proper caution, assumed that the data on which the subsequent analyses are made were obtained from children who seem to be less certain or serious about their knowledge about themselves.

SOMETHING ABOUT THE "OTHERS"

Person perception is influenced by the degree to which that person is known and liked (e.g., Livesley & Bromley, 1973). In the present study in addition to the self, four significant others were used. As a consequence, it is likely that most respondents knew and generally liked these persons well. This was verified by two Likert-scales, on which the subjects had to rate how well they knew and how much they liked their parents, peers, and selves. The Likert-scales ranged from not at all (score 1) to very much (score 5). With the exception of a few cases, all children were able to mention two parents or caretakers and a male and female friend, and to rate them and themselves. The few exceptions were children from divorced parents, who refused to include the parent they had not seen for years and for whom no substitute caretaker was present and a single child who refused to mention a peer of the opposite gender. An ANOVA with repeated measurements on all the rating scores revealed significant effects for age-group [$F_{(5,139)} = 12.47$, $p < .0001$], person [$F_{(4,556)} = 7.47$, $p < .0001$], age by person [$F_{(20,556)} = 13.39$, $p < .0001$], and age by person by knowing versus liking [$F_{(20,556)} = 3.96$, $p < .0001$]. By means of contrast analyses a decrease in the rating scores from the first to the fourth age-group could be demonstrated [$F_{(1)} = 41.07$, $p < .0001$]. The rating scores for the parents and the self were approximately identical and significantly higher than for the peers, especially the male friend. The rating scores for the parents and the self tended to decrease more with age than for the peers and to decrease more for familiarity than for likeability. Nevertheless, the lowest mean score still exceeded the 3.8 level. For gender, the only significant interaction effect was with wave and person [$F_{(8,1112)} = 2.30$, $p < 05$]. For the girls in the second wave the familiarity with their male friends was lower than for the boys. For the boys the familiarity with their female friends was lower than for the girls. As indicated above, this result was found for all ages. In addition, the lowest mean rating score was 3.5, indicating that the opposite-gender friend was still known and liked at an above "average" level (i.e., score 3).

In conclusion, the children indicated that they know and like their parents, friends, and themselves at an above average level. The parents and the self were known and liked somewhat better than the friends. With increasing age, though, the children seem to become increasingly aware of the relativity of the likeability of, and familiarity (i.e., knowledge about) of their parents and themselves, in particular. That is, frequent or lengthy interactions as an index for familiarity seemed no longer to be interpreted as meaning that the interaction partner was really very well known. Similarly, the children became aware that knowing somebody closely does not imply that this person is also automaticaly liked. In addition, there were some indications showing that the children, as well as adolescents, were less close to their opposite-gender friend than to their same-gender friend.

THE CIRCLES AS BALLS:
THE ABSTRACTNESS AND CLEARNESS
OF THE DESCRIPTIVE DIMENSIONS

Abstractness of Self-Descriptions

In chapter 2, it was argued that the descriptive dimensions that were used in the Repertory Grid procedure should be obtained from the children themselves to assure the personal relevance and age-appropriateness of the dimensions. The descriptive dimensions were elicited by dyadic comparisons between the children and their parents and peers. It was also argued that these descriptive dimensions should be rated for their level of abstractness, because the abstractness of the descriptive dimensions might influence the organization of the self-system.

Within the age-range studied (i.e., from 6 to 18 years), a shift from more concrete to more abstract descriptive dimensions is expected (e.g., Damon & Hart, 1982; Oppenheimer et al., 1990). This shift in abstraction may influence the relationship between the self-concepts, independent of the ability to differentiate. Hence, it could be expected that the more concrete the descriptive dimension (e.g., "I have blond hair and blue eyes"), the more unambiguous its applicability would be to the elements. For the more abstract and consequently more ambiguous descriptive dimensions the answer is less clear (e.g., "I am smart" or "I am popular"). For instance, if a child mentions the descriptive dimension Boy versus Girl, no differentiation between one's own real concept and the perceived real concepts of others on this dimension will be present. If, however, the dimension Intelligent versus Stupid is offered, considerably more varied interpretations could be possible. This possible influence of the descriptions on the relationship between the concepts was assessed by a content analysis on the present data (Noom, 1989) and an additional study by Van de Poel (1990).

According to Oppenheimer et al. (1990), the shift from concrete to abstract self-definitions or descriptive dimensions can be perceived as a shift from material and physical descriptions to descriptions based on activities and competencies, psychological, and social-relational characteristics, respectively. Two independent raters categorized the descriptions used in the first wave of the present study according to these four categories. The Cohen's Kappa reliability

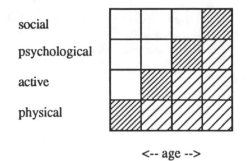

FIG. 3.2. A schematic representation of the development in
the use of categories. Age increases from the left to the right.

between the raters was .71. Incongruent scores were reconsidered in
consultation. On the basis of these scores a modal score for each child was
determined to permit loglinear analyses of the data (for a more extensive
description see Noom, 1989). Chi-square tests revealed a significant association
between the use of categories and age [$\chi^2(20) = 504.46$, $p < .001$ for the raw
scores; $\chi^2(15) = 117.60$, $p < .001$ for the modal scores]. The most parsimonious
model for the modal scores in the loglinear analysis (Green, 1988) was the
saturated linear model represented by AGE + CATEGORY + AGE * CATEGORY
($\chi^2(15) = 117.60$, $p < .001$). A prediction analysis was used to compare a
divergent against a synchronic developmental model (Wohlwill, 1973). A
synchronic developmental model predicts development to occur along the
diagonal of an age by category matrix. At any one period in development only
one particular category of descriptions is used. A divergent developmental
model predicts not only a progression along the diagonal of the matrix but also
an increase in the simultaneous use of different categories (Fig. 3.2). The results
of the prediction analyses indicated that the association between age and category
was slightly better represented by a synchronic than by a divergent model:

raw scores

divergent model: $Vp = .27$ ($z = 11.67$; $p < .001$) $Prec = .34$
convergent model: $Vp = .33$ ($z = 18.05$; $p < .001$) $Prec = .49$

modal scores

divergent model: $Vp = .39$ ($z = 5.99$; $p < .001$) $Prec = .34$
convergent model: $Vp = .45$ ($z = 9.32$; $p < .001$) $Prec = .49$

In sum, these data corroborated previous results showing an increase in the
level of abstractness of self-descriptions with progressive age. With increasing
age new and more abstract categories were used. However, although the

emphasis was on development along the diagonal of this descriptive matrix, representing the new categories, an increase in the simultaneous use of different categories was also observed.

Van de Poel (1990) administered the Repertory Grid to 40 first-year psychology students to test whether the level of abstraction of the categories affect the degree of differentiation. It was expected that abstract categories might result in more differentiation between real and ideal self-concepts than concrete categories. Twenty students scored the Grid according to the five most common descriptions of each category in the first wave of the main study. Twenty students mentioned their own descriptions for each category. Thus, each student completed a Repertory Grid, representing one's own and perceived real and ideal concepts, according to 25 descriptions, equally divided over the physical, active, psychological, and social category. Because of their age, the students were expected to be able to handle all categories. One-way ANOVAs, with the five categories as factors and the differentiations scores as dependent measure were done to examine the presence of any effect for category on the differentiation scores for the parents and the peers separately. These analyses demonstrated significant effects for category on the differentiation score for parents [i.e., $F_{(4,30)} = 5.24$, $p < .005$ for the same-gender parent and $F_{(4,32)} = 5.11$, $p < .005$ for the opposite-gender parent]. This effect was found for the preselected, as well as for one's own descriptions. No significant effect was found for peers. Contrast analysis on the data obtained with respect to parents showed that, whereas active and psychological descriptions resulted in identical levels of differentiation, physical as well as social descriptions resulted in a significantly lower level of differentiation. In addition, when one's own descriptive dimensions were used, they were rated higher in personal relevance than when the preselected dimensions were used [$F_{(4,34)} = 8.36$, $p < .0001$].

In sum, with increasing age, children use more abstract and also more varied categories of descriptions. The categories affect the relationship between the concepts but not because of their level of abstraction. Whereas the data showed that the descriptive dimensions affect differentiation between the perceived real and ideal concepts of the parents, this effect was larger for the middle categories (i.e., descriptions in terms of activities and psychological traits) than for the lowest and highest categories (i.e., descriptions in terms of physical features and social traits). If this effect had been due to the level of abstraction, a linear increase for differentiation from the physical to the social descriptions should have been observed. In addition, no effects for category on the differentiation between the perceived real and ideal concepts of the peers could be demonstrated. Consequently, it appears that the descriptive dimensions affect differentiation in a more subtle way. Whereas physical characteristics of children are predominantly related to the parents, social characteristics are features not only of the children but also of their environment. As Van de Poel (1990) remarked, parents may comment more on activities and psychological traits of their children because these may be changed and are within the control of children. It is obviously much more problematic to insist on a change in children's physical appearance, such as being small, or to demand from children that they find more friends if they are actually rejected or neglected by their peers. In contrast, it is much easier to comment on the loudness of music, the roughness of a game, or the desirability of a sport or some other interest. Many children are also regularly ordered to clean their room or do their homework. Parents may consider it desirable and realistic to criticize activities and psychological traits of their children, in particular, but unfair to criticize physical appearance and social characteristics. Consequently, children may experience a larger differentiation between self-descriptions based on active and psychological than on physical and social characteristics, because their parents act toward their children in this way.

Clearness of Self-Descriptions

In chapter 1, we described how the clearness of self-descriptions is related to self-esteem (Baumgardner, 1990; Campbell, 1990) and the degree to which people resist information that is inconsistent with the content of their self-concept (Chaiken & Baldwin, 1981; Markus, 1977). Based on the former relationships, it was expected that self-concepts that consist of well-defined self-descriptions are more easily differentiated than self-concepts that include less well-defined self-descriptions. If the self-descriptions themselves are vague and ambiguous for the individual, it will be hard to tell exactly how they differ from each other. Although little is known about the development of clearness for the definitions of self-descriptions, some possibilities can be generated. For instance, it might be that concrete self-descriptions are easier to define than abstract self-descriptions. Because the level of abstractness for self-descriptions was found to develop with age, younger children may define their self-descriptions more clearly (i.e., in more concrete concepts) than older children. On the other hand, older and more experienced children may be more articulate about who and what they are than younger and less experienced children. By analyzing the definitions of the self-descriptions, the effects for age on the clearness of the self-descriptions can be explored.

A self-description is considered here to be well comprehended by children if they are able to explain what the self-description implies for them. That is, if a

TABLE 3.2

Categories and Matching Scores for Clearness
of Definition of Self-Description

Description	score
"I don't know," or no response	1
synonyms and/or repetitions and/or very obvious implications	2
different synonyms, or one example, implication, or generalization	3
more than one example, implication, or generalization; or one elaborate example, implication, or generalization; or a combination of examples, implications, or generalizations	4
more than one elaborate example, implication, or generalization; or the explicit reflection, for instance, on the origin, desirability, or consequences of the self-description	5

dictionary definition of a description is given, it does not necessarily imply that the children are aware of its meaning in terms of its consequences for their being as defined by the specific self-description. However, if implications, consequences, and associations are given, it is assumed that the self-description is meaningful for the child. Consequently, the definitions of the self-descriptions were categorized and scored according to the procedure shown in Table 3.2, irrespective of the raters' judge of correctness of the definitions.

Two independent raters were involved in this categorization procedure, one scoring all, and the other 67% of the definitions. Cohen's Kappa (Cohen, 1960) for these double-rated definitions reached .90, indicating a high interrater reliability. An ANOVA revealed no main effect for either age or type of self-description (i.e., category). However, a significant effect was evident for the interaction between both variables [$F_{(40,1584)} = 1.66$, $p < .01$]. ANOVA's with age as factor and the self-descriptions as dependent measure showed that the significant interaction was due to an effect for age on the self-descriptions that indicated a difference with regard to the same-gender parent [$F_{(5,198)} = 2.65$, $p < .05$] and on the self-descriptions that indicated a similarity with respect to the same-gender peer ($F_{(5,198)} = 2.52$, $p < .05$). Contrast analyses revealed that the self-descriptions, indicating a difference between the self and the same-gender parent, became better defined from age 6 to 8 and again from age 12 to 16. The self-descriptions, indicating a similarity between the self and the same-gender peer became better defined from age 6 to 8, followed by a regression back to the level at age 6, and became better defined again from age 12 to age 16 (see Table 3.3).

TABLE 3.3

Means and Standard Deviations for Scores of
Clearness by Age-Group and Self-Description

		Self-Descriptions								
		1	2	3	4	5	6	7	8	9
		pasg	pasg	paog	paog	pesg	pesg	pesg	peog	peog
Age-group		sim.	diff.	sim.	diff.	sim.	diff.	-	sim.	diff.
1	m	2.89	2.95	2.92	3.16	3.08	3.27	3.27	3.49	3.19
	sd	1.02	1.00	.83	1.01	.89	.77	.90	.87	.94
2	m	3.16	3.30	3.34	3.25	3.46	3.14	3.25	3.23	3.25
	sd	.94	.77	.80	.94	.90	.91	.87	.94	.75
3	m	3.39	3.28	3.28	3.36	3.42	3.39	3.42	3.53	3.22
	sd	.69	.70	.74	.64	.60	.73	.60	.61	.90
4	m	3.11	3.07	3.18	3.25	3.07	3.21	2.93	3.21	3.04
	sd	.83	.77	.72	.65	.77	.63	.77	.63	.69
5	m	3.32	3.50	3.27	3.24	3.12	3.18	3.41	3.24	3.35
	sd	.77	.75	.75	.89	.81	.83	.82	.86	.77
6	m	3.44	3.52	3.32	3.32	3.60	3.68	3.20	3.32	3.32
	sd	.77	.71	1.07	.80	.76	.63	.87	.80	.75

Note. pasg: parent, same gender; paog: parent, opposite gender; pesg: peer, same gender; peog: peer, opposite gender; sim.: similarities; diff.: differences.

In conclusion, neither age, nor the way self-descriptions were obtained influenced the clearness by which self-descriptions were defined. Younger children defined their self.descriptions as clearly as did older children, irrespective of procedure by which the self-descriptions were obtained. Even though younger children used more concrete self-descriptions than older children (see earlier), they were able to define these more concrete self-descriptions as well as the older children were able to define the more abstract self-descriptions which they used. That is, if older children were better able to define their self-descriptions than younger children and if concrete self-descriptions were defined more easily than abstract self-descriptions, these effects balanced out each other. Exceptions were found, however, for the self-descriptions that presented differences between the self and the same-gender parent and similarities between the self and the same-gender peer. Both were defined more clearly at age 8 than at age 6. In addition, both types of self-descriptions showed a second definitional refinement from age 12 to 16. The latter refinement was most evident with the self-descriptions indicating differences between the self and the same-gender parent. This process, in which children become increasingly more aware of differences between themselves and their same-gender parent, may reflect the increasing independence of the children from their major "identification parent." The self-descriptions showing similarities between the self and the same-gender peer also showed a second refinement from the base-line between age 12 and 16. That is, following a first refinement (i.e., between 6 and 8 years), children become more aware of similarities between themselves and their same-gender peer during the early years of adolescence (i.e., between the ages of 12 and 16 years). The increasing awareness of similarities between the children themselves and their peers nicely parallels the decreasing identification with the same-gender parent, and suggests a shift in attention or identification from parents to peers. This increasing awareness of similarities between the children themselves and their peers is, however, less consistent. The decrease in clearness for these self-descriptions between the ages of 8 and 12 years, back to the level of clearness evident at the age of 6 years, is likely the result of the presence of interfering processes. Within the Dutch educational system, the change from the elementary to the secondary school is made at the age of 12 years. Consequently, 12-year-olds are confronted with changes in their social environment and peers (i.e., new friends). The need to compare oneself to a new friend could explain the decrease in the clearness of self-descriptions that present similarities between the self and the same-gender peer at that age. Although these children may be well aware of the existing similarities, they will have to get better acquainted with their new friends before these similarities become well defined.

CONCLUSIONS

In the present chapter, the reliability of the Repertory Grid procedure used in this study, as well as data on some additional measurements, were analyzed. Besides the reliability of the Repertory Grid procedure itself, the effect of drop-out on this reliability was also assessed. In addition, the degree of likeability and familiarity of the parents and peers from whom the perceived self-concepts were considered, the abstractness of the self-descriptions that were used, as well as their clearness of definition were reviewed. In all cases, special attention was given to the presence of age effects in the measurements.

The findings demonstrated an adequate reliability for the Repertory Grid. An increase in the reliability was observed with increasing age and the continuation of participation in the study, that is, the data become more reliable with increasing age, as well as time (i.e., the continuation of participation in the study involving three repeated measurements with intervals of approximately 1 year). The latter test-effect suggests that the children became more thoughtful about their self-concepts and the questions that were asked during the procedure. The reactions of the children who dropped out of the study were even more reliable than those of the children who continued their participation. Although this finding decreases the generalizability of the present data to children who are apparently less sure or certain about their self-concepts, it also strengthens the validity of the findings. The finding that the children became more careful and certain about their self-concepts suggests that the procedure followed in the present study appeals to their real inner feelings.

The validity of the present procedure is also confirmed by the findings from the additional measurements. The assessment of the familiarity and likeability of the parents and peers, for whom the perceived self-concepts were assessed, demonstrated that all children report that they like and know their parents, their peers, as well as themselves at an above average level. In addition, a slight decrease in familiarity and likeability could be observed with increasing age, the parents and selves were liked and known somewhat better than the peers, and the decrease with age was larger for the parents and self than for the peers. That is, although all peers became *relatively* known and liked more, there was a tendency to know the same-gender peer better than the opposite-gender peer. Besides these findings the data suggest that knowing and liking become increasingly better differentiated; that is, the scores for familiarity decreased more than the scores for likeability. The decrease in familiarity with age may suggest that children become increasingly aware of the lack of relationship between frequent interactions with an individual and the extent to which that person is really known. That is, the relationship between knowing somebody and liking that person appears to be reconsidered.

The initial findings that children know and like their parents better than their friends, the relative increase in familiarity and likeability for their peers with increasing age, as well as the tendency to know and like the same-gender peer more than the opposite-gender peer reflect often-reported shifts in the significance of others from family-members to persons outside the family (see chapter 1) and the preference, especially with younger children and adolescents, for peers of the same gender in contrast to peers of the opposite gender (e.g., Hartup, 1983).

In addition to these findings with respect to the more formal aspects of the Repertory Grid, the contents of the assessed self-concepts were also evaluated; that is, the levels of abstractness for the descriptive dimensions that were obtained and the clearness of their definitions. The level of abstractness for the self-descriptions was demonstrated to increase with age according to the model of Damon and Hart (1982) and adapted by Oppenheimer et al. (1990). As children became older, the emphasis in their self-descriptions shifted from physical descriptions, through activety and psychologically oriented descriptions, to descriptions in terms of social relationships, in this developmental order. In addition, with the appearance of new categories as a function of age the earlier categories did not disappear, leading to an increase in the simultaneous use of the various categories. As a result the self-concepts were not only described in increasingly more abstract terms but also by increasingly more diverse categories.   The expectation that the level of abstractness for the self-descriptions would affect the degree to which the self-concepts were differentiated was not confirmed. The concrete category of physical self-descriptions, as well as the most abstract self-descriptions based on social relationships, resulted in less differentiation for the perceived real and ideal self-concepts of the parents than the two middle categories involving active and psychological self-descriptions. No effects were demonstrated for the descriptive categories on the differentiation between the real and ideal perceived self-concepts for the peers. Consequently, it was argued that the content rather than the level of abstractness of the self-definitions affect the degree to which self-concepts are differentiated. The differentiation between the self-concepts is then not interpreted as a mere function of the level of abstractness of the self-descriptions within these self-concepts, but by their psychological meaning. Because the procedure employed in this study was designed to obtain idiosyncratic, personally relevant self-descriptions, the contents of these self-descriptions cannot be standardized. Not only are different self-descriptions used by different children but, because these self-descriptions become increasingly more abstract with the age, they show a skewed distribution over the categories (i.e., physical, active, psychological, and social self-descriptions) and age groups. Although this can be interpreted as a shortcoming of the procedure employed, it has no consequences for the purpose of the present study, that being to examine the structural organization of the self-system in terms of the interrelationships between self-concepts. Actually, the finding that the obtained self-descriptions involve idiosyncratic, psychological meanings within each individual self-concept that differentiate between them but that cannot be analyzed within the scope of this study, supports the conclusion that the the relationships between the self-concepts studied are based on the most salient, age-appropriate, and personally relevant self-descriptions.

Finally, the data, described in the present chapter indicate that the self-descriptions that were used in the study were relatively clearly defined. The observed shift from parents to peers again served to help confirm the validity of the procedure. Whereas the self-descriptions pertaining to differences between the self and the same-gender parent (i.e., the identification parent) become more clearly defined with increasing age, this developmental course was paralleled by greater clarity of definition for self-descriptions denoting similarities between the self and the same-gender peer. There was no significant main effect evident, however, for either age or type of self-description.

In sum, it is concluded that the method described in chapter 2 offers sufficiently reliable and valid information and is sensitive to several aspects of social and cognitive development.

4 Differentiation between Intraindividual Self-Concepts

The present chapter reports on the relationships observed between the intraindividual self-concepts (i.e., one's own and perceived real and ideal concepts) by means of the procedure that was described and discussed in chapters 2 and 3. Special attention will be paid to the relative distance between the self-concepts and age-related changes in such distances.

It was observed in chapter 1 that the distances between the intraindividual self-concepts diverge and converge in an ongoing dynamic process of differentiation and integration. Changes in the distances between the self-concepts were thought to result from changes in the self-concepts, due to personal or situational circumstances. That is, changes will be induced by a cognitive reinterpretation of the self because of new experiences. Though the global dynamic summarized above could be deduced from the literature, little is known about the actual distances between the self-concepts and the changes in these distances in relation to each other. This is especially the case with children.

The cognitive character of the process suggests that the level of cognitive development of children may present a complicating factor in the relative distance between the pairs of concepts. According to the orthogenetic principle of Werner (1957), the several concepts should develop from one global concept, to integrate at a later stage in an hierarchically organized self-system. Harter (1983; see also chapter 1) described such a dynamic with respect to the self-descriptions within the self-concept. In addition, she noted that differentiation between the real and ideal self-concepts does not occur before age 5 (Harter, 1985). Hence, no differentiation between the real and ideal self-concepts should be expected until approximately that age as well.

DIFFERENTIATION STUDIES

Among the few studies dealing with the development of differentiation between intraindividual self-concepts, the studies of Zigler and Leahy and their colleagues are especially relevant. According to Zigler, cognitive-developmental factors exert a fundamental influence on the degree of differentiation and integration between these concepts, one that may even overrule the influence of personal experiences (Glick & Zigler, 1985). In a series of studies (Katz & Zigler, 1967; Katz et al., 1975; Phillips & Zigler, 1980; Zigler et al., 1972; for an overview of the former studies see Glick & Zigler, 1985; Rosales & Zigler, 1989), Zigler and his colleagues looked at differences between one's own real and ideal self-concepts and between one's own real and the perceived real self-concept of a generalized other using several groups of children with different levels of cognitive maturity and/or different experiences. The main instruments were a six-alternative questionnaire and a two-alternative checklist that were scored for each self-concept, both instruments counting the number of differences between the self-concepts. Comparison of the results from both instruments made it possible to control for the degree of differentiation.

In the first part of this series, Katz and Zigler (1967) studied the differentiation (i.e., distance) between one's own real and ideal self-concepts and between one's own real concept and the perceived real self-concept of a generalized other at three grade levels (5th, 8th, and 11th grade), and two levels of intelligence (low and high). In this study the older children were observed to attain a higher level of differentiation for both comparisons on both questionnaires than the younger children. The more intelligent children showed significantly more and larger differentiations between the real and ideal self-concepts than the less intelligent children. No difference between one's own and preceived real self-concepts was evident between both of these groups. In another study, Zigler et al. (1972) compared the influence of cognitive development on the differentiation between the real and ideal self-concept to the influence of life-history experiences. In order to study the influence of cognitive development on the distance between real and ideal self-concepts, cognitively retarded boys were compared to nonretarded boys. The nonretarded, normal boys were of two different age-groups, matching the retarded boys in, either the level of cognitive development, or chronological age. To study the influence of life-history on the degree of differentiation, half of each group came from an institutionalized population, although the other half came from a noninstitutionalized population. For both the institutionalized and noninstitutionalized group, higher differentiation scores were found for the older normal boys than for the younger normal and retarded boys. However, independent of their cognitive level, the institutionalized boys showed more differentiation between the self-concepts than the noninstitutionalized boys.

In a following study, Katz et al. (1975) compared 80 boys from four age-levels (i.e., from the fifth grade: 9.6 years to the eighth grade: 14.6 years). These children were either maladjusted (i.e., from a school-class for emotionally disturbed children) or not (i.e., from a school for nondisturbed children), and either classified as action or as thought oriented (externalizers and internalizers). No difference in real–ideal differentiation was found between the emotionally disturbed and nondisturbed children. However, older children differentiated more than younger children, and boys with action-oriented symptoms differentiated less than boys with thought-oriented symptoms. Phillips and Zigler (1980) also studied the interaction of Social Economical Status (SES), ethnicity, and gender with developmental status for real–ideal differentiation. The children in this study were younger than in the former studies: 40 second graders and 40 fifth graders served as subjects. Except in the case of lower SES boys, again older children showed more differentiation than younger children. Finally, Rosales and Zigler (1989) divided 34 seventh graders according to high and low role-taking ability. High role-takers scored higher on real–ideal differentiation both on the six-alternative questionnaire and on the checklist.

Leahy and Huard (1976), using 10- to 12-year olds, also found a positive relationship between role-taking abilities and real–ideal differentiation as measured by the six-alternative questionnaire of Zigler and his colleagues. Based on their own and others' research, Leahy and Shirk (1985) proposed a model for the development of the relationship between real, ideal, and perceived concepts within the self-concept. At the first level, apparent in 5-year-olds, no differentiation was assumed to be evident between one's own self-concepts and the perceived self-concepts of others. Children were expected instead to describe themselves in terms of objective, external characteristics. Though subjective experiences or value judgements are possible, no conflicts between them were expected. In short, it was assumed that there would be little real–ideal differentiation. At the second level, at 10 years of age, Leahy and Huard (1976) expected the subjective self to develop. By these lights, the self's performance is now thought to be judged by means of social comparison, and the sharing of one's own view by others verified by role-taking. Children at this level judge their behavior in terms of their perceived expectations of others in an attempt to conform to these expectations. A hidden private self is also thought to develop. The differentiation between the real and ideal as well as between one's own versus perceived self-concepts increases. At the third level, which is predominant during adolescence, self-chosen principles are preferred to stereotypic role-expectations. An increasing awareness arises that others may have inaccurate impressions of the self, as well as the recognition that different others may have different impressions of oneself. During this level the possibility of conflicts between the several perspectives may be experienced.

Even though the data from the Zigler-studies demonstrated that the distances among the self-concepts are affected by subjective life-histories, the role of cognitive development was very persistent. Based on these studies and the developmental model of Leahy and Shirk (1985), there should be an increasing degree of differentiation between the real and ideal self-concepts with age, because increases in cognitive maturity (with age) ought to overrule the effect of personal life-histories. With respect to one's own and perceived self-concepts, the expectations are more ambiguous. Zigler and colleagues omitted this relationship from their studies because no age-related differences were found between one's own and the perceived real self-concept of a generalized other. Leahy and Shirk, on the other hand, predict – in accordance with Werner's (1957) orthogenetic principle – an increase in the differentiation between one's own and perceived self-concepts, as well as among perceived self-concepts from different others. However, they predict that the former differentiation occurs later than the differentiation between the real and ideal self-concepts (see also Higgins, 1989).

Besides the fact that no decisive conclusion about the development of the differentiation between one's own and perceived real self-concept is apparent, it should be noticed that Zigler studied the relationship between one's own real self-concept and the perceived real self-concept of a generalized other. That is, no data on the development of this relationship are available with regard to particular others. The distinction between generalized others and particular others could account for the different expectations of Zigler and Leahy. More important, however, is that particular others have been found to influence the self-concepts differently (see chapter 1). In addition, the above findings deal with the relationship between one's own real and ideal self-concepts and with the relationship between one's own and perceived real self-concept, only. No data are provided about the other half of the self-system, as it was described in chapter 1, that is, about the development of differentiation between the perceived real and ideal self-concepts of others and between one's own and perceived ideal self-concepts. There are also no data available dealing with the relative size of the distances between two intraindividual self-concepts as compared to the distances between the remaining pairs of intraindividual self-concepts. In the present chapter, data are presented that deal with each of these problems.

To study the differentiation between the self-concepts within the self-system, the developmental course of the distances between one's own real and ideal self-concepts, the perceived real and ideal self-concepts, one's own and perceived real self-concepts, and one's own and perceived ideal self-concepts are assessed. In doing so, the perceived self-concepts of four particular others (i.e., both parents and a peer from the same and opposite gender; see chapters 2 and 3) are considered. Though it is expected that each of these distances will increase with age, differences in degree of differentiation between the different pairs of self-concepts are also expected. Before such age- or type of differentiation-related differences can be considered, it should first be determined if differentiation occurs at all, at the ages under study.

RESULTS

Does Differentiation Actually Occur?

In chapter 2, the Repertory Grid procedure for assessing one's own and perceived real and ideal self-concepts was described. The degree of differentiation was calculated on the basis of this procedure by means of the absolute differences between the self-descriptions within the self-concepts. These absolute differences were averaged by comparison, resulting in a mean difference score for each pair of concepts. In addition to the above assessment of the self-concepts, two of the self-concepts were rated a second time. The comparison of these measurements resulted in test–retest scores. In order to analyze the degree of differentiation for the several combinations of self-concepts (see chapter 2), their mean scores for difference were compared to the mean score for test–retest, which functioned as a baseline (see chapter 3). This procedure was followed because it was assumed that the difference between a self-concept and itself would not equal zero. That is, uncertainty or carelessness in the rating procedure may result in biased scores that incorrectly indicate differences between the self-concepts. As was shown in chapter 3, this possibility was confirmed, especially for the youngest age-groups. By comparing the difference scores with the test–retest measure, which is uncommon in the use of the Repertory Grid, reliability is automatically secured when the differentiation scores are computed.

Because an analysis of variance on the indices for differentiation failed to demonstrate gender effects, the data for boys and girls were combined. The effect for age-group on test–retest reliability, however (chapter 3), implies that the several difference-scores per group should not be compared to the general test–retest mean but to the test–retest mean per age-group. This has been done by t test (two-tailed).

Differentiation for each combination of concepts was apparent for each age-group, except for the 6- and 8-years olds. When differentiation was present, the mean difference between two self-concepts was larger than the mean test–retest score. At the age of 6, children did not differentiate between their own and perceived real self-concepts of both parents and the same-gender peer ($S \times O$). Cross-sectionally, this lack of differentiation in the first wave lasted until the age of 8, if the perceived real self-concept of the same-gender parent was considered. As the data for the second wave indicate, however, the same children were perfectly able to differentiate between one's own and perceived real self-concepts at the age of 7. In the third wave, these children again did not show differentiation between one's own real self-concept and the perceived real self-concepts of both parents. In addition, no differentiation was evident between one's own real self-concept and the real self-concept of the opposite-gender peer for the 8-years-olds in this wave.

In summary, differentiation between the real and ideal self-concepts and between one's own and perceived *ideal* self-concepts appears to be well-established at age 6. Differentiation between one's own and perceived *real* self-concepts becomes well established only from age 8. A less consistent differentiation pattern is evident until that age. Though children between age 6 and 8 may succeed in differentiating between one's own and perceived real self-concepts, their succes is still fluctuating. Self–other differentiation between real self-concepts is a more difficult type of differentiation than self–other differentiation between ideal self-concepts and differentiation between real and ideal self-concepts. The former type of differentiation is not consistently mastered until age 9.

Relative Distance Between the Concepts

The effects for age on the several intraindividual differentiation measures and the relative distance between the self-concepts are analyzed by ANOVAs with repeated measurements. Because such analyses require a crossed design with an equal amount of identical repeated levels, the data were split into two analyses with congruent levels. The first ANOVA, in which the differentiation scores were the dependent measure and age and wave the factors, concerned the differentiation between one's own real and ideal self-concept ($S \times S'$) in each wave. No effect could be demonstrated for either age or wave. The second, $6 \times 3 \times 3 \times 4$ (age x wave x type of differentiation x other) ANOVA considered the differentiation between the perceived real versus ideal concept ($O \times O'$) and the differentiation between one's own and the perceived self-concepts of others for both the real ($S \times O$) and ideal condition ($S' \times O'$) separately and for age and each wave. Here a main effect for type of differentiation [$F_{(2,248)} = 132.26$,

TABLE 4.1

Means and Standard Deviations for Differentiation Between One's Own
Real and Ideal Self-Concept (S x S'), the Perceived Real and Ideal Self-Concepts of
Others (O x O'), One's Own and Perceived Real Self-concepts (S x O),
and One's Own and Perceived Ideal Self-Concepts (S' x O')

differentiation	mean	sd
S x S'	.82	.43
O x O'	.97	.47
S x O	.59	.38
S' x O'	.76	.45

$p < .0001$] and for the other [$F_{(3,372)} = 5.37$, $p < .005$] were found. Interaction effects occurred for type of differentiation by other [$F_{(6,744)} = 43.90$, $p < .0001$], type of differentiation by age [$F_{(10,248)} = 3.36$, $p < .0005$], other by age [$F_{(15,372)} = 2.12$, $p < .01$], and type of differentiation by other by age [$F_{(30,744)} = 2.60$, $p < .0001$].

Contrast analyses for the degree of differentiation demonstrated a significant difference between each of the three types of differentiation. Differentiation was highest between the perceived real and ideal self-concepts (O x O'). The mean differentiation between one's own and perceived ideal self-concepts (S' x O') was smaller than between the real and ideal self-concepts, but larger than between one's own and perceived real self-concepts (S x O). F values and probability for O x O' versus S x O, SxO versus S' x O', and O x O' versus S' x O' were $F_{(1)} = 261.55$, $p < .0001$; $F_{(1)} = 43.51$, $p < .0001$; and $F_{(1)} = 91.71$, $p < .0001$, respectively. Consequently, although the children showed relatively little self–other differentiation (S x O ; S' x O') as compared to real–ideal differentiation (O x O'), they experienced a larger distance between their own ideal self-concept and the perceived ideal concept of others (S' x O') than between their own real self-concept and the perceived real self-concepts of others (S x O; Table 4.1).

Contrast analysis for the others revealed that only for the peer of the same gender, differentiation was significantly lower than for both parents and the peer of the opposite gender [parents and opposite-gender peer versus same-gender peer: $F_{(1)} = 13.81$, $p < .0005$]. In other words, the highest congruence was perceived between the several concepts of the same-gender peer.

A closer inspection of the interaction effect between type of differentiation and other revealed that the differentiation for both parents was approximately equal for all types of differentiation. Significant differences were present between the peers, and between parents and peers. For the perceived real versus ideal

TABLE 4.2

Means, Standard Deviations, F values (df=1), and Probability for Type of Differentiation by Other (pa: parents; pe: peers; sg: same gender; og: opposite gender)

Other	OxO' mean	sd	SxO mean	sd	S'xO' mean	sd
pasg	1.06	.47	.51	.34	.73	.43
paog	1.08	.48	.54	.35	.75	.44
pesg	.86	.44	.61	.36	.74	.46
peog	.88	.43	.69	.42	.82	.48
contrasts: F	135.39		52.55 / 50.13		11.04	
p	.0001		.0001		.001	
contrasts:	OxO' vs. SxO		SxO vs. S'xO'		OxO' vs. S'xO'	
parents F	1264.97		164.70		516.79	
p	.0001		.0001		.0001	
peer sg F	119.36		29.55		30.14	
p	.0001		.0001		.0001	
peer og F	69.86		22.98		12.70	
p	.0001		.0001		.0005	

self-concepts ($O \times O'$) a lower degree of differentiation was present for peers than for parents. In contrast, a larger differentiation for the peers than for the parents was evident [$F_{(1)} = 52.55$, $p < .0001$] for the differentiation between one's own and perceived real concepts ($S \times O$), with a larger differentiation for the opposite-gender peer than for the same-gender peer [$F_{(1)} = 50.13$, $p < .0001$]. That is, for the peer of the opposite gender a larger differentiation between one's own and perceived ideal self-concepts was found than for the parents and the same-gender peer ($S' \times O'$). The significant effects, the means for differentiation, and the standard deviations are to be found in Table 4.2.

From these data it can be concluded that children perceive the real and ideal self-concepts of their peers ($O \times O'$ peers) to be closer (i.e., more similar) than the real and ideal concepts of their parents ($O \times O'$ parents). At the same time, they perceive their own real self-concept to be more similar to the perceived real self-concept of their parents than to that of their peers ($S \times O$ parents $< S \times O$ peers). Finally, their own ideal self-concept was perceived to resemble the ideal self-concept of the opposite-gender peer less than the ideal self-concepts of the other three others ($S' \times O'$ parents, pesg$< S' \times O'$ peog).

Because separate analyses were run for the differentiation between one's own real and ideal self-concepts ($S \times S'$), an extra analysis was neccessary to determine the position of this differentiation among the other differentiations.

TABLE 4.3

The Means, Standard Deviations for Each of the Differentiation Measures, F Values and Probabilities for Contrasts Between the Differentiation Measure for One's Own Real and Ideal Self-Concept ($S \times S'$) and Each of the Remaining Differentiation Measures ($df=1$)

Type of differentiation	mean	sd	F value	probability
SxS'	.82	.43		
x OxO'pasg	1.09	.51	$F =$ 53.45	$p <.0001$
x OxO'paog	1.09	.49	$F =$ 52.70	$p <.0001$
x OxO'pesg	.90	.45	$F =$ 4.39	$p <.05$
x OxO'peog	.92	.49	$F =$ 6.78	$p <.01$
x SxOpasg	.49	.32	$F =$ 74.00	$p <.0001$
x SxOpaog	.56	.38	$F =$ 45.91	$p <.0001$
x SxOpesg	.61	.36	$F =$ 31.09	$p <.0001$
x SxOpeog	.69	.40	$F =$ 11.49	$p <.001$
x S'xO'pasg	.71	.44	$F =$ 7.43	$p <.01$
x S'xO'paog	.74	.46	$F =$ 4.00	$p <.05$
x S'xO'pesg	.75	.46		ns
x S'xO'peog	.84	.51		ns

An analysis of variance (ANOVA) with repeated measurements was run on each of the 13 intraindividual differentiations. This analysis revealed a significant effect for type of differentiation [$F_{(12,2400)} = 47.60$, $p < .0001$]. Contrast analyses revealed that the distance between one's own real and ideal self-concept differed from almost all other intraindividual differentiations. The distance between one's own real and ideal self-concept ($S \times S'$) was smaller than the distance between the perceived real and ideal self-concepts ($O \times O'$) but larger than the distance between one's own and perceived real self-concepts ($S \times O$). The distance between one's own real and ideal self-concept was larger than the distance between one's own and perceived ideal self-concepts of the parents, but identical to the distance between one's own and perceived ideal concepts of the peers ($S' \times O'$; see Table 4.3). Like the ideal self-other differentiation, the real–ideal differentiation for one's own self-concepts falls in between the real self–other differentiation and the perceived real–ideal differentiation.

Effects for Age-Group

In order to assess the interaction effects with age found in the overall analysis, further analyses of the data were performed. This resulted in ANOVAs with repeated measurements for each type of differentiation and each other.

TABLE 4.4

Means and Standard Deviations by Age-Group for Each Type of Differentation for All
Waves Combined; F Values, Degrees of Freedom, and Probabilities for Age-Effects

	SxS' pasg		OxO' paog		OxO' pesg		OxO' peog		OxO'	
	m	sd	m	sd	m	sd	m	sd	m	sd
Group 1	.71	.39	.93	.44	.87	.44	.89	.46	.92	.48
Group 2	.79	.41	1.08	.41	1.06	.40	.92	.52	.86	.48
Group 3	.86	.40	1.11	.46	1.15	.46	.99	.39	1.01	.38
Group 4	.89	.42	1.08	.43	1.19	.53	.88	.40	.85	.36
Group 5	.78	.45	1.18	.56	1.16	.52	.78	.35	.83	.39
Group 6	.83	.34	1.14	.59	1.21	.54	.68	.33	.77	.34
F					3.26		3.09			
df	ns		ns		5,134		5,134		ns	
p					.01		.05			

	SxO pasg		SxO paog		SxO pesg		SxO peog	
	m	sd	m	sd	m	sd	m	sd
Group 1	.51	.36	.55	.38	.60	.40	.65	.51
Group 2	.47	.33	.52	.37	.58	.37	.77	.44
Group 3	.45	.33	.46	.31	.57	.40	.70	.48
Group 4	.52	.27	.59	.29	.70	.32	.80	.36
Group 5	.60	.42	.59	.37	.63	.34	.84	.41
Group 6	.56	.30	.57	.33	.57	.27	.68	.38
F								
df	ns		ns		ns		ns	
p								

	S'xO' pasg		S'xO' paog		S'xO' pesg		S'xO' peog	
	m	sd	m	sd	m	sd	m	sd
Group 1	.81	.49	.79	.48	.77	.53	.88	.55
Group 2	.79	.44	.80	.48	.81	.53	.96	.57
Group 3	.65	.38	.68	.38	.73	.39	.85	.36
Group 4	.63	.34	.72	.34	.62	.32	.65	.40
Group 5	.72	.41	.75	.42	.71	.37	.76	.35
Group 6	.72	.45	.70	.44	.63	.36	.62	.35
F							3.95	
df	ns		ns		ns		5,128	
p							.005	

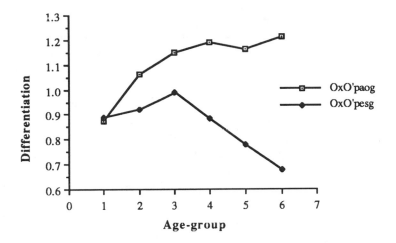

FIG. 4.1. Mean differentiation scores for the perceived real and ideal self-concepts of the opposite-gender parent (paog) and the same-gender peer (pesg) by age-group for all waves.

The results of these analyses are presented in Table 4.4. Significant effects for age are only present for the perceived real versus ideal self-concepts of the opposite-gender parent ($O \times O'$ paog) and the same-gender peer ($O \times O'$ pesg), and for one's own versus perceived ideal self-concepts of the opposite-gender peer ($S' \times O'$ peog).

Between the first and fourth age-group (including children from age 6 to 8 and 12 to 14), the differentiation between the perceived real and ideal self-concept of the opposite-gender parent increases, although this differentiation remains stable after the fourth age-group. Between age-group one and three (including children from age 6 to 8 and 10 to 12), the differentiation between the perceived real and ideal self-concept of the same-gender peer also increases. However, in contrast to the data for the opposite-gender parent, this differentiation decreases after the latter age-group (see Fig. 4.1).

The children in the first age-group are, respectively, 6, 7, and 8 years old in the first, second, and third wave. That is, possible effects for the youngest age-group in the first wave (i.e., 6 years of age) may be affected by the increase in age in the subsequent waves. Preliminary analyses (Oosterwegel & Oppenheimer, 1990) revealed that the contrast in developmental pattern for the differentiations between the perceived real and ideal self-concepts of the parents and peers is more salient if only the first wave is considered. Here, the effect for the opposite-gender parent was also found for the same-gender parent

$[F_{(5,197)} = 3.07, p < .05]$. Similarly, the differentiation for the opposite-gender peer revealed a similar though non-significant pattern as compared to the same-gender peer $[F_{(5,196)} = 1.93, p < .09]$. In addition, no significant differences in the trend for both parents or in the trend for both peers were found.

Consequently, the data for all three waves, and for the first wave in particular, suggest different age-effects on the perceived real versus ideal differentiation for parents and peers. After age 6, an increase appears in differentiation both for the parents and the peers between what they are perceived to think about the children and what they are perceived to expect from them. Although during adolescence this differentiation decreases with regard to the peers, it remains stable with respect to the parents.

Finally, the differentiation between one's own and perceived ideal self-concept of the opposite-gender peer is larger for the first three age-groups than for the latter three and decreases from the second to the fourth age-group. As the children grow older a decrease in differentiation between one's own ideal self-concept and the perceived expectancies of the opposite-gender peer is observed. That is, from pre- to early adolescence the role of the opposite-gender peer becomes more similar to the role of the same-gender peer.

Cohort and Drop-Out Effects

In the time-sequential model, cohort effects can be tested by comparing a particular age-group in the first wave with the group of that same age in the third wave. In the present design, this means that the 8-, 10-, 12-, 14-, and 16-year-olds of the first wave (group 2, 3, 4, 5, and 6) are compared to the 8-, 10-, 12-, 14-, and 16-years-olds in the third wave (group 1, 2, 3, 4, and 5). Because no main effect for age or wave were found in the overall analysis of variance, none or only small differences between the age-groups over wave were expected. Indeed, separate t tests (paired, two-tailed) revealed some, but small differences. Most discontinuities or differences between the groups occur around age 12 and 14. In particular, such differences were present for the self–other differentiation with regard to the real self-concept ($S \times O$), and with regard to the ideal self-concept for the peers ($S' \times O'$).

One reason for these discontinuities may be traceable to the children who dropped out of this study. In the previous chapter it was concluded that those children who dropped out were more certain about their answers than the children who continued their participation. In addition, it was hypothesized that these children would demonstrate higher degrees of differentiation than the children who continued their participation in this study. Consequently, further

ANOVAs examining the effects of the drop-outs on the differentiation scores were done. The analysis for effects of drop-out from the first to the second wave on the differentiation between one's own real and ideal self-concept ($S \times S'$) revealed that the children who dropped out demonstrated a significantly higher differentiation score than children who continued to participate [$F_{(1,202)} = 6.56$, $p < .05$]. An ANOVA for drop-out effects from the first to the second wave on the remaining differentiation scores ($O \times O'$; $S \times O$; $S' \times O'$) revealed an interaction effect for differentiation by drop-out [$F_{(2,398)} = 14.22$, $p < .0001$]. Because of this interaction effect, separate analyses were done for each type of differentiation. These analyses revealed that a significant effect for drop-out was evident [$F_{(1,199)} = 16.96$, $p < .0001$] only for the perceived real versus ideal differentiation ($O \times O'$). Children who discontinued their participation in the study perceived more distance between the perceived real and ideal concepts of others than children who continued their participation in the study. In other words, children who discontinued participation from the first to the second wave differentiated more between their perceived real and ideal self-concepts and were more sure about this differentiation. Analyses of variance for the effect of drop-outs from the second to the third wave on the differentiation measures (i.e., for $S \times S'$, $O \times O'$, $S \times O$, and $S' \times O'$, respectively) revealed an interaction effect for others by drop-out [$F_{(3,474)} = 6.65$, $p < .0005$], and for type of differentiation by others by drop out [$F_{(6,948)} = 2.77$, $p < .05$] for the comparisons $O \times O'$, $S \times O$, and $S' \times O'$. Separate one-way ANOVAs on type of differentiation by other revealed that the effect for drop-out from the first to the second wave was only weakly repeated from the second to the third wave for the perceived real and ideal concepts of the parents only [$O \times O'$; $F_{(1,166)} = 3.83$, $p = .0519$ for the same-gender parent; and $F_{(1,165)} = 3.59$, $p = .0599$ for the oppsite-gender parent]. A significant effect in the opposite direction [$F_{(1,161)} = 4.46$, $p < .05$], however, was present for the opposite sex peer. In the present analysis, children who dropped out perceived less differentiation between the real and ideal self-concept of their opposite-gender peer. Consequently, despite these contrasting results, it must be concluded that the absence of the scores in the latter waves of the children who dropped out of the study affected the mean scores of the remaining participants in the real versus ideal comparisons.

Because of the effects of drop-out on the differentiation scores, the scores for these children were excluded from the data for the 8-, 10-, 12-, 14-, and 16-years-olds of the first wave (i.e., Group 2, 3, 4, 5, and 6). The thus corrected scores were again compared to the 8-, 10-, 12-, 14-, and 16-years-olds in the third wave (i.e., Group 1, 2, 3, 4, and 5). In the reanalysis of the corrected data, the cohort effects for the real versus ideal comparisons disappeared. That is, the apparent cohort effects found by the first analysis were due to the drop-out effects.

With the exclusion of the data for the drop-outs, the time-sequential data for real versus ideal differentiation can be accepted as longitudinal. During childhood, an increase in differentiation between the perceived real and ideal self-concepts of the parents and the peers is evident. During adolescence, this difference remains stable for the parents but decreases for the peers. As could be expected, the cohort effects for self–other differentiation remained. The effects for drop-out had no significant influence on these scores. It could be argued, however, that a period of 2 years is too short to result in real cohort effects. There is also no special reason to expect cohort effects within this 2-year period. In addition, with the exception of the comparison between one's own and perceived ideal self-concept of the opposite-gender peer, no age-effects for self–other differentiation were found. Consequently, instead of real cohort effects, it appears that it is idiosyncracies between participant differences in self–other differentiation that account for the present discontinuities in the longitudinal data.

CONCLUSIONS

The purpose of this chapter was to assess and discuss the developmental dynamics between the four intraindividual self-concepts (i.e., one's own real and ideal self-concept and the perceived real and ideal self-concepts of others) with children from 6 to 18 years old. The perceived self-concepts of others were assessed in relation to four persons, that is, both parents, and a peer of the same and the opposite gender. The developmental dynamic between these self-concepts (for the self and each of the others) was studied from three different perspectives. The first of these involved the question of whether children from the age of 6 years differentiate between the different intraindividual self-concepts. The second vantage on these data dealt with the relative distance between each pair of concepts. Finally, age-related changes in the relationships between each pair of concepts were assessed.

The data revealed that a real–ideal differentiation and a self–other differentiation for the ideal self-concepts was already established at age 6 and remained at older ages. Self–other differentiations for the real self-concepts, however, revealed a less consistent developmental pattern. Although children between 6 and 8 years sometimes succeeded in differentiating between one's own and perceived real self-concepts, this success was unstable. Self–other differentiation between real self-concepts apparently is a more difficult type of differentiation, which is only completely mastered at 9 years of age.

With regard to the relative distance between the self-concepts, it was found that children showed relatively little self–other differentiation compared to real–ideal differentiation, but experienced more distance between their own ideal self-concept and the perceived expectancies of others than between their own and others' real self-concepts. At the individual level, the data indicated that the children experienced the real and ideal self-concepts of their peers as closer to one another than the real and ideal self-concepts of their parents. At the same time, they perceived their own real self-concept as closer to the real self-concepts of their parents than to those of their peers. Finally, their own ideal self-concept was considered to resemble the ideal of their same-gender peer more than the ideal of the other three. In general, most congruence was perceived between the several concepts for the same-gender peer. The role of the opposite-gender peer became more similar to the role of the same-gender peer in adolescence.

The comparisons of the age-groups from Wave 1 and 3 warrants a longitudinal interpretation of the data on real–ideal differentiation, but not for the data on self–other differentiation. In addition, a developmental trend was found only for the differentiation between the perceived real and ideal concepts. During childhood, an increasing difference is perceived between the real and ideal self-concepts of both the parents and the peers. This difference, however, stays large for the parents but decreases again for the peers during adolescence. For self–other differentiation there were no significant developmental patterns and no justification for a longitudinal interpretation. These findings suggest that self–other differentiation is primarily an individualized process.

Together these data indicate the complexity of the developmental process in self-conception. Though differentiation between the self-concepts is present, the amount and course of this differentiation are different for different pairs of self-concepts and others involved. Clearly, an eventual consideration of *the* differentiation between concepts within the self-concept presents an undesirable reduction of reality. The children in this study showed very little self–other differentiation, and they identified more with the perceived opinion of their parents than of their peers. Their ideal self-concept, though, was relatively independent of eventual preferences in the environment. Except for the peer of the opposite gender, no consistent development of self–other differentiation was found with increasing age. That is, rather than an explanation in terms of cognitive development, a more affective explanation seems warranted here. In such terms, children seem not unwilling to listen to descriptions of themselves as they are *now*, but they keep their private ideas about how they would like to *become*. Although they do not try to deny or run away from the impression they make right now, they save some room for their private dreams in their future self (see chapter 1). The still small difference between one's own and perceived ideals (less than 1 point at a 5-point scale), though, suggests that the private dreams of the children are probably not unrealistic, or that the others under consideration are perceived as close by the child. In this respect, the data show that the opposite-gender peer has to fight his or her way in.

The absence of a major age-effect in the self–other differentiation in the present data confirms the data of Zigler and colleagues. In contrast, this absence, as well as the presence of an opposite trend for the peer of the opposite gender, contradicts the model of Leahy and Shirk. Although it is done somewhat hesitantly in the beginning, children do differentiate between one's own and perceived self-concepts, and this differentiation does not increase in adolescence. The opposite applies to the data on real–ideal differentiation. In contrast to the data of Zigler, the present data do not show a significant age-effect in the real–ideal differentiation as far as the child's own self-concepts are concerned. For the perceived concepts of others, though, a significant developmental trend is evident. Children up to the age of approximately 12 years become more and more aware that from the perspective of others the expectancies are not met. This awareness increases with respect to the perceived self-concepts of their parents as well as their peers. After age 12, this idea remains with regard to the parents but disappears more and more for the peers. That is, as the adolescents grow older, their perception of how they meet their parents' expectancies in the eyes of their parents does not change, although their perception of the relationship between their peers' ideas and wishes makes them feel more and more comfortable. This different pattern for parents and peers reflects the recognition of adolescents that different others may have a different impression of them, confirming Leahy and Shirk's model.

Several reasons can be proposed to explain the different results in real–ideal differentiation as obtained by Zigler and colleagues and the present data, the methodological differences between the studies being most obvious among them. In most of their studies, Zigler and colleagues only assessed one's own real and ideal self-concept. Thus, it might be that in the real and ideal self-concept, as measured by their instrument, one's own perspective and perceived perspective of others are combined. Unfortunately, in such a case it would remain unclear which others are considered, although the present study indicates that this information is of crucial importance. This possibility would explain the fact that, in the present study, an effect was found only for the real–ideal differentiation between the perceived self-concepts, as well as the fact that this effect was different from the effect in the Zigler studies.

Further, Zigler offered his participants ready-made items, in which the self-descriptions were fixed. In the Repertory Grid procedure, as used in this study, each participant chose his or her own characteristics. This not only increases the likelyhood that the items were optimally adapted to the children's individual cognitive level, but also that the characteristics were almost certainly of personal relevance to the child. Thus, it may be that the difference in results reflects the difference between an experimental study and a field study. Though the adolescent's ability to differentiate probably still grows, in the real-life situation, on items that really matter to the child, this ability may not be warranted.   As Rosales and Zigler argued, some degree of real–ideal differentiation is neccessary as a source of motivation to act in a goal-directed way. However, this surely has its limits, above which a difference no longer motivates. That is, the increase of differentiation has to stop at some point. Probably this happens in adolescence, when the child also learns to integrate information (e.g., Barenboim, 1977; Bernstein, 1980; Harter, 1985; see chapter 1). The ability to integrate appears to be the tool that allows the adolescent to stop a process that starts as an advantage but may grow into a burden. According to the present data, adolescents use this tool – at least with regard to the opinion of their peers.

A more theoretical explanation for the difference in findings comes from the work of Rosenberg (1979; see also Harter, 1985). Rosenberg differentiated not only between a real and ideal self-concept, but also between an ideal self-concept as a pleasant kind of fantasy, and an ideal self-concept for which one actually strives: the committed image. That is, although one can have some ideal of which one only dreams, one may also have some more concrete aims to which one is committed and will attempt to really reach. A possible explanation for the difference in findings may be differences in the employed methods. Whereas the method used by Zigler and colleagues may to a larger extent tap the "fantasy" type of self-concept, the Repertory Grid procedure may be more related to a more concrete type of self-concept.

Finally, despite the influence of cognitive factors on the degree of differentiation, the affective reaction to a certain amount of distance between the real and ideal self-concepts should not be neglected. That such a distance causes emotional reactions appears from the data of the children who dropped out. Those children seemed to be more certain about their answers and scored higher on differentiation than the children who stayed. If it are the most mature participants who experience the most distance between their concepts, then it should be concluded that it was the most sincere and mature children who left the study. This is not how dropping out generally is explained. A more acceptable explanation seems to be that the children who dropped out found the emotional burden too heavy for a situation in which they participated voluntarily.

The next chapter deals with cognitive maturity in terms of role-taking ability, situating the self-concepts of children in the perception of the actual environment about them.   The affective component of the relationship between the domain-specific intraindividual self-concepts comes under discussion in chapters 6 and 7.

5 Differentiation between Interindividual Self-Concepts

In chapter 4 the relationships between the intraindividual self-concepts and their dynamics were assessed. This chapter is directed towards the dynamics in the relationship between the interindividual concepts, that is, the person's intraindividual self-concepts and the actual concepts of the self provided by others. Also, the relative size of the relationship between the interindividual concepts and the relationship between the intraindividual concepts is explored. Whereas in the previous chapter it was argued that a *larger* difference between *intraindividual* self-concepts should be considered as an indicator for cognitive maturity, in the present chapter the presence of *smaller* differences between *interindividual* concepts is thought to be an indicator for cognitive maturity.

THE SELF IN ENVIRONMENTS

Self-concepts develop in the interaction between the person and the environment. Individuals communicate self-relevant information by self-presentation (Baumeister, 1982) and receive feedback from the environment. Feedback from the environment can be more or less consistent, depending on factors like the favorability and credibility of the environment and the multi- or unidimensionality of the situation (Rosenberg, 1979; Rosenholtz & Simpson, 1984; Van Lieshout, 1987). Baumgardner (1990) argued that people seek information about the self because it permits a sense of control that will heighten their self-esteem (self-enhancement). However, the motive for self-enhancement and for a sense of continuity also prompt people to use self-serving biases in their perception and processing of the information (e.g., Gollwitzer & Wicklund, 1985; Krosnick & Sedikides, 1990; Schlenker, Weigold, & Hallam, 1990). Strategies for such biases are extensively described by Backman (1988), Caspi, Bem, and Elder (1989), and Swann (1983, 1987) (see also Markus & Wurf, 1987, and chapter 1).

From these studies it can be concluded that some level of defensiveness, as expressed in self-serving attributional biases, is a healthy phenomenon (cf. Greenwald, 1980; see also chapter 1). Defenses, when they work, serve to protect the person (Lane, Merikangas, Schwartz, Huang, & Prusoff, 1990). However, the maintenance of defences requires energy, and a serious lack of agreement between the person and the environment will result in conflicts and misunderstanding. The larger the agreement, the less conflicts and misunderstanding, and consequently the fewer defenses required. Hence, in addition to some degree of defensiveness, a certain degree of agreement between the intraindividual self-concepts and the concepts about the individual held by others in the environment should be present.

It can be argued that children do not possess the neccessary social cognitive abilities to attain optimal agreement between their self-concepts and the environment's or others' actual opinion about them. The fit between children's own and perceived self-concepts and the actual concepts of others about them depends on children's accuracy in self-assessment and their ability to understand and infer the perspective of the others correctly. It is frequently reported that in respect to actual competencies, younger children make less realistic self-appraisals than older children (e.g., Harter, 1982; Pintrich & Blumenfeld, 1985; Rosenholtz & Simpson, 1984). For instance, Pintrich and Blumenfeld found less accurate self-assessments for cognitive competence with children younger than 8 years, as compared to older children. Results from Harter's study involving children from the third to the ninth grade show that the agreement between the children's own ratings of their cognitive competencies, the teachers' ratings, and the actual scores increased continuously from the sixth to the ninth grade, with a temporary drop in the seventh grade. According to Harter (1985), this is due to children's increasing ability to understand how their competence is perceived and evaluated by others and to their familiarity with the situation. Although the participants in her study were becoming progressively insightful with regard to how they were being evaluated, entrance into a new school system (i.e., in the seventh grade) resulted in a temporary handicap because of the novelty and unfamiliarity of the situation.

Children's abilities to infer the perspectives (i.e., thoughts) of others (i.e., to take the role or perspective of others) develop during childhood (Selman, 1980). Chandler and Boyes (1982) argued, however, that only that information will be used that is understood, In other words, information of a cognitive complexity that surpasses that of the child will not be incorporated into the current perspective of the child. Conversely, the fact that a particular ability is acquired does not necessarily guarantee that it will always be used. Harter ascribed this phenomenon, particularly in adolescence, to the complexity of the situations.

This phenomenon may also be due to a shift in interests. For instance, according to Elkind (1967), adolescents become so involved with their newly acquired cognitive skills that they do not acknowledge the fact that others have interests that differ from their own. Thus, although adolescents have mastered the ability to take the perspective of others, their involvement with the changes that happen to and with themselves may prevent them from using this ability.

In summary, it can be expected that the fit between the perceived intraindividual self-concepts (S, S', O, and O') and the environmental concepts (RO and RO') will increase during childhood. Because of experiences due to the awareness of one's own developmental achievements, and/or changes in the complexity of the environment, the fit between these concepts may remain stable or even decrease during adolescence.

RESULTS

Degrees of Fit and Effects of Age-Group

Fit was defined as the distance between one's own and perceived real and ideal self-concepts (i.e., the intraindividual self-concepts, S, S', O, O', respectively) and the actual real and ideal concepts of others (i.e., the environmental concepts about the self, RO and RO', respectively). Difference scores, reflecting this distance, were calculated for one's own real self-concept versus the actual real concept of each of the parents ($S \times RO$; two comparisons), one's own ideal self-concept versus the actual ideal concept of each of the parents ($S' \times RO'$; two comparisons), the perceived real concept of the parents and their actual real concept ($O \times RO$; two comparisons), and the perceived ideal concept of the parents and their actual ideal concept ($O' \times RO'$; two comparisons). Relative distances and effects for age-group were assessed by analysis of variance (ANOVA).

The number of pairs of parents in each age-group and wave who completed the material for the real as well as the ideal concept of their child are shown in Table 5.1. Because of the decreasing number of parents who participated in each wave, an overall ANOVA would result in cell sizes between four and nine. These cell sizes are too small to obtain reliable results. Consequently, the analyses were run by each wave in order to maintain the largest number of participants possible in the analysis. For the first wave, the ANOVA with age as factor and the distances between self-concepts as dependent measures revealed no significant effects. For the second age-group, however, the comparison between one's own real versus actual real self-concept for the opposite-gender

TABLE 5.1

Number of Pairs of Parents Who Both Scored Their Actual Ideas and
Expectations Concept of Their Child by Age-Group and Wave

Group	Wave 1	Wave 2	Wave 3
Group 1	21	17	13
Group 2	20	16	13
Group 3	17	6	8
Group 4	16	15	13
Group 5	16	12	6
Group 6	18	10	6

parent ($S \times RO$ og) produced a standard deviation that exceeded several times those of the other comparisons. Closer examination revealed that this extreme standard deviation was not due to a single score of one individual, but reflected the actual range of scores of all children in the second age-group. Such a large standard deviation may mask otherwise significant effects. In addition, the respective mean was also very high; none of the other comparative means for the distances within the second age-group were out of range when compared to those for the first and third age-group. Therefore, the data of the first wave were analyzed in two ways: (a) omitting the second age-group from the analysis and (b) including the second age-group, but with the omission of the comparison between one's own real self-concept and the actual ideas about the child by the opposite-gender parent ($S \times RO$ og).

In the first analysis, when the second age-group was omitted, several significant effects appeared. Main effects were found for age [$F_{(4,83)} = 5.14$, $p < .001$] and for the distance measures between one's own and actual self-concepts ($S \times RO$ and $S' \times RO'$) versus the perceived and actual self-concepts [$O \times RO$ and $O' \times RO'$; $F_{(1,83)} = 8.24$, $p < .01$). An interaction effect was present for one's own-actual versus perceived-actual comparison by real versus ideal self-concepts [$F_{(1,83)} = 7.59$, $p < .01$).

To assess contrasts within the main effect for age, the eight distance measures were summed and averaged. A one-way ANOVA with age as factor and distance as dependent measure was done. This analysis, resulting in a significant effect for age [$F_{(4,83)} = 4.86$, $p < .005$], showed a significant decrease of the distance from the first to the third age-group [see Fig. 5.1; $F_{(1)} = 11.78$, $p < .001$]. From the third age-group onwards, that is, from the age of 10 years, the distance between one's own and perceived concepts versus the actual concepts of the parents remained stable.

The main effect for the distance between one's own self-concepts and the actual concepts of the parents about their child ($S \times RO$ and $S' \times RO'$) versus the

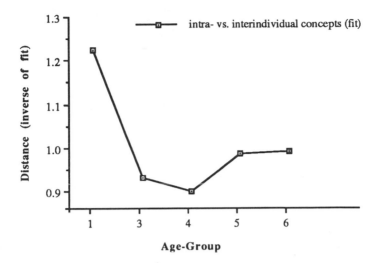

FIG. 5.1. Mean scores of fit for the first, third, fourth, fifth, and sixth age-group for the combined comparisons ($S \times RO$, $S' \times RO'$, $O \times RO$, and $O' \times RO'$).

perceived self-concepts and actual concepts of the parents about their child ($O \times RO$ and $O' \times RO'$) was due to a larger difference between the former compared to the latter. That is, the distance between one's own self-concepts and the actual concept of the parents was larger than the distance between the perceived self-concepts and actual concepts of the parents. Examination of the interaction effect for these distances with the real and ideal self-concepts condition revealed that this effect was primarily due to the difference scores for the ideal self-concept versus the actual expectancies of the parents ($S' \times RO'$). Only for the $S' \times RO'$ comparison were significantly higher difference scores found as compared to the other three comparisons [i.e., $S \times RO$, $O \times RO$, and $O' \times RO'$; $F_{(1)} = 18.81$, $p < .0001$; see Fig. 5.2).

The second analysis, in which only the comparison between one's own real self-concept versus the actual ideas about the child by the opposite-gender parent was omitted instead of the total second age-group, revealed similar results. To balance the data following this omission, the data for both parents in the other conditions were averaged. An additional ANOVA again revealed main effects for age [$F_{(5,102)} = 3.63$, $p < .005$) and the distance between one's own self-concepts and the actual ideas of the parents ($S \times RO$ and $S' \times RO'$) versus the distance between the perceived self-concepts and actual ideas of the parents [$O \times RO$ and $O' \times RO'$; $F_{(1,102)} = 4.99$, $p < .05$], as well as the interaction effect between one's own-actual versus perceived-actual comparison and the real

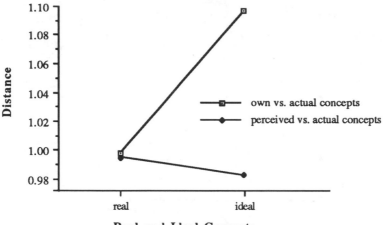

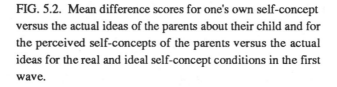

Real and Ideal Concepts

FIG. 5.2. Mean difference scores for one's own self-concept versus the actual ideas of the parents about their child and for the perceived self-concepts of the parents versus the actual ideas for the real and ideal self-concept conditions in the first wave.

versus ideal self-concepts were found $[F_{(1,102)} = 10.02,\ p < .005)$. The directions of these effects were identical to the effects described for the first analysis.

The results reported above are partly replicated for the second and third wave. The main effects for the distance measure own-actual versus perceived-actual were both significant [Wave 2: $F_{(1,70)} = 8.16,\ p < .01$; Wave 3: $F_{(1,53)} = 13.85$, $p < .0005$, respectively) and in the same direction. A smaller fit was evident between one's own self-concepts and the actual ideas of the parents than between the perceived self-concepts and actual ideas of the parents. The interaction effect for own-actual versus perceived-actual by real versus ideal self-concepts was replicated in the data of the third wave $[F_{(1,53)} = 11.79$, $p < .005]$. In this wave, not $S' \times RO'$ but $O' \times RO'$ differed significantly from the other scores $[F_{(1)} = 26.52,\ p < .0001,\ mean = .79,\ sd = .33$; for the other comparisons: $S \times RO$: $mean = .93$, $sd = .36$; $S' \times RO'$: $mean = .99$, $sd = .34$; $O \times RO$: $mean = .93$, $sd = .34]$. Despite this difference, the interaction pattern was identical. The smaller degree of fit for the perceived self-concepts as compared to one's own self-concepts was due to the comparatively high degree of fit for the perceived ideal concepts of the parents and the comparatively low degree of fit for one's own ideal self-concept. The fit for one's own real self-concept and the perceived real self-concept was equal (compare Fig. 5.2).

As a result of the smaller number of subjects in the second and third wave of the study, a main effect for age could not be demonstrated. In both waves, however, a significant effect for the interaction between age and the comparisons for the real versus ideal self-concept condition was evident [$F_{(5,70)} = 3.79$, $p < .005$ and $F_{(5,53)} = 5.29$, $p < .0005$, respectively]. In the second wave, the interaction effect for age and the real versus ideal self-concepts was due to a significant effect for age on the fit for the ideal self-concepts [$F_{(5,70)} = 3.51$, $p < .01$], whereas such an effect was absent for the real self-concepts. In the third wave, the interaction effect involved a significant effect for age on the fit for the real self-concepts [$F_{(5,55)} = 3.78$, $p < .01$] but not on the fit for the ideal self-concepts. The developmental patterns for the ideal concepts were similar between the waves; that is, there was a decrease from the first to the third age-group, with a stabilization following this age in the ideal self-concept condition. Results for the real self-concept condition were less clear. The significant effect for age on the fit of the real self-concepts in the third wave indicated an oscillating pattern.   This pattern involved an increase in differentiation from the first to the second age-group, a decrease from the second to the third age-group, an increase from the third to the fourth group, and a final decrease from the fourth to the sixth group. Closer examination of the mean in the first and second wave revealed that these waves also produced a difference score for the second age-group in the real self-concept condition that exceeds the other difference scores, though not significantly. No evidence for this excess was found at the fourth age-group. Consequently, the latter excessively high difference score can be interpreted as an artifact due to the small number of participants in the third wave (see Table 5.1). In contrast, the excessive score for the second age-group required a different interpretation. Keeping in mind the extreme standard deviation for the second age-group in the first wave, it becomes obvious that something exceptional happened for this age-group. As a result of the excessive score for the second age-group, a different developmental pattern emerged for the fit of the real as opposed to the ideal self-concepts. In the ideal self-concept condition an increasing level of fit was found during childhood with a stabilization during adolescence. These findings correspond to results reported in the literature on perspective taking. In the real self-concept condition a less stable and clear pattern of development appeared. It may be that the role of perspective taking is minor in the real self-concept condition.

The interaction effect of age-group with the gender of the parent [$F_{(5,53)} = 3.95$, $p < .005$] that appeared in the third wave was not found in the first or second wave. Closer examination of the data by means of contrast analysis only revealed a significant decrease from the second to the third age-group for the same-gender parent. This effect will not be discussed further.

In summary, the data showed that the degree of fit is higher for the perceived self-concepts of the parents than for the children's own self-concepts for all age-groups. This finding is due to one's own ideal self-concept, which shows significantly less fit as compared to the actual ideas of the parents than the other self-concepts. The ideal self-concept of children and adolescents is different from their parents' actual ideal for their children. The fit for each of the self-concepts increases, that is, the distance between the intraindividual self-concepts of the children and the actual concepts of the parents about their children decreases, however, until approximately the age of 11 years. This is especially true for the fit for the ideal concepts. Although the data from the first wave indicate that the same pattern exists for the real concepts, the data for the third wave suggest that some caution is needed here. Extreme scores between approximately the age of 8 and 10 years old indicate the appearance of possibly lower fits.

Cohort Effects

An ANOVA with drop-outs and remaining children as factor and the interpersonal distance scores as dependent measure showed a significant effect for drop-out between the second and third wave $[F_{(1,74)} = 4.33, p < .05]$. The children who remained in the study had higher distance scores on the interpersonal comparisons $(S \times RO, S' \times RO', O \times RO,$ and $O' \times RO'$ for both parents) than the children who dropped out. That is, the children who dropped out showed a higher fit.

To test for cohort effects, the data of the second to sixth age-group in the first wave were compared to the data of the first to fifth age-group in the third wave (i.e., by means of paired, two-tailed t test). Because of the former effect of drop-out, the data of the drop-outs were omitted from these comparisons. Some cohort effects were evident for the same-gender parent in the ideal self-concept condition. Differences were found between the fourth age-group in the first wave and the third age-group in the third wave for the distance between one's own ideal self-concept and the actual expectancies of the same-gender parent $[S' \times RO'; t_{(7)} = 2.40, p < .05]$ and between the perceived ideal self-concept and actual expectancies of the same sex parent $[O' \times RO'; t_{(7)} = 3.82, p < .01]$. In addition, a difference was found between the fifth age-group in the first wave and the fourth age-group in the third wave for the distance between the perceived ideal self-concepts and the actual expectancies of the same-gender parent $(O' \times RO'; t_{(4)} = 4.03, p < .05)$. No other cohort effects were evident.

Consequently, the results for the real self-concept condition can be interpreted longitudinally. The observed cohort effects, however, should be considered with caution because of the large number of t tests, which results in a high capitalization on probability. This, in combination with the relatively small number of subjects in each age-group in the last wave, makes the reliability of the t tests questionable.

Relative Distance Between the Actual Concepts of Others

An ANOVA with age and parents as factors and the difference between the actual ideas of the parents and their expectancies (RO x RO') for each wave separately did not reveal any significant effects. The data for the parents did not indicate any change in the distance between how they perceive their children and how they would like them to be. This is in contrast to how the children themselves perceive the ideas and expectancies of their parents (O x O'; see chapter 4).

Interindividual Versus Intraindividual Differentiation

To test the relationship between the intra- and interindividual comparisons, all distance scores for the child's self-concepts and the ideas of the parents were analyzed together in one analysis of variance by each wave separately. To permit the inclusion of the difference between one's own real and ideal self-concepts, which has only one level, the data for both parents were combined. Thus, the analysis included the comparison between one's own real versus ideal self-concept (S x S'), the perceived real and ideal self-concepts of the parents (O x O'), the actual ideas and expectancies of the parents (RO x RO'), one's own and perceived real self-concepts (S x O), one's own and perceived ideal self-concepts (S' x O'), one's own real self-concept versus the actual ideas of the parents (S x RO), one's own ideal self-concept versus the actual expectancies of the parents (S' x RO'), the perceived real self-concepts and the actual ideas of the parents (O x RO), and the perceived ideal self-concepts and the actual expectancies of the parents (O' x RO'). The between subject factor age-group had five levels in the first wave (the second age-group was omitted) and six levels in the second and third wave. In each wave a significant main effect for type of comparison was evident [i.e., $F_{(8,664)} = 26.96$, $p < .0001$; $F_{(8,552)} = 18.93$, $p < .0001$; and $F_{(8,400)} = 17.24$, $p < .0001$ for the first, second, and third wave, respectively)]. Although the single effects were slightly different among the waves (i.e., by means of contrast analysis), the main pattern of the relationships was similar for each wave (see Fig. 5.3).

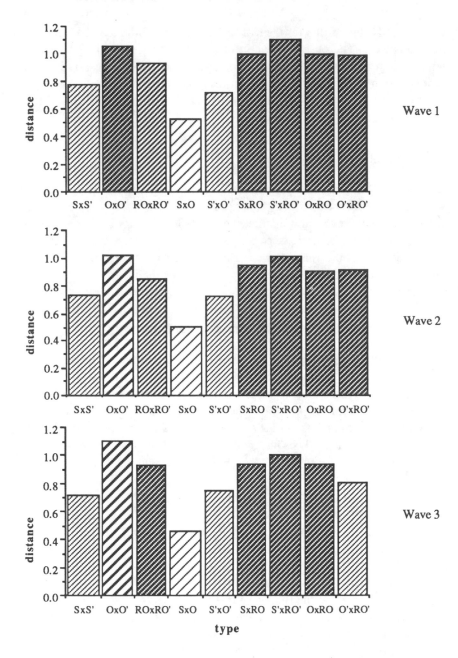

FIG. 5.3. Mean distance scores for each type of comparison by wave. Approximately identical means are depicted by similar shades. All differences are at a $p < .05$ level of significance.

As can be inferred from Fig. 5.3, the distance between one's own real and ideal self-concept $(S \times S')$ is smaller than between either the perceived self-concepts $(O \times O')$ or the actual ideas and expectancies of the parents $(RO \times RO')$; that is, most coherence exists between one's own real and ideal self-concepts. The distance between the actual ideas and expectancies of the parents $(RO \times RO')$ is smaller than the distance between the perceived real and ideal self-concepts of the parents $(O \times O')$. This finding suggests either that the children overestimate the distance between their parents' ideas and expectancies about themselves, or that the parents report less distance between their ideas and expectancies with respect to their children than they really experience.

As was shown in chapter 4, the distance between one's own and the perceived ideal self-concepts $(S' \times O')$ is similar to the distance between one's own real and ideal self-concept $(S \times S')$, whereas the distance between one's own and the perceived real self-concepts is smaller $(S \times O)$. In addition, the distance scores for the self–other differentiation $(S \times O; S' \times O')$ are small as compared to the distance-scores for the interindividual differentiation $(S \times RO, S' \times RO', O \times RO, O' \times RO')$. In general, then, the distances between the interindividual comparisons are larger than for any of the intraindividual comparisons. That is, the intraindividual congruence between the self-concepts is stronger than the fit of the self-concepts within the environment.

CONCLUSIONS

The purposes of the present chapter were (a) to assess the relationships between the interindividual concepts relating to the self for six different ages, and (b) to assess the size of these relationships as compared to those of the relationships between the intraindividual self-concepts. Except for the middle age-groups in the ideal self-concept condition, the results indicate that the data are age graded. Although these results should be interpreted with caution, the consistency between the developmental course that was indicated by the present data as compared to earlier findings (cf. Harter, 1982; Pintrich & Blumenfeld, 1985; Rosenholtz & Simpson, 1984) justifies such a conclusion.

Confirming expectations, the distance between the interindividual self-concepts decreased as the children became older (i.e., until approximately the age of 11 years). That is, from age 6 to approximately the age of 11, the intraindividual concepts of the child and the actual concepts of the environment about the child became more equal. In contrast to what might be expected, this finding was stronger for the ideal self-concepts than for the real self-concepts. What children like from life as well as what they believe that their parents expect from them becomes more and more equal to what the parents actually want from them. That is, not only do the children become better able to take the perspective of their parents, but they also adjust their own ideals in accordance with their perceived parental views. In contrast, when the concern is with their real self-concept, some children around age 8 to 10 show a sudden impulse to perceive themselves relatively differently from how their parents perceive them. A sudden increase in distance for the 8 year olds and an excessively large standard deviation for the comparison with the parent of the opposite gender in the first wave suggest the presence of an event with a strong developmental impact on some children. The large size of this standard deviation in the first wave indicates that the effect does not apply to all children. In addition, there is no other special situational complexity that is known around this age. Consequently, this sudden movement away from the parents is caused by affective rather than by cognitive factors. Following the age of 11 years, the fit for the intraindividual self-concepts stabilized. Finally, as far as the relationship is concerned between the actual ideas of the parents about and their expectancies with respect to their children, no changes could be demonstrated for any of the ages present. At each age, the parents' responses suggest a stable distance between their actual image and their expectancies of and for their child.

Among the interindividual self-concepts, the distances between one's own and environmental concepts are larger than between the perceived and environmental concepts. The parents' actual ideas were closer to the children's perceived self-concepts of their parents than to one's own self-concepts of the child. This was primarily due to the tendency for the distance between the ideal own and actual concepts to be larger, and the tendency for the distance between the ideal perceived and actual concepts to be smaller than both the distance between the real own and actual and perceived and actual concepts, which were about equal. In other words, whereas the children were aware of their parents' expectancies and adjusted their own ideals toward these expectancies (see above), they were also particularly aware of a distinction between these expectancies and their own private ideals.

Between the inter- and intraindividual concepts, intraindividual concepts were generally closer than interindividual concepts, except in the case of the perceived real versus ideal self-concepts of the parents. That is, relatively large differences between the perceived real and ideal self-concepts of the parents were experienced as compared to the distances between the remaining intraindividual self-concepts. The higher congruence between the intraindividual concepts than between the interindividual concepts corroborates earlier findings with adults (cf. Edwards & Klockars, 1981; Shrauger & Schoeneman, 1979) and adds consensual validity to the study. The intraindividual concepts are processed by one single person, whereas the interindividual concepts are processed by two different persons, each introducing their own biases. More striking was the finding that the real and ideal concepts of the parents about their children were perceived by the children to be larger than the parents themselves indicated. If the difference between a real and ideal concept is interpreted as a measure for self-acceptance, children accept themselves more than their parents do. However, although parents accept their children less than the children accept themselves, they accept their children more than the children believe that they do.

If the findings of chapter 4 are included, a picture arises in which children, through childhood, become more and more able to take the perspective of their parents and bring their self-concepts into harmony with the concepts of their parents. At the same time, though, these children become more and more aware that in the eyes of their parents, they do not meet the expectations of these parents. The parents, though, not only indicate more acceptance of their children than their children perceive, but also indicate that this acceptance was equal at all ages. Not only does this pattern point to a psychologically important misunderstanding between children and their parents, but it also raises the question of how this misunderstanding appears. Either the parents were answering in a socially desired way, or some adolescent negativism was interfering with children's perception, or both children and parents were right. That is, one possibility is that the parents set modest but achievable standards for their children, when compared to how they perceive their children, but communicate these standards more strictly to the children for purposes of education. The other possibility is that parents truly believe that they are satisfied with their children and that they accept them almost as they are, but forget about their secret wishes, which, in turn, are perceived more strongly by their children. Thus, parents may have two ideals for their children: one ideal that is reasonable and within the limits of the child, and one ideal that has not as much to do with their child as much as with the parents themselves. Further research is necessary to explain the misperception between parents and children. Regardless of the reasons why, this misunderstanding will motivate the child to try harder as well as cause feelings of alienation and depression. The following chapters deal with this topic.

In the present chapter the remaining question concerns the use of self-serving biases in children. Put more succinctly, is the amount of fit during childhood and adolescence already influenced by self-enhancing and self-verifying motives? The literature suggests that this may well be the case, in particular when motives for self-enhancement are concerned. Although the motive for self-consistency may not yet be completely present in childhood (see chapter 1), children develop during this period a sense of self-continuity, that will prompt them to become motivated towards self-consistency (Chandler, Boyes, & Oppenheimer, 1983; Damon & Hart, 1982; Oppenheimer & De Groot, 1981). Motives for self-enhancement have been argued to be present in children as early as from 7 to 11 years old (Ruble & Flett, 1988). Consequently, whereas their increasing abilities to understand the perspective of others allows children to reduce the difference between their and others' concepts, they may also become motivated to do so to greater or lesser degrees in order to keep or raise their self-esteem or experience consistency during this age. The latter assumption could explain the sudden decrease in fit between the real concepts in age-group two. In addition, given the finding that during adolescence a considerable difference is experienced between the real and ideal concept of the parents, it may be that the degree of fit that is reached in this period is not caused by a ceiling in the children's ability to take the perspective of their parents, but that it is moderated by self-enhancing motives (cf. chapter 1). However, as becomes clear in chapter 7, keeping the actual opinion of your parents at a distance does not help you as long as you are aware that they have such an opinion.

6

Discrepancies between Intraindividual Self-Concepts

In the earlier chapters, the differences between domain-specific self-concepts were analyzed in terms of differentiation. In this chapter, it is argued that with regard to personal functioning a distinction should be made between differentiation and *discrepancies*. Whereas *differentiation* represents the distance between intra- and interindividual self-concepts from different domains, *discrepancies* involve distances that exceed the average distance between two self-concepts or present incompatibility between those self-concepts. In addition, besides discepancies *between* concepts, discrepancies *within* concepts are also thought to be of psychological relevance. More specifically, the purpose of this chapter is to assess the development of *discrepancies between* and *within* the intraindividual self-concepts. That is, within and between one's own real self-concept; one's own ideal self-concept; and the perceived real and ideal concepts of both parents and the best male and female friend.

RESEARCH ON DISCREPANCIES

The assumption regarding the psychological meaning of discrepancies between the intraindividual self-concepts within the self-system is known from the work of Rogers (e.g., Rogers, 1951). Whereas in the fourth chapter *differentiation* (i.e., distance) between domain-specific self-concepts was regarded as an indicator for cognitive maturity (Glick & Zigler, 1985), *discrepancies* (as presented in this chapter) between the real and ideal self-concept are thought to be an indicator for emotional maladjustment. This assumption was confirmed empirically with adults by Higgins (1987; Higgins et al., 1986; Higgins et al., 1985; Strauman, 1989). Higgins studied the discrepancies between one's own and perceived real and ideal, and real and ought-to-be self-concepts. Each of these discrepancies was found to result in different, but negatively experienced emotions.

Research dealing with discrepancies between domain-specific self-concepts in childhood and adolescence primarily focusses on the development of children's and adolescents' abilities to differentiate between these concepts (i.e., as an indicator of cognitive maturity). Glick and Zigler's (1985) emphasis on cognitive maturation was corroborated by the findings of Leahy and Shirk (1985), who reported that the ability to differentiate between the real and ideal self-concepts during *childhood* is related to the acquisition of role-taking skills. Hauser (1976; Hauser & Shapiro, 1973) studied the presence of differences between domain-specific self-concepts with *adolescents*. He reported, in agreement with Higgins's (1987) findings with *adults*, and in contrast to the argument of Zigler and Leahy, that the difference between the real and ideal self-concepts is larger with emotionally maladjusted adolescents (i.e., adolescents with psychiatric complaints) as compared to adolescents without any such problems.

These contradictory findings suggest that the presence of differences among domain-specific self-concepts may be the result of different developmental processes during childhood and adolescence. Though the presence of discrepancies always implies differentiation, the presence of differentiation may not be sufficient for the presence of discrepancies. Differentiation indicates a difference, whereas discrepancy implies not only a difference but also incompatibility. A discrepancy in terms of incompatibility between two self-concepts or self-descriptions within one self-concept implies that they are mutually exclusive.

It is argued here that the cognitive developments in adolescence play an important role in the distinction between differentiation and discrepancies. This importance can be observed with the organization of social perceptions. Livesley and Bromley (1973), for instance, reported that between 8 and 12 years children become aware that people may possess contradictory personality characteristics. Contrary to adolescents, however, they are not able to resolve these contradictions, that is, to integrate these characteristics within one unified personality. The ability to integrate or simultaneously deal with such contradictory information requires new organizing principles, which, according to Barenboim (1977), develop between the ages of 10 and 16 years. As the result of this development the use of separate and nonintegrated psychological statements when describing another person disappears between the ages of 14 and 16 years. Similar findings are reported by Selman (1980) with respect to conflicting motives. Between the ages of 10 and 15 years children become aware that conflicting motives, thoughts, or feelings can exist within one and the same person. However, it is only from the age of approximately 12 years that attempts are made to integrate these conflicting elements into an "integrative core" (p. 135). Consequently, the ability to integrate and abstract personality characteristics develops primarily during adolescence, although the main improvement occurs between the ages of 15 and 20 years (Bernstein, 1980; see also chapter 1).

Based on these findings it can be expected that during childhood it is the differentiation, and during adolescence the integrative processes that will be predominant (cf. Harter, 1986). With respect to self-concept discrepancies an increase will be expected during childhood and a decrease during adolescence. However, children will lack the organizing principles to integrate contradictory characteristics and, consequently, may not even be aware of their contradictory nature. This might result in a dominant relationship between differentiation and cognitive maturity. With adolescents, however, the newly developed organizing (i.e., integrative) principles will urge them to increase the coherence between the domain-specific self concepts. These integrative processes will emphasize the presence of contradictory self-concept characteristics. The extent to which adolescents are able to deal with these contradictions will determine the degree of negative emotional consequences. It could be expected that to deal with these contradictions either the real ideas, the expectations, or the perceived ideas of others will have to be modified, or the discrepancies between particular self-concepts will continue to exist, leading to a wide range of emotional maladjustments (see also chapter 7). Indeed, Harter (1986) found an increase in contradictions within the self-system until age 15, followed by a slight decrease, whereas at the age of 15 also emotional conflict was experienced mostly.

In the research mentioned earlier, the focus is on discrepancies *between* domain-specific concepts. However, each domain-specific self-concept will also consist of knowledge about the self in different contexts. Consequently, it is also possible to study discrepancies *within* one domain-specific self-concept. Such a discrepancy within one domain-specific self-concept might occur if two self-descriptions relating to different context-related self-concepts are contradictory. For instance, such a discrepancy in the real self-concept can be experienced by a woman who is convinced that she gives her full attention to her growing children, although she is simultaneously occupied in realizing an academic career. A similar discrepancy within the ideal self-concept, prior to the decision to have children, can consist of the realization that the expectation to pay full attention to the children and the expectation to realize an academic career are probably incompatible. Even more disturbing is the possibility of a discrepancy between self-descriptions related to one and the same context-related self-concept (e.g., the academic or social self-concept). Such a discrepancy may occur when, for instance, someone considers herself or himself a successful academician, though no publication has yet appeared, whereas, at the same time, knowing that successful academics publish. Because discrepancies between domain-specific self-representations in adolescence and adulthood lead to emotional problems, it is expected that discrepancies within domain-specific concepts will result in similar emotional problems. That is, if a discrepancy between the ideal self-concept and the perceived ideal self-concept of others results in conflict and stress within the individual (e.g., Higgins et al., 1985), the same might be expected from two contradictory self-descriptions within the same ideal concept. In fact, this is what was reported by Emmons and King (1988), Nurius and Majerus (1988), and Van Hook and Higgins (1988).

Little is known about the development of such discrepancies within self-concepts. Higgins (1989) suggested that discrepancies within self-concepts will not be evident before age 13 to 16, due to the younger children's inability to relate different perspectives on the self. However, no empirical research dealing with the development of discrepancies within one domain-specific concept is available.

The purposes of the present analyses are to examine the presence and development of discrepancies between and within domain-specific self-concepts with children and adolescents (i.e., from 6 to 18 years). It is expected that both types of discrepancy will appear in childhood as a consequence of increasing skills to differentiate (chapter 4). Next, the discrepancies are expected to disappear somewhat in adolescence as a consequence of increasing skills to integrate and the subsequent awareness of discrepancies.

METHOD

As was described in chapters 2 and 3, the self-concept of the children and adolescents was assessed by means of a Repertory Grid procedure. In total the Repertory Grid included 10 elements, that is, for the real self-concept (S) 1 element; for the perceived real self-concept of others (O) 4 elements (i.e., both parents, a friend of the same, and a friend of the other gender); for the ideal self-concept (S') 1 element, and for the perceived ideal self-concept of others (O') again 4 elements. The descriptive statements had to be scored on a 5-point scale (i.e., from 1 to 5) in terms of their correctness. A score of 5 indicated that the left statement was completely correct, a score of 1 meant that its opposite was completely applicable.

In addition to this Repertory Grid, children were required to compare each of one's own descriptive statements as well as their opposites with all the other descriptive statements in order to obtain the children's evaluation of the degree to which these statements are compatible. This comparison was again made by a 5-point Likert-scale (i.e., from totally incompatible [1] to totally compatible [5]). The obtained compatibility scores were recorded in a 18 x 18 matrix.

Finally, the children had to score each descriptive statement and its opposite for its personal relevance (i.e., importance) by means of a 5-point Likert-scale. A score of 1 indicated that the characteristic was relatively irrelevant; a score of 5 indicated that the characteristic was very relevant.

A discrepancy between two domain-specific self-concepts was operationalized as a difference of 3 or 4 points (on the Likert-scale) between two questions, based on a characteristic with a relevance-score of 3 to 5, with respect to different self-concepts in the grid. These differences were summed for each self-concept comparison (i.e., real vs. ideal self-concept $[S \times S']$, real versus perceived real self-concept of others $[S \times O]$, ideal versus perceived ideal self-concept of others $[S' \times O']$, and perceived real versus ideal self-concept of others $[O \times O']$) and averaged, resulting in a discrepancy score for each pair of self-concepts.

For a discrepancy within one domain-specific self-concept to be present three conditions had to be satisfied:

1. The two descriptive statements (i.e., characteristics) had to be incompatible, that is, a score of 1 or 2 in the matrix of comparisons should be present;
2. The two descriptive statements (i.e., characteristics) had to be relevant; that is, a relevance-score of 3 to 5 for the two characteristics should be present, as an indication that both characteristics are approximately equally and highly relevant; and
3. The two descriptive statements (i.e., characteristics) had to apply to a particular self-concept, that is, a score of 4 or 5 (i.e., with respect to the nine characteristics), or a score of 1 or 2 (i.e., with respect to their opposites) on one question in the grid, as an indication that both characteristics apply, although they are incompatible.

Discrepancies of this sort were added for each domain-specific self-concept (i.e., the real $[S]$ and ideal $[S']$ self-concepts and the perceived real $[O]$ and ideal $[O']$ self-concept of others).

RESULTS

Relations Between Within and Between Self-Concept Discrepancies

To determine if there was any relationship among the between and within self-concept discrepancies the correlations were calculated. In Table 6.1 the correlation coefficients for the comparison between the discrepancies are presented. The correlation coefficients in Table 6.1 indicate that, although most

TABLE 6.1

Correlation Coefficients for the Discrepancies Between and
Within Domain-Specific Self-Concepts

Discrepancies	SxS'	OxO'	SxO	S'xO'	S	O	O'
OxO'	0.53**	-					
SxO	0.28**	0.41**	-				
S'xO'	0.04	0.54**	0.29**	-			
S	0.10	0.06	0.16*	0.07	-		
O	0.04	0.10	0.12*	0.06	0.90**	-	
O'	0.01	0.05	0.04	0.03	0.80**	0.88**	-
S'	0.07	0.03	0.08	0.04	0.81**	0.82**	0.86**

Note. ** $p < .001$; * $p < .05$
The between self-concept discrepancies involve those between the real and ideal
self-concepts ($S \times S'$), the perceived real and ideal self-concepts ($O \times O'$), the real and
perceived real self-concepts ($S \times O$), and the ideal and perceived ideal self-concepts
($S' \times O'$). The within self-concept discrepancies involve those within the real (S), the
perceived real (O), the perceived ideal (O'), and the ideal self-concepts (S').

between self-concept discrepancies and all within self-concept discrepancies
correlate highly with each other, the between and within self-concept
discrepancies rarely correlate with each other. To study whether all
discrepancies are related to one and the same latent factor (i.e., the self-concept)
or represent two different factors (i.e., comparisons between and within
domain-specific self-concepts), a one- and two-factor model were fitted with
LISREL (i.e., LInear Structural RELations). In order to use the Chi-square and
t values obtained by this procedure as indices of fit, the Maximum Likelihood
(henceforth, ML) procedure was followed. To control for skewness of the data
(within a range from 1.43 to 4.25), the Ordinary Least Square (henceforth,
OLS) solution was compared to the best fitting ML solution. Neither a one-, nor
a two-factor model fit the data when the ML procedure was used. The
Chi-square values, however, dramatically decreased from a one-factor
[$\chi^2_{(20)} = 983.34$] to a two-factor model ($\chi^2_{(20)} = 96.27$), indicating a better fit.
The two-factor solution showed significant t values for all factor-loadings
($p < .05$). The introduction of a regression-coefficient, indicating a relationship
between the factors, did not significantly improve the model's fit. The OLS
solution for the two-factor model was comparable to the ML solution and
showed an adjusted goodness of fit index of .98 with a residual variance of .05.
These data indicate that the discrepancies based on differences between
domain-specific self-concepts and those between context-related self-concepts
within particular domain-specific self-concept reflect different constructs.

Between Self-Concept Discrepancies

To assess the effect for age with the between self-concept discrepancies, two ANOVAs with repeated measurements were executed. The first analysis involved the discrepancy scores between one's own real and ideal self-concepts as the dependent measure and age and wave as the factors concerned. No effect was found, either for age or for wave. The second analysis included the discrepancies between the perceived real and ideal self-concepts, between one's own and perceived real self-concepts, and between one's own and perceived ideal self-concepts for each wave as dependent measures and age, wave, and other as factors. Main effects were found for wave $[F_{(2,282)} = 3.86,\ p < .05]$, type of discrepancy $[F_{(2,282)} = 62.68,\ p < .0001]$, and other $[F_{(3,423)} = 9.72,\ p < .0001]$. Interaction effects were found for discrepancy by age $[F_{(10,282)} = 2.04,\ p < .05]$, other by age $[F_{(15,423)} = 3.8,\ p < .0001]$, wave by other $[F_{(6,846)} = 2.17,\ p < .05]$, type of discrepancy by other $[F_{(6,846)} = 15.02,\ p < .0001]$, and type of discrepancy by other by age $[F_{(30,846)} = 1.89,\ p < .005]$.

Contrast analyses revealed that the discrepancies decreased from the first to the third wave [Wave 1 to Wave 3: $F_{(1)} = 7.40,\ p < .01$]. Consistent with the findings for differentiation between the self-concepts, the number of discrepancies between the perceived real and ideal self-concepts ($O \times O'$) was significantly larger than the number of discrepancies between (a) one's own and perceived real self-concepts $[O \times S;\ F_{(1)} = 115.19,\ p < .0001]$ and (b) one's own and perceived ideal self-concepts $[O' \times S';\ F_{(1)} = 66.07,\ p < .0001]$. The number of discrepancies between one's own and perceived real self-concepts ($O \times S$) was smaller than between one's own and perceived ideal self-concepts $[O' \times S';\ F_{(1)} = 6.78,\ p < .01]$. The number of discrepancies was identical among parents and among peers, but more discrepancies were evident for the parents than for the peers $[F_{(1)} = 26.47,\ p < .0001]$.

Contrast analyses on the interaction effect between wave and other showed that a significant decrease in discrepancy from the first to the third wave was evident only for the parents [same-gender parent: $F_{(1)} = 4.66,\ p < .05$; opposite-gender parent: $F_{(1)} = 8.81,\ p < .005$]. For the opposite-gender parent no difference between the second and third wave was found (for the means and standard deviations see Table 6.2). Contrast analyses on the interaction effect between type of discrepancy and other revealed that for the perceived real versus ideal self-concepts a difference between the parents occurred: The number of perceived real–ideal discrepancies for the same-gender parent was smaller than for the opposite-gender parent $[O \times O';\ F_{(1)} = 6.52,\ p < .05]$. As with the main effect, the numbers of perceived real–ideal discrepancies of the parents were larger than those of the peers [opposite-gender parent vs. same-gender peer

TABLE 6.2

Means and Standard Deviations for Other by Wave and

for Type of Discrepancy by Other

Average for Comparisons by:	parent same gender		parent opposite gender		peer same gender		peer opposite gender	
	mean	*sd*	*mean*	*sd*	*mean*	*sd*	*mean*	*sd*
Wave								
Wave 1	.34	.65	.42	.77	.26	.56	.28	.54
Wave 2	.30	.66	.26	.59	.24	.66	.26	.69
Wave 3	.26	.68	.30	.76	.20	.49	.20	.50
Type of Discrepancy								
OxO'	.54	.85	.60	.96	.33	.73	.32	.70
OxS	.14	.45	.12	.37	.17	.42	.19	.48
O'xS'	.24	.55	.26	.59	.21	.53	.22	.53

$F_{(1)} = 79.74$, $p < .0001$]. The latter finding was also true for the discrepancies between one's own versus perceived ideal self-concepts [$S' x O'$; opposite-gender parent vs. same-gender peer $F_{(1)} = 4.09$, $p < .05$], but not for one's own versus the perceived real self-concept discrepancies ($S x O$). In addition, these analyses revealed that for the peers the discrepancies between one's own and perceived real and ideal self-concepts were identical ($S x O = S' x O'$). This finding stands in contrast to the main effect for type of discrepancy.

Because of the significant effect for the interactions between age and type of discrepancy and between age and other, as well as between age and type of discrepancy and other, the analysis was split into ANOVAs to assess these effects. This resulted in twelve ANOVAs with the discrepancies as dependent measure and age and wave as factors. Only for the discrepancies between the perceived real and ideal self-concepts of the parents were significant effects for age observed [$F_{(5,14)} = 2.70$, $p < .05$, for the same-gender parent, and $F_{(5,14)} = 2.42$, $p < .05$, for the other-gender parent; see Fig. 6.1]. Neither for the self–other discrepancies, nor for discrepancies between one's own real and ideal self-concepts or the perceived real and ideal self-concepts of the peers could an age effect be demonstrated. The discrepancy between the perceived real and ideal concept of the same-gender parent increased from the first to the second age-group [$F_{(1)} = 8.27$, $p < .005$]. The discrepancy between the perceived real and ideal self-concept of the opposite-gender parent also increased, though more

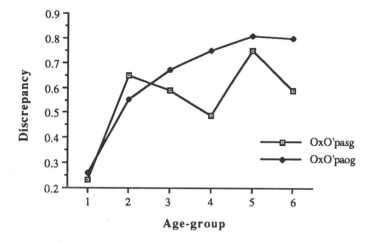

FIG. 6.1. Mean self-concept discrepany scores between the perceived real and ideal self-concepts of the parents by age-group.

gradually, from the first to the third age-group [$F_{(1)} = 4.97$, $p < .05$]. Both discrepancies stabilized following this increase.

In summary, the data indicate that the wave, the type of *between* self-concept discrepancy and the significant other involved clearly influence the number of discrepancies. The children demonstrated a decrease in discrepancies for the subsequent waves when the concepts were those of their parents. More discrepancies were shown between the perceived real and ideal self-concepts and between one's own and perceived ideal self-concepts with regard to their parents than with regard to their peers. The number of discrepancies between the perceived real and ideal self-concept of the opposite-gender parent was larger than for the same-gender parent. Age only affected the number of discrepancies between the perceived real and ideal self-concepts of the parents. This discrepancy increased from the first to the second and third age-groups and remained stable afterwards. The age effects for discrepancies between self-concepts were in general comparable to those for the difference scores between the intraindividual concepts (see chapter 4), which is due to the fact that discrepancy scores form a special category of difference scores.

Within Self-Concept Discrepancies

The data for the discrepancies *within* self-concepts were assessed by means of a 6 x 3 x 2 x 5 (age x wave x [real-ideal self-concept] x [other + self]) ANOVA with repeated measurements. Main effects were found for age [$F_{(5,144)} = 4.60$,

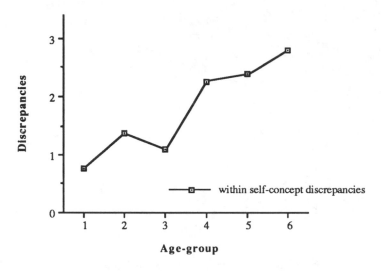

FIG. 6.2. Within self-concept discrepancies by age-group.

$p < .001$], type of self-concept [i.e., real vs. ideal self-concepts; $F_{(1,144)} = 163.81$, $p < .0001$], and person involved [$F_{(4,576)} = 82.05$, $p < .0001$]. Interaction effects were present for person by age [$F_{(20,576)} = 10.17$, $p < .0001$] and for wave by real versus ideal self-concepts by age [$F_{(10,288)} = 19.84$, $p < .001$].

Contrast analysis for age revealed a significant effect for the first, second, and third versus the sixth age-group. Though no differences between the former three age-groups occurred, from the third to the sixth age-group a significant increase in the discrepancies within self-concepts was apparent [contrast analysis on age-group 1, 2, and 3 against age-group 6: $F_{(1)} = 12.35$, $p < .001$; see Fig. 6.2]. The number of discrepancies within the real self-concepts was larger than that within the ideal self-concepts. Significantly more discrepancies were found within the perceived self-concepts of the parents than within the perceived self-concepts of the peers [$F_{(1)} = 41.07$, $p < .0001$]. However, even more discrepancies could be observed within the subjects' own self-concepts than in either the self-concepts of their parents or their peers [$F_{(1)} = 40.66$, $p < .0001$]. In other words, these findings suggest that more discrepancies are present within the children's own self-concepts than within the perceived self-concepts.

To assess the interaction effects between the person involved and age, and between wave, real versus ideal self-concepts, and age, separate ANOVAs for age-group on the summed scores by each person (five analyses) and on thesummed scores by wave and real versus ideal self-concepts (six analyses) were run (for the means and standard deviations see Table 6.3). Contrast

TABLE 6.3

Means and Standard Deviations of Within Self-Concept Discrepancies for Person by
Age-Group and Wave by Real Versus Ideal Self-Concepts by Age-Group

	parent same gender		parent opposite gender		peer same gender		peer opposite gender		self	
	m	sd	m	sd	m	sd	m	sd	m	sd
Group 1	.81	2.24	.70	2.14	.83	2.69	.67	2.11	.84	2.42
Group 2	1.71	3.57	1.49	3.07	1.08	2.22	.71	1.77	1.91	3.75
Group 3	1.18	2.55	1.18	2.87	.85	1.85	1.08	2.62	1.15	2.30
Group 4	2.12	3.01	2.19	3.23	2.27	3.14	1.76	2.79	2.89	4.42
Group 5	2.57	3.55	2.55	3.58	2.15	3.07	1.96	2.90	2.76	3.96
Group 6	2.98	4.35	3.37	4.68	2.16	2.83	2.11	3.40	3.45	4.43

	Wave 1				Wave 2				Wave 3			
	real		ideal		real		ideal		real		ideal	
Group	m	sd	m	sd	m	sd	m	sd	m	sd	m	sd
1	.57	1.22	.56	1.35	1.14	3.03	1.21	3.71	.76	2.21	.38	.97
2	1.76	3.65	1.33	3.14	2.11	3.65	1.91	3.60	.64	1.08	.51	1.17
3	.96	1.61	1.01	1.81	2.17	3.53	.84	1.85	.73	2.29	.81	2.84
4	2.50	3.57	1.83	2.81	2.46	3.72	1.38	2.63	2.85	3.67	2.46	3.55
5	2.20	3.02	2.31	3.75	2.68	3.36	2.87	4.26	2.67	3.48	1.65	2.36
6	4.25	6.05	2.82	3.88	2.49	3.07	2.69	3.35	2.69	3.72	1.93	3.01

analyses indicated that for the perceived self-concepts of the parents the above
main effect was repeated; though the discrepancies were stable until the third
age-group, a gradual increase from this age to the sixth age-group was present
[third to sixth age-group, same-gender parent: $F_{(1)} = 6.91$, $p < .01$; opposite-
gender parent: $F_{(1)} = 9.43$, $p < .005$]. For the perceived self-concepts of the
same-gender peer and one's own self-concept an increase from the third to the
sixth age-group was also evident. Here, however, the significance was due to
an increase from the third to the fourth age-group only; that is, from the first to
the third age-group the number of discrepancies was stable, from the third to the
fourth age-group this number increased, whereas from the fourth to the sixth
age-group the number of discrepancies remained stable again [Age-group 3 to 4,
self: $F_{(1)} = 5.42$, $p < .05$; same-gender peer: $F_{(1)} = 7.49$, $p < .01$]. The
discrepancies within the perceived self-concepts of the opposite-gender peer
gradually increased from the first to the sixth age-group [$F_{(1)} = 8.34$, $p < .005$].

When wave and real or ideal self-concepts were considered, the following
results were found. In contrast to the first and third wave, no significant effect
for age-group was evident in the second wave. In the first wave, both the

discrepancies for the real and ideal self-concepts increased from the third to the sixth age-group [real self-concepts: $F_{(1)} = 28.39$, $p < .0001$; ideal self-concepts: $F_{(1)} = 16.06$, $p < .0001$]. Although in the third wave the same effect was found, it was due to an increase between the third and fourth age-group only [real self-concepts: $F_{(1)} = 8.99$, $p < .005$; ideal self-concepts: $F_{(1)} = 7.45$, $p < .01$], indicating that the main increase in discrepancies within self-concepts occurs between late childhood and middle adolescence.

In conclusion, discrepancies within self-concepts gradually increased from the third to the sixth age-group. Only in the case of one's own self-concepts and those of the same-gender peer did this increase occur abruptly between the third and fourth age-group. Whereas in the first wave general, gradual increases in the discrepancies from the third to the sixth age-group were observed, in the third wave more abrupt increases from the third to the fourth age-group were evident. No such increases could be demonstrated in the second wave. In addition, more discrepancies were present within the real self-concepts than within the ideal self-concepts. Finally, most discrepancies were present within one's own self-concepts as compared to the perceived self-concepts of others. Among the latter self-concepts of others, a larger number of discrepancies was found within the perceived self-concepts of the parents than of the peers.

Additional Inquiries for Between as well as Within Self-Concept Discrepancies

At the beginning of this chapter, it was argued that discrepancies *between* and *within* intraindividual self-concepts might be affected by changing cognitive abilities. Because of the growing ability to differentiate between self-concepts a subsequent increase in the number of discrepancies during childhood was expected. Conversely, because of the increasing ability to integrate information, a decrease in the number of discrepancies in adolescence was predicted. Consequently, the previous analyses had as their purpose the comparison of mean scores. However, besides age-related changes in the mean discrepancy scores, other indications for either stage transitions or developmental accelerations are present in continuous processes (Van der Maas & Molenaar, in press). Such indications are, among others, a lack of homogeneity of variance and a bimodality of the scores. Small standard deviations, for instance, indicate little variance in children's reactions to the assessment procedure. Large standard deviations, however, suggest a different phenomenon. At a particular age when a change in information-processing strategies occurs, children are expected to react differently. Children who are still in the former stage will react with a response based on the strategy characterizing that stage (n), whereas

TABLE 6.4

F Values for Hartley's Tests and *F* Tests for Homogeneity at an *a* = .05
for the Differences Between Variances

		between OxO' parent sg	between OxO' parent og	between OxO' peer sg	between OxO' peer og	between SxS'	between SxO parent sg	between SxO parent og
Hartley's Test	*F*	4.25	4.64	10.24	3.82	4.54	8.63	5.81
Group 1-2	*F*	2.44	2.03	1.62	2.32	4.60	2.19	*ns*
Group 2-3	*F*	*ns*	1.64	*ns*	*trend*	*ns*	2.69	4.00
Group 3-4	*F*	*ns*	*ns*	3.58	1.95	*ns*	*ns*	2.27
Group 4-5	*F*	*ns*	*ns*	*ns*	10.24	*ns*	7.19	2.56
Group 5-6	*F*	1.69	*ns*	2.18	*ns*	1.76	4.91	*ns*

		between SxO peer sg	between SxO peer og	between S'xO' parent sg	between S'xO' parent og	between S'xO' peer sg	between S'xO' peer og	within concepts
Hartley's Test	*F*	2.17	3.35	2.66	2.98	3.90	5.10	2.99
Group 1-2	*F*	*ns*	*ns*	1.71	*ns*	*ns*	*ns*	1.63
Group 2-3	*F*	1.69	2.47	2.23	*ns*	1.78	1.59	1.49
Group 3-4	*F*	*ns*	3.15	*ns*	*ns*	2.19	3.22	1.89
Group 4-5	*F*	*ns*	1.82	*ns*	*ns*	*ns*	1.75	1.04
Group 5-6	*F*	*ns*	1.84	*ns*	2.98	*ns*	1.74	1.37

children who are already in the new stage will react with a response based on the strategy characterizing the new stage (*n+1*). In addition, children who are in a transitional stage show unstable responses based on either strategy (i.e., characterizing either stage *n* or stage *n+1*). As a consequence, a transitional stage is indicated by an increased variance in the responses, which follows and will be followed by smaller variances. In other words, the transition from one stage to the next higher stage, through a transitional stage, can be defined as a shift in distribution scores. Whereas for stage *n* and stage *n+1* a unimodal frequency distribution (i.e., peak) is expected, for the transitional stage a bimodal frequency distribution (i.e., two peaks) is predicted. That is, a unimodal distribution will shift to a bimodal distribution, and again be followed by a new unimodal distribution.

For the discrepancies *between* as well as *within* self-concepts, age-related shifts in standard deviations occurred. Hartley's *F* tests (Winer, 1971) revealed that these shifts were significant for each type of discrepancy. Separate *F* tests for the homogeneity of variance between two age-groups demonstrated several significant increases and decreases in homogeneity (see Table 6.4). With regard

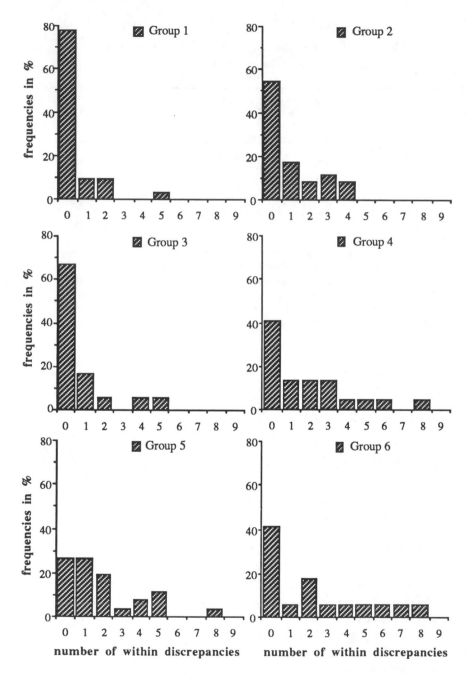

FIG. 6.3. Percentage of children with discrepancies within
their self-concepts by number of discrepancies and age-group.

to the discrepancy between real and ideal self-concepts, an increase in variance is evident from the first to the second age-group. For the following age-groups as well as the discrepancies between one's own and perceived self-concepts of others, little regularity was apparent. That is, there was no consistent pattern presenting an increase and subsequent decrease in the standard deviations for the discrepancies *between* self-concepts. Such a pattern is present for the discrepancies *within* self-concepts. From the first to the second age-group the variance for the discrepancy scores within self-concepts increases, from the second to the third age-group the variance decreases, after which it increases again until the sixth age-group. This age-related pattern suggests the onset and completion of a transitional stage, and the onset of a new and larger transitional stage.

Although no formal analyses were done on these data, the frequency tables for the discrepancies between and within self-concepts for each age-group corroborate the data for changes in variance of the discrepancy scores. Here also, the pattern for the discrepancies between self-concepts is too equivocal to allow even cautious conclusions. The pattern for discrepancies within self-concepts is more promising. As can be seen in Fig. 6.3, a shift from a one-peak frequency distribution in the younger age-groups to a bimodal distribution in the fifth and sixth age-group is present. In contrast to the more traditional tests for cognitive ability, higher scores in the older age-groups are represented by the small number of discrepancies (i.e., comparable to the scores for the lower levels in the younger age-groups). Following the bimodal distribution, a shift to new unimodality around the higher scores was expected, that is, in the present case, a shift from bimodality back to unimodality around the lower scores. This was not the case, preventing clear conclusions about the onset of a new stage. The high frequency of scores larger than zero, in combination with the increasing variance, indicate that the adolescents in the sixth age-group are still in a transitional stage. It may be that the integration of discrepancies within self-concepts is a task that is not yet completed by the end of adolescence, or that some discrepancies cannot be integrated at all.

Drop-Out and Cohort Effects
for the Between Self-Concept Discrepancies

A possible explanation for the absence of consistent patterns for the standard deviations of the discrepancies between self-concepts may be that the different waves in the present study disturb the actual pattern. A combination of waves implies an overlap in ages between the subsequent age-groups. For instance, the 8-year-olds in the first wave (i.e., the second age-group) are overlapping the

8-year-olds in the third wave (i.e., the first age-group). Because a significant difference was found for the discrepancy between self-concepts between the first and third wave, it may again be useful to examine the data for drop-out effects.

Analysis of variance for drop-out effect on the discrepancy scores between self-concepts showed that the children who dropped out of the study following the first wave scored a larger number of discrepancies than the children who remained in the study [$F_{(1,202)} = 5.42$, $p < .05$]. Interaction effects revealed that this was primarily for the discrepancies between the real and ideal self-concepts of the parents and the discrepancies between one's own and the perceived ideal self-concepts of the peers. No such effects were found for the children who dropped out following the second wave.

Because of this finding, the data for the children who left the study following the first wave were omitted from the reanalysis of the data. In this reanalysis the discrepancy scores of the second, third, fourth, fifth, and sixth age-group of the first wave were compared to the scores of the first, second, third, fourth, and fifth age-group of the third wave. That is, the 8-year-olds from the first wave were compared to the 8-year-olds from the third wave, the 10-year-olds from the first wave to the 10-year-olds of the third wave, and so on. Only five significant differences out of 65 comparisons were found (i.e., less than 10%). These were for the 8-year-olds, differences for the discrepancy scores between one's own real and ideal self-concepts [$S \times S'$; $t_{(31)} = 2.27$, $p < .05$], the discrepancy scores between the perceived real and ideal self-concept of the same-gender parent [$O \times O'$pasg; $t_{(31)} = 3.62$, $p < .001$] and between one's own and the perceived real self-concept of the opposite-gender peer [$S \times O$peog; $t_{(31)} = 2.74$, $p < .01$] were present. In addition, a difference was present between one's own and perceived real self-concepts for the same-gender parent with the 14-year-olds [$S \times O$pasg; $t_{(21)} = 2.16$, $p < .05$], and for the opposite-gender parent with the 16-year-olds [$S \times O$paog; $t_{(16)} = 2.75$, $p < .05$]. Although these cohort effects may be spurious because of their small number, they may represent indicators for an absence of a regular developmental course for discrepancies between self-concepts until the age of 10 years. This assumption would be consistent with the findings for the children's ability to differentiate between self-concepts, which is also unstable until the same age (see chapter 4).

Because of the disruptive character of these cohort effects, the data from the first and third wave can be combined, which permits the analysis for a more extended pattern of development. The means and standard deviations for the discrepancies between the real and ideal self-concepts of the overlapping age-groups were avaraged over the first and third wave to explore this pattern (Table 6.5). With the exception of the discrepancies for the opposite-gender parent, the developmental pattern for all discrepancies between the real and ideal

TABLE 6.5

Means and Standard Deviations for the Discrepancies Between Real and Ideal
Self-Concepts for the 6-Year-Olds from Wave 1, the 8-Year-Olds from Waves 1 and 3,
the 10-Year-Olds from Waves 1 and 3, the 12-Year-Olds from Waves 1 and 3, the
14-Year-Olds from Waves 1 and 3, the 16-Year-Olds from Waves 1 and 3,
and the 18-Year-Olds from Wave 3, Averaged Over Wave

	SxS'		OxO' parent sg		OxO' parent og		OxO' peer sg		OxO' peer og	
	m	sd	m	sd	m	sd	m	sd	m	sd
age 6	.27	.51	.38	.76	.27	.73	.30	.52	.27	.45
age 8	.41	.63	.47	.65	.47	.73	.39	.67	.35	.61
age 10	.59	.73	.70	.88	.79	.93	.58	.88	.53	.89
age 12	.48	.82	.50	.79	.83	1.19	.29	.58	.32	.57
age 14	.43	.82	.64	1.19	.89	1.34	.30	.55	.27	.52
age 16	.43	.91	.79	1.13	.77	1.06	.16	.58	.21	.51
age 18	.11	.32	.50	.71	1.06	1.16	.22	.55	.11	.32

self-concepts is characterized by an inverted u-shaped curve. The largest
number of discrepancies is found at approximately the age of 10 years. Abrupt
decreases in the number of the discrepancies are not found before the age of 16
years. The abruptness of these decreases is affected by the finding that the
difference scores from the age of 8 years onward are depressed by the tendency
to score lower in the third than in the first wave, that is, due to the drop-out of
high discrepancy participants. In fact, the increase from 6 to 8 years should be
more pronounced, and the abrupt decrease from 16 to 18 years should be less
pronounced. Also the variance (i.e., the standard deviations) follows the same
inverted u-shaped pattern.

In summary, the number of discrepancies between the real and ideal
self-concepts, though apparently unstable between the ages of 6 to 8 years,
increases during childhood and decreases during (late) adolescence, confirming
expectations. It is thought that these age-related changes are due to differing
underlying cognitive processes such as differentiation and integration. These
changes were significant only for the discrepancies between the perceived real
and ideal self-concepts of the parents.

Drop-Out and Cohort Effects
for the Within Self-Concept Discrepancies

No difficulties were encountered in the interpretation of the data on the
development of the discrepancies within self-concepts. Neverthelesss, the data

of the age-groups with the same age were compared to determine whether the cross-sectional data with respect to the development of the discrepancies within the self-concepts were or were not affected by cohort effects. Analysis of variance for the effect of drop-out on the discrepancy scores within self-concepts revealed no significant effects. Therefore, no corrections of the data were neccessary to compare the age-groups of the same age from the first and third wave. As with the discrepancies between the self-concepts, little differences could be demonstrated for the discrepancies within the self-concepts between the age-groups. Of the 50 comparisons, only 5 showed a significant difference. In all cases, the differences were present for the 12-year-olds only. Differences were present for four of the five types of discrepancies within the real self-concepts [i.e., one's own real self-concept (S): $t_{(24)} = 2.29$, $p < .05$; the perceived real self-concept of the same sex parents $(O\text{pasg})$: $t_{(24)} = 2.165$, $p < 05$; of the opposite-gender parents $(O\text{paog})$: $t_{(24)} = 2.36$, $p < .05$; and of the same-gender peer $(O\text{pesg})$: $t_{(24)} = 2.72$, $p < .05$], and for the discrepancy within one's own ideal self-concept $[(S'); t_{(24)} = 2.08, p < .05]$. As was previously discussed, the number of discrepancies within self-concepts increased from the third to the sixth age-group in the first wave, although in the third wave this happened primarily between the third and fourth age-group. Consequently, the only differences found for that age-period were those in which the most obvious changes in the number of discrepancies were evident.

In summary, there is sufficient reason to assume that the cross-sectional data regarding the development of discrepancies within self-concepts presents longitudinal data. Discrepancies within self-concepts are stable but low during childhood and abruptly increase in early adolescence.

CONCLUSIONS

The purposes of the present chapter were to report on the presence and development of discrepancies *between* and *within* domain-specific self-concepts with children and adolescents. Discrepancies were defined as contradictions between the self-descriptions within the self-concepts. Discrepancies *between* self-concepts were thought to be present if highly personally relevant self-descriptions within different self-concepts were incompatible. Discrepancies within self-concepts were thought to be present if highly personally relevant self-descriptions within one self-concept were incompatible. Although the results of this study demonstrated the presence of discrepancies *between* as well as *within* domain-specific self-concepts, little if any relationship was evident between both types of discrepancies. Age-related changes in the discrepancies *between* the self-concepts were only present for the discrepancy between the perceived real and ideal self-concepts of the parents. For the discrepancies *within* the self-concepts, age-related changes could be demonstrated for all four domain-specific self-concepts (i.e., one's own and perceived real and ideal self-concepts).

The discrepancy between the perceived real and ideal self-concepts of the parents was characterized by increases until approximately age 10, followed by stability and a tendency to decrease. This trend is in accordance with the assumption that in middle and late childhood (i.e., from 6 to 10 years) children become increasingly more aware of contradictory information with respect to themselves. They are, however, not yet able to cope with this contradictory information. The growing ability to integrate this information is reflected by a decrease in the discrepancies in late adolescence. However, because children may not yet be able to solve all contradictions in an acceptable way, and because these contradictions will be consciously present, the level of discrepancy in adolescence may remain higher than that in early childhood. The increase in standard deviations from middle to late childhood suggests large individual differences in the developmental progress with respect to the above cognitive abilities. The decrease in discrepancies in late adolescence may represent the end of a transitional period from an inability to integrate contradictory information to the ability to do so. The inconsistent standard deviations in adolescence also reflect these individual differences in children's abilities to cope with contradictory information; that is, whereas some adolescents experience such discrepancies, others do not. In other words, the developmental as well as emotional progress from the inability to the ability to integrate is more pronounced for one person than for another. Finally, although significant age-related changes in the discrepancies were present between the perceived real and ideal self-concepts of the parents, no such changes could be observed for the discrepancies between one's own real and ideal self-concepts or the perceived real and ideal self-concepts of the peers.

Significant age-related changes could be demonstrated for all the discrepancies *within* the domain-specific self-concepts (i.e., one's own real and ideal, and the perceived real and ideal self-concepts of others). These changes, however, are different from those found for the discrepancies *between* the perceived real and ideal self-concepts. For all discrepancies within self-concepts an increase is observed between the ages of 10 and 18 years, and between the ages of 10 and 14, in particular. This increase suggests a growing awareness during adolescence of conflicting characteristics within the various self-concepts.

The more pronounced and delayed occurrence of developmental changes for the discrepancies within self-concepts, as compared to the discrepancies between real and ideal self-concepts in the age-range studied may be due to a delayed developmental awareness of discrepancies within self-concepts (cf. Higgins, 1989). Another explanation, however, may involve the operationalizations used in this study for the two different types of discrepancy (i.e., the discrepancies *between* and the discrepancies*within* self-concepts). It was assumed that the awareness of conflicting or contradictory characteristics in self-descriptions or self-understanding is a developmental prerequisite for discrepancies to be experienced. In the operationalizations employed in the present study, the awareness of contradictory characteristics was implied by the procedure to assess discrepancies *within* domain-specific self-concepts, but not in the procedure used to assess discrepancies *between* domain-specific self-concepts. The discrepancies *between* the self-concepts were inferred from the children's and adolescents' answers in the Grid. There was no control for whether these children and adolescents were aware of any discrepancy. The discrepancies *within* self-concepts, however, were based on the children's and adolescents' responses following the prior awareness (i.e., experience) of the contradictory nature of the various self-characteristics. Consequently, although the developmental changes for discrepancies *between* self-concepts may be directly based on underlying cognitive processes such as the differentiation between, and integration of self-concepts, the age-related changes for the discrepancies *within* self-concepts may be the result of the experimentally induced awareness of such discrepancies and the children's and adolescent's abilities to deal with these.

7 Discrepancies and Emotional Functioning

In chaper 6 the occurence of discrepancies between and within self-concepts was discussed. It was found that the number of discrepancies between the perceived real and ideal self-concepts of the parents increased from the first to the third age-group and remained stable thereafter. In contrast, the number of discrepancies within each of the self-concepts remained low and stable until the third age-group and increased afterwards. The purpose of the present chapter is to study the relationship between both types of discrepancy and affect. That is, whether discrepancies *between* and *within* concepts are related to negative affects, and whether this relationship is present at all ages.

SELF-CONCEPTS AND EMOTIONS

As was already noted in chapters 1 and 6, discrepancies between real and ideal self-concept are thought to be related to negative emotions (e.g., Higgins, 1987) in adults. In a series of studies, Higgins and colleagues (Higgins, 1987; Higgins et al., 1985; Higgins et al., 1986; Strauman, 1989) found strong evidence for this relationship. Discrepancies between one's own real self-concept and either one's own or the perceived ideal concept of others resulted in dejection-related emotions. The more such discrepancies were present, the stronger the emotion (Higgins et al., 1985). In addition, a causal relation could be demonstrated between such emotions and discrepancies (Higgins et al., 1986), and discrepancies distinguished between disorders in a clinical situation (Strauman, 1989). Similarly, Keeton, Cash, and Brown (1990) found that discrepancies between real and ideal body-concepts and a negative attitude towards the body were related to eating problems. Flett, Hewitt, and Dyck (1989) reported that the individuals' tendency to possess high goals and standards for themselves (i.e., the ideal self-concepts) directly predicts anxiety and neuroticism (life-stress functions as an additional mediating variable).

Although less is known about discrepancies *within* one domain-specific self-concept, indications about their consequences can be inferred from studies on self-regulation dealing with conflicts between personal strivings (i.e., discrepancies within the ideal self-concept). Van Hook and Higgins (1988) reported that conflicts between self-guides (i.e., between self-descriptions) within a possible self, such as the ideal self-concept, result in: confusion, a more frequent occurrence of such incompatible self-descriptions in free descriptions of the real self-concept, and more moderate scores for personal relevance for these self-descriptions than other, compatible, self-descriptions. Emmons and King (1988) reported that conflicts within a personal striving or between strivings (i.e., within or between context-related concepts within a possible self like the ideal self-concept) were related to negative affects, depression, neuroticism, and psychosomatic complaints. The conflicts were predictive for psychosomatic complaints 1 year later. In addition, participants who reported such conflicts tended to be less active and to reflect more on the incompatible self-descriptions than participants without such conflicts (for a case-study see Nurius & Majerus, 1988).

Higgins (1989) proposed a model for the development of discrepancies in children that is based on his self-discrepancy theory (Higgins, 1987; cf. chapter 1). Accordingly, children are able to experience discrepancies between real and ideal self-concepts between the ages of 4 and 6 years. During this age-period, children shift from egocentric to nonegocentric thinking and acquire the ability to take the perspective of others. Children become, then, able to go beyond immediate actions and to interpret their actions in reference to "internally represented standards or guides that others hold for them. Towards the end of this period, there is a shift from concern with the direct consequences of one's actions to a concern with social approval, to living up to what one believes are the expectancies others hold for oneself" (p. 416). The feelings that are expected to be associated with the discrepancies during this period are feelings of guilt and embarrassment. Discrepancies within self-concepts and discrepancies between one's own and the perceived ideal self-concepts of others should not occur until age 13 to 16. It is not until that age that the adolescent is able to relate two distinct possible selves. Once such possible selves are consciously experienced, the double approach–avoidance conflict that results from discrepancies should result in feelings of uncertainty and confusion. The model of Higgins was partly confirmed by the findings in chapter 6, which offered evidence for an earlier increase in discrepancies *between* the real and ideal perceived self-concepts for the parents than in discrepancies *within* these self-concepts and revealed an absence of any age-related effect for the discrepancies between one's own and perceived self-concepts.

Furthermore, based on her research on emotional development, Harter (1986) argued that none of the discrepancies within the self-system causes any conflict until adolescence because of children's inability to integrate conflicting attributes (see also chapters 1 and 6). Harter and colleagues found that the experience of conflicts in the self-system dramatically increased from early to middle adolescence, after which it decreased again. More important, they reported that the percentage of adolescents who reported that the discrepancy made them feel confused followed the same developmental pattern. Unfortunately, in this study no distinction was made between   discrepancies *between* and *within* self-concepts.

In the present study, the assumption examined was that children will not experience any negative emotions as a result of discrepancies prior to adolescence, because of the absence of integrative abilities. To test this assumption, the 'Amsterdamse Biografische Vragenlijst voor Kinderen' (ABV-K; Van Dijl & Wilde, 1982) was added to the assessment instruments in the third wave of the time-sequential study. The ABV-K is a Dutch questionnaire for emotional (in)stability for children and adolescents from 9 to 17 years of age. Based on the guiding hypothesis in this chapter, it was expected that even if discrepancies were present, they would not affect emotional functioning until adolescence. During adolescence, discrepancies *between*, as well as *within* self-concepts were expected to result in negative emotional effects, such as neuroticism and psychosomatic complaints. Thus, an interaction between age, discrepancy, and emotional affects was expected. Because to date little is known about the emotional effects of discrepancies *within* self-concepts, the data analysis dealing with these discrepancies is exploratory.

METHOD

The 'Amsterdamse Biografische Vragenlijst voor Kinderen' (ABV-K; Van Dijl & Wilde, 1982) consists of four scales, assessing neuroticism expressed by psycho-neurotic complaints (N), neuroticism expressed by physical complaints (NS), extraversion (E) related to social competence, and test-attitude (T), that is, defensiveness against self-criticism. In a series of studies the relevance of neuroticism and psychosomatic complaints in relation to discrepancies between self-concepts has been demonstrated (Emmons & King, 1988; Flett et al., 1989). For instance, Emmons and King found that conflicts between and within personal strivings (i.e., possible selves) were associated with negative affect, depression, neuroticism, and psychosomatic complaints. Flett et al. reported that people with high goals showed neuroticism and anxiety. Neuroticism has

TABLE 7.1

Correlation Coefficients Between the Four ABV-K Scales for Boys and Girls,
as Reported for the Normative Sample (Van Dijl & Wilde, 1982, p. 43)
and as Found in the Present Study

		N		NS		E	
		norm	study	norm	study	norm	study
NS	boys	.55	.55				
	girls	.53	.57				
E	boys	-.33	-.42	-.21	-.21		
	girls	-.22	-.30	-.16	-.19		
T	boys	-.35	-.22	-.26	-.26	.08	-.24
	girls	-.36	-.25	-.16	-.26	-.02	-.19

Note. N: psycho-neurotic complaints; NS: neuroticism expressed by physical complaints;
E: extraversion; T: test-attitude

also been shown to correlate negatively, and extraversion and test-attitude positively with life-satisfaction (Heaven, 1989). The validity and reliability of the ABV-K have been sufficiently demonstrated (Visser, Van Vliet-Mulder, Evers, & Ter Laak, 1982). The ABV-K consists of 115 precoded items with the response possibilities yes and no. The raw scores were translated in percentile scores according to the norms of the ABV-K.

The discrepancy scores were obtained and calculated according to the procedure followed in chapter 6. These scores were then classified into two categories: "no discrepancies" and "discrepancies." In addition, in order to increase the number of subjects in each "discrepancy" cell, the six age-groups were handled pairwise. Thus, the first and the second group, the third and the fourth group, and the fifth and the sixth group were combined, resulting in a group for late childhood (8- to 10-year-olds), a young adolescents group (12- to 14-year-olds), and a late adolescents group (16- to 18-year-olds).

RESULTS

The Scores on the ABV-K

Correlation coefficients for boys and girls were calculated between the four scales of the ABV-K. The interscale correlation coefficients did not significantly differ from the coefficients in the normative sample (see Table 7.1). The subjects also scored largely within the normal range of the scales, with the

TABLE 7.2

Frequency Distribution of Scores on the Four ABV-K Scales
in Percentage Over Five Categories

	% N	% NS	% E	% T
very low	7.55	6.92	.63	5.06
low	13.21	18.87	.00	19.62
average	39.62	32.08	2.53	43.04
high	18.87	28.93	5.70	18.99
very high	20.76	13.21	91.14	13.29

Note. N: psycho-neurotic complaints ; NS: neuroticism expressed by physical complaints; E: extraversion; T: test-attitude

exception of the extraversion scale. The scores on the latter scale indicate that the present sample was highly extrovert (see Table 7.2).

Effects of Discrepancy and Age-Group on Emotional Functioning

The relationship between discrepancies, age-group, and emotional functioning was tested by means of ANOVAs for each type of discrepancy and ABV-K scale. That is, analyses were done on the 13 different types of discrepancies between self-concepts. These were: the discrepancies between one's own real and ideal self-concept ($S \times S'$), the perceived real and ideal self-concepts ($O \times O'$), one's own and perceived real self-concepts ($S \times O$), and one's own and perceived ideal self-concepts ($S' \times O'$). In addition, analyses were done on the 10 discrepancies within self-concepts, that is, one's own real self-concept (S), one's own ideal self-concept (S'), the perceived real concept of two parents and two peers (O), and the perceived ideal self-concept of parents and peers (O'). Because the affect of a discrepancy could be mediated by the role of the other involved, as well as by the gender of the other (e.g., Siegal, 1987), analyses were done with the others organized by gender (i.e., same gender, opposite gender) and role (i.e., mother, father, female best friend, male best friend). However, despite the reduction of the number of age-groups from six to three, hardly any children mentioned discrepancies between one's own and perceived self-concepts (i.e., the number of participants was usually smaller than 10). Analyses on these discrepancies will, therefore, not be discussed.

A first review of these analyses confirmed the expectation that discrepancies *between* self-concepts affected primarily neuroticism, though neuroticism expressed by psycho-neurotic complaints rather than physical complaints (see

TABLE 7.3

Results of the Analyses of Variance of Age and Between
Self-Concept Discrepancy on Four Scales of the ABV-K

discrepancy	N			NS		
	age	dis.	int.	age	dis.	int.
SS'	ns	p=.07	ns	ns	ns	ns
OO'pasg	ns	*	p=.07	ns	ns	ns
OO'paog	ns	*	*	ns	ns	ns
OO'pesg	ns	ns	ns	ns	ns	ns
OO'peog	ns	ns	ns	ns	ns	ns
OO'mother	ns	*	*	ns	*	ns
OO'father	ns	*	ns	ns	ns	ns
OO'female friend	ns	ns	ns	ns	ns	ns
OO'male friend	ns	ns	ns	ns	ns	ns

Note. * : significant at p < .05; N: psycho-neurotic complaints; NS: neuroticism expressed by physical complaints; dis.: discrepancy; int.: interaction between age and discrepancy; SS': own real–ideal discrepancies; OO': supposed real–ideal discrepancies of others; pasg: parent same gender; paog: parent opposite gender; pesg: peer same gender; peog: peer opposite gender.

Tabel 7.3). No effects for discrepancies *between* self-concepts on extraversion and test-attitude were observed. Discrepancies between the real and ideal self-concepts showed a significant main effect on neurotic complaints when the perceived self-concepts of the parents were involved ($O \times O'$) and a trend when one's own self-concepts were involved ($S \times S'$). Children with discrepancies between these real and ideal self-concepts scored higher on neurotic complaints than children without such discrepancies. Discrepancies between the perceived real and ideal self-concepts of the peers did not affect the scores on any of the scales. A significant interaction between discrepancy and age could not be demonstrated for one's own self-concepts, although the mean scores are in the expected direction (Table 7.3). The interaction was significant for the opposite-gender parent and showed a nonsignificant trend for the same-gender parent. If the parents were considered according to their role (and not gender), the effect was significant for the perceived self-concepts of the mother, but absent for the perceived self-concepts of the father. Hence, with regard to the influence of discrepancies between the perceived real and ideal self-concepts of the parents, the role rather than the gender of the parent is important. The mean scores for neuroticism increased with age when discrepancies between the

TABLE 7.4

Number of Subjects, Standard Deviations, Means, F Values and Probablitities
for Scores on Four Scales of the ABV-K by the Absence (No) and
Presence (Yes) of Discrepancies Between Real and Ideal Self-Concepts

Discrepancies		N SxS' no	N SxS' yes	N OxO'mother no	N OxO'mother yes	N OxO'father no	N OxO'father yes	NS OxO'mother no	NS OxO'mother yes
Age-group:									
1+2	n	44	22	44	23	47	20	44	23
	sd	29.55	33.51	30.25	6.65	31.08	31.33	30.01	29.63
	m	64.41	60.82	64.55	59.44	61.77	65.20	59.61	61.26
3+4	n	29	18	31	17	29	19	31	17
	sd	24.96	30.62	31.74	4.57	30.39	21.34	25.79	35.21
	m	49.93	66.83	53.29	67.12	50.83	69.42	48.84	55.18
5+6	n	36	8	25	19	22	22	25	19
	sd	27.56	20.25	25.24	4.15	26.20	27.72	29.50	25.70
	m	58.06	74.25	44.80	76.47	52.73	64.23	44.88	69.32
total	n	109	48	100	59	98	61	100	59
	m	58.46	65.31	56.12	67.14	56.50	66.16	52.59	62.10
	F	3.41		8.41 (5.55)		5.45		4.93	
	df	1,151		1,153 (2,153)		1,153		1,153	
	p	.07		.005 (.005)		.05		.05	

perceived real and ideal self-concepts of the mother are experienced. The small standard deviations for this discrepancy, as compared to the other discrepancies between self-concepts give an indication of the strength of this effect (see Table 7.4).

In summary, there is reason to suggest that neurotic complaints will be observed with children and adolescents when discrepancies are present between their own real and ideal self-concepts and between the perceived real and ideal self-concepts of the parents. Discrepancies between the perceived real and ideal self-concepts of the peers do not result in similar neurotic complaints. As far as the discrepancies between the perceived real and ideal self-concepts are concerned, it is the fact that the "others" are parents (i.e., the role) rather than their gender that seems important.

For the discrepancies *within* self-concepts, no interaction effects with age could be demonstrated. Contrary to the findings for discrepancies *between* self-concepts, no effects for discrepancies *within* self-concepts were observed on neuroticism expressed by psycho-neurotic complaints. The main effects for

TABLE 7.5

Results of Two-Way Analyses of Variance of Age-Group and
Within Self-Concept Discrepancy on Four Scales of the ABV-K

Discrepancy	N			NS			E			T		
	age	dis.	int.	age	dis.	int.	age	dis.	int.	age	dis.	int.
S	ns	ns	ns	ns	p=.08	ns	ns	ns	ns	ns	ns	ns
O pasg	ns	ns	ns	ns	*	ns	ns	ns	ns	ns	ns	ns
O paog	ns	ns	ns	ns	*	ns	ns	*	ns	ns	ns	ns
O pesg	ns	ns	ns	ns	ns	ns	ns	ns	ns	ns	ns	ns
O peog	ns	ns	ns	ns	ns	ns	ns	ns	ns	ns	ns	ns
O mother	ns	ns	ns	ns	*	ns	ns	p=.05	ns	ns	ns	ns
O father	ns	ns	ns	ns	p=.05	ns	ns	*	ns	ns	ns	ns
O female friend	ns	ns	ns	ns	ns	ns	ns	ns	ns	ns	ns	ns
O male friend	ns	ns	ns	ns	ns	ns	ns	ns	ns	ns	ns	ns
S'	ns	ns	ns	ns	ns	ns	ns	p=.08	ns	ns	ns	ns
O' pasg	ns	ns	ns	ns	ns	ns	ns	p=.08	ns	ns	ns	ns
O' paog	ns	ns	ns	ns	ns	ns	ns	p=.07	ns	ns	*	ns
O' pesg	ns	ns	ns	ns	ns	ns	ns	ns	ns	ns	ns	ns
O' peog	ns	ns	ns	ns	ns	ns	ns	ns	ns	ns	ns	ns
O' mother	ns	ns	ns	ns	ns	ns	ns	ns	ns	ns	ns	ns
O' father	ns	ns	ns	ns	ns	ns	ns	p=.05	ns	ns	p=.06	ns
O' female friend	ns	ns	ns	ns	ns	ns	ns	ns	ns	ns	ns	ns
O' male friend	ns	ns	ns	ns	ns	ns	ns	p=.08	ns	ns	ns	ns

Note. * : significant at p < .05; N: psycho-neurotic complaints; NS: neuroticism expressed by physical complaints; E: extraversion; T: test-attitude; dis.: discrepancy; int.: interaction between age and discrepancies; S: own real discrepancies; O : supposed real discrepancies of others; S' : own ideal discrepancies; O' : supposed ideal discrepancies of others; pasg: parent same gender; paog: parent opposite gender; pesg: peer same gender; peog: peer opposite gender.

discrepancies within self-concepts were observed on neuroticism as expressed by physical complaints and extraversion and to a lesser extent on test-attititude (see Table 7.5). Interesting in these data are the consistent patterns for the effects. A nonsignificant trend was present for discrepancies within one's own real or ideal self-concept (*S* and *S'*). The discrepancies within the perceived self-concepts showed significant effects for the parents, but not for the peers. One exception was a non-significant trend on extraversion for the perceived ideal self-concept of the male peer. Discrepancies within real self-concepts (i.e., one's own and perceived real self-concepts; *S* and *O*) influenced the scores on neuroticism expressed by physical complaints (i.e., psychosomatic complaints)

TABLE 7.6

Number of Participants, Standard Deviations, Means, F Values
and Probablitities for Scores on Four Scales of the ABV-K
by Discrepancies Within Real and Ideal Self-Concepts

		NS S		NS O parent sg		NS O parent og		E O parent og	
Discrepancy		no	yes	no	yes	no	yes	no	yes
Age-group									
1+2	n	42	21	45	18	42	21	42	21
	sd	29.74	30.71	29.46	32.00	29.71	31.57	6.09	5.53
	m	62.19	52.57	61.29	53.22	60.52	55.91	96.60	95.57
3+4	n	22	18	23	17	23	17	22	17
	sd	29.68	30.90	30.30	30.80	29.35	31.76	16.27	3.64
	m	56.55	44.56	54.96	46.00	55.61	45.12	91.09	97.12
5+6	n	13	20	9	24	10	23	10	23
	sd	28.19	33.58	23.66	32.46	24.97	31.58	28.01	3.25
	m	58	50.15	68.11	47.67	69.70	46.09	88.60	97.13
total	n	77	59	77	59	75	61	74	61
	m	59.87	49.31	60.20	48.88	60.24	49.20	93.88	96.59
	F	3.12		4.58		5.17		4.87	
	df	1,130		1,130		1,130		1,129	
	p	.08		.05		.05		.05	

		E S'		E O' pasg		E O' paog	
Discrepancy		no	yes	no	yes	no	yes
1+2	n	46	17	48	15	50	13
	sd	5.85	6.05	6.01	5.64	5.62	6.75
	m	96.61	95.29	96.38	95.87	96.72	94.46
3+4	n	22	17	24	15	26	13
	sd	15.69	7.29	15.16	6.97	15.18	0
	m	92.32	95.53	92.17	96.20	91.58	98.00
5+6	n	12	21	13	20	13	20
	sd	25.55	1.09	24.69	1.54	24.69	1.54
	m	88.92	97.76	90.00	97.50	90.00	97.50
total	n	80	55	85	50	89	46
	m	94.92	96.76	94.21	96.62	94.24	96.78
	F	3.07		3.14		3.40	
	df	1,129		1,129		1,129	
	p	.08		.08		.07	

Table 7.6 continued

discrepancy		E O' father no	E O' father yes	E O' male friend no	E O' male friend yes	T O' paog no	T O' paog yes	T O' father no	T O' father yes
1+2	n	51	12	51	12	50	13	51	12
	sd	5.84	6.24	6.27	4.04	28.78	32.94	29.15	33.11
	m	96.47	95.33	96.12	96.83	54.14	39.00	53.31	41.25
3+4	n	24	15	25	14	26	13	24	15
	sd	15.70	0	15.39	4.01	24.03	30.26	24.93	28.08
	m	91.04	98.00	91.92	96.93	59.42	52.15	59.96	52.27
5+6	n	15	18	18	15	13	20	15	18
	sd	23.03	1.62	21.02	1.29	24.94	27.78	27.26	27.85
	m	91.07	97.44	91.94	97.67	68.31	50.35	63.67	52.22
total	n	90	45	94	41	89	46	90	45
	m	94.12	97.07	94.20	97.17	57.75	47.65	56.81	49.31
	F	3.77		3.23		6.13		3.64	
	df	1,129		1,129		1,129		1,129	
	p	.06		.08		.05		.06	

and extraversion. Discrepancies within the ideal self-concepts influenced the scores on extraversion and test-attitude. The more unequivocal results obtained for the real self-concepts for the parents when differentiated by gender instead of by role suggest that the gender of the parent is more important here.

The observed effects were contrary to the expectations. Children *with* discrepancies within their own real self-concept had a lower psychosomatic score than children *without* such discrepancies (see Table 7.6). Children with discrepancies within their perceived real self-concepts of their parents showed a lower psychosomatic score and a higher extraversion score than children without such discrepancies. Extraversion occurred in particular when the perceived real self-concept of the opposite-gender parent was considered, but not when the perceived real self-concept of the same-gender parent was considered. Children with discrepancies within their own ideal self-concept scored higher on extraversion than children without such discrepancies. Discrepancies within the perceived ideal self-concepts of the parents tended to lead to high scores on extraversion (except for the mother) and to a more self-critical attitude when the perceived ideal self-concept of the opposite-gender parent was concerned.

In summary, discrepancies *within* one's own self-concept as well as in the perceived self-concepts of the parents had a positive instead of a negative effect. Children with discrepancies within real self-concepts scored lower on psychosomatic complaints and higher on extraversion than children without such discrepancies. Children with discrepancies within ideal self-concepts tended to be more extravert and less defensive (more self-critical) than children without such discrepancies. Discrepancies within the perceived self-concepts of their peers had little effect. In addition, the effects for discrepancies within self-concepts were not affected by age.

CONCLUSIONS

In this chapter the relationship between discrepancies *between* and *within* self-concepts and emotional functioning in children and adolescents (i.e., as measured by the ABV-K) was examined. From the available literature indications were obtained that discrepancies between self-concepts as well as within self-concepts would exert a negative influence on emotional functioning. In addition, the mediating role of age on this relationship was discussed. According to Higgins' (1989) theoretical model dealing with the development of discrepancies and their relation to affect, discrepancies *between* real and ideal self-concepts were assumed to occur prior to discrepancies *within* these self-concepts. Once a discrepancy is present, a negative emotional response was thought to follow. According to Harter (1986), however, the ability to integrate conflicting information about the self (i.e., conflicting self-descriptions) was a neccessary prerequisite for the negative emotional effects of discrepancies to occur. This ability is only mastered in adolescence. Therefore, although discrepancies might occur prior to adolescence, they should not relate to any negative emotional effect until adolescence.

In the present study little interaction between age, discrepancy, and emotional functioning could be demonstrated, with an exception for the discrepancy between the perceived real and ideal self-concepts of the mother. Although this effect could only be demonstrated for one's own and perceived self-concepts of the parents, once such a discrepancy is present, an effect on the emotional functioning of the child was observed. In chapter 6 it was noted that the number of discrepancies between the real and ideal self-concepts increases earlier than the number of discrepancies within the self-concepts. Consequently, the findings of the present study favor Higgins' model over Harter's arguments.

The findings of the present study, however, do not fit Higgins' model completely. According to Higgins, discrepancies *between* self-concepts and *within* self-concepts both affect the emotional functioning in a negative way. Adults showing discrepancies demonstrate more dejection-related emotions and neuroticism than adults without discrepancies (e.g., Higgins, 1987). These findings are corroborated by the present study for discrepancies between real and ideal self-concepts, but only when one's own self-concepts or the perceived self-concepts of the parents are concerned. If a discrepancy between the real and ideal self-concept of a peer was present no serious consequences for emotional functioning could be observed. Because the children in the present study demonstrated hardly any discrepancies between one's own and perceived self-concepts of others, no conclusions about the effects of these discrepancies on emotional functioning could be drawn. That is, although children differentiate between their own and perceived self-concepts of others (chapter 4), they appear not to be bothered by discrepancies between their own and the perceived real and ideal self-concepts of others. More important, however, is the finding that *within* self-concept discrepancies do not have a negative effect on emotional functioning. On the contrary, when discrepancies within one's own real and ideal self-concepts or within the perceived self-concepts of the parents (i.e., again, no effects could be demonstrated for discrepancies within the perceived self-concepts of the peers) were experienced, more positive scores on emotional functioning were present than if the child experienced no discrepancies.

An explanation for the latter finding showing that discrepancies within self-concepts have a positive effect on emotional functioning can be found in the work of Rosenholtz and Simpson (1984) and Linville (1985). Rosenholtz and Simpson remarked that multidimensional, inconsistent feedback about children's abilities enables self-enhancement, whereas unidimensional, consistent feedback leads to more objective self-knowledge. Children who receive negative feedback for one ability can shift their attention and priority towards another ability that had been evaluated more positively. Linville reported that, in contrast to a low distinctness between self-relevant aspects within a self-concept, high distinctness has positive consequences for mental health. In contrast to low distinctness, high distinctness prevents the generalization of negative affect from one aspect to the other. Conflicting self-descriptions within one self-concept can be interpreted as multidimensional feedback and as being highly distinctive. Consequently, if one of the discrepant self-descriptions results in a negative emotional reaction, the child can shift its attention to the conflicting self-description and feel more positive. Children are probably better able to use this strategy than adults, because their self-system will be less extensively differentiated and integrated and possess less alternative connections between the self-descriptions over a variety of possibly overlapping self-concepts. Also, children may be less scrupulous than adults in the use of such self-protecting techniques, that is, to turn a conflict into an advantage.

More research will be necessary to refine the present findings and conclusions. For instance, in the present study, children were free to mention self-descriptions from different contexts (e.g., the social, athletic, and academic contexts) and from as many contexts as they wished. No control for contexts was used. Knowledge of whether conflicting self-descriptions are derived from one and the same or from different contexts could add information to the above argument. In other words, the emphasis of positive evaluation of self-descriptions and neglect (i.e., rejection) of a negative evaluation of the same self-description is more likely when the discrepant self-descriptions are derived from different contexts or from different areas within the context.

Information about the contexts from which the self-descriptions are derived could also clarify the effect on emotional functioning for the discrepancies between the real and ideal self-concepts. In the present study, this effect is significant, but not strong. Research from Cantor, Norem, and Brower (1987), Edwards and Klockars (1981), and Koestner, Bernieri, and Zuckerman (1989) suggests that such a small effect may in part be caused by mixed contexts. Cantor et al. (1987) reported that American students demonstrated negative affects from discrepancies between the real and ideal self-concepts in the academic context, but positive affects from similar discrepancies in the social context. Edwards and Klockars (1981) noted that the correlations between own and perceived real self-concepts are differentially related to self-descriptions. Similarly, Koestner et al. (1989) found that discrepancies between one's own and perceived real self-concepts showed more cross-situational consistency if the discrepancies were operationalized in a description-specific way than if the results were averaged over traits.

In addition, the meaning of a discrepancy seems to be mediated by the personality of the individual. For instance, pessimists have been found to report larger discrepancies between their real and ideal self-concepts than optimists. However, in contrast to optimists, pessimists appear to use these larger discrepancies as a source of motivation; that is, large discrepancies were related to higher school-grades for pessimists but not for optimists (Cantor et al., 1987). Furthermore, some people seem to be primarily oriented toward and influenced by the perceived self-concepts of others, whereas others are primarily oriented toward their own self-concepts (Barnes et al., 1988; see also Snyder's theory on self-monitoring, e.g., Snyder, 1979, or chapter 1). Therefore, some controls of personality characteristics may also be necessary to further refine the findings of the present study.

Furthermore, discrepancies in this study were operationalized as products. It could be argued, however, that discrepancies between self-concepts should be studied as processes instead of products. The idea of a discrepancy as a process was elegantly discussed by Carver and Scheier (1990). They introduced this process in terms of a meta-discrepancy and argued that besides the size of a discrepancy at a particular moment in development, the perceived speed and direction of the discrepancy might be of particular relevance. A discrepancy that is large at one moment, but was even larger prior to it, might result in a positive instead of a negative affect, simply because the individual realizes that the situation is improving. Conversely, a negative affect may be the consequence of a deteriorating situation, that is, an increasing discrepancy. In addition, the judgement of such processes as being as quick or slow as desired or intended may mediate the accompanying positive or negative affect.

Finally, in additional studies on discrepancies with children and adolescents, there should be controls for the developing ability to integrate self-concepts as well as self-descriptions. Though the present research shows that the study of discrepancies *between* and *within* self-concepts with children is promising, much more research on such discrepancies in general, and on discrepancies with children, in particular, is required for the formulation of unequivocal conclusions.

8 Conclusions: The Model and the Data

In chapter 1, a theoretical model on the organization of the self-system was proposed. In the subsequent chapters, empirical findings on several aspects of the development of this organization were reported. The purpose of the present chapter is to integrate all that has come before. Following a summary of the model, the findings are discussed more explicitly in the framework of the assumptions and considerations in chapter 1. Based on this discussion, two general factors explaining the mechanisms that were evident are considered. Subsequently, some remaining as well as new questions are discussed and suggestions for future studies are presented based on the present research and recent literature. The chapter ends with a specification of the model.

THE MODEL

The self-system was depicted as a multidimensional construct that develops in interaction between the person and the social environment. Besides the context-related self-concepts, domain-related self-concepts within the self-system were distinguished. Though *context-related self-concepts* reflect different aspects of the content of the self-system, *domain-related self-concepts* refer to different perspectives on the self. Among the domain-related self-concepts a distinction was made between the *real self-concept* and several *possible selves*, such as, for instance, the *ideal self*. Real self-concepts were considered to be evaluated in the light of the possible selves, which serve a motivating function. People were thought to strive to reach their positive possible selves and to avoid negative ones. Possible selves were argued to be more private than real self-concepts. The real self-concept as well as the possible selves were thought to be perceived from one's own *perspective* as well as from the perspective of others. The *perceived perspectives of others* mediate between the individual's own perspective and the *actual perspectives of others*. They could be considered in a generalized way, as the perspectives of a generalized other, or in a more differentiated way, as the perspectives of several differentiated others. Specific others were each thought to exert their own particular influence on the individual's own self-concepts, depending on the characteristics of the other in question and the situation, as well as the age and gender of the individual. The influence of the environment was considered to be modified by the active role of the individual, who tends to selective interactions and biased perceptions, because of the motive to reach positive possible selves and avoid negative ones, or the motive to keep the real self-concept consistent.

Due to the reciprocal interaction between the individual, the social environment, and the situation, the self-concepts were thought to develop from one global self-concept in a dynamic process of differentiation and integration. This process was thought to reflect initially increasing distances, followed by changing relationships between the several self-concepts. The temporary configuration of relationships between the self-concepts, representing their *organization*, was thought to be defined by several *structural characteristics*. These structural characteristics were considered to affect the subsequent organization of the self-system and the emotional functioning of the individual. The structural characteristics were defined in terms of relationships between the domain-related self-concepts, perceived from several perspectives, and the context-related self-descriptions within these self-concepts. The *temporary state of organization* of the self-concepts was thought to be represented by the complexity, clearness, internal consistency, distinctness, and validity of the self-system. Though the *complexity* of the self-system refers to the degree of differentiation as well as the degree to which the self-system was elaborated, its *clearness* refers to the degree of differentiation between the self-concepts as such. *Clearness* could either occur *between real and possible selves*, or between one's own and perceived perspectives, that is, in terms of *distinctness. Internal consistency* refers to the absence of incompatibilities or *discrepancies* between or within the self-concepts. Finally, two types of *validity* were distinguished: validity of the self-concepts in comparison to the actual behavior; and validity in comparison to the actual opinion of others about the person, or *fit*. In addition, the characteristics *flexibility* and *stability* or continuity of the self-system were considered to reflect the *process of organization* of the self-concepts. The *clearness, positiveness, abstractness*, and *personal relevance* of the self-descriptions within the self-concepts were considered to influence the organization of the self-concepts according to the former characteristics.

THE MODEL THROUGH THE LENSES
OF THE DATA: CONFIRMATION AND NEED
FOR FURTHER DIFFERENTIATION

In the present study the phenotype of the self-system dynamics in childhood and adolescence was examined. This was done through its temporal organization as defined by the characteristics clearness, distinctness, internal consistency, and fit. To measure these characteristics, age-appropriate, personally relevant self-descriptions were used that were examined for their clearness and abstractness. The data confirmed the general dynamics in the model. An interaction between the individual and the environment as well as a process of differentiation and integration of the self-concepts were found. However, the specific developmental course as well as the general framework for the model have to be differentiated and adapted. In what follows, the conclusions for the separate structural characteristics are considered first. Following this, the more general conclusions regarding the dynamics of the self-system are discussed.

The Onset of Clearness Between Self-Concepts

In accordance with Werner's (1957) orthogenetic principle, the various self-concepts within the self-system were argued to develop through differentiation from one global self-concept. Because of this development, increasing distances between the self-concepts were expected during childhood. The data from the present study only partly confirm the expectation of increasing differentiation and are not decisive with regard to the expectation that the self-concepts develop from one global self-concept. In accordance with the expectations, the distance between the real and ideal self-concepts were found to increase until about age 12. However, no such increase was similarly evident for the subjects' own versus perceived self-concepts. Additionally, children were found to already be able to differentiate clearly between most self-concepts at the youngest age (i.e., age 6) under study. It is possible that differentiation from one global self-concept into real, ideal, own, and perceived self-concepts occurs *before* age 6. However, these age-groups were not represented in the study. Obviously, additional data with younger age-groups are required to examine this possibility. The present data indicate that if a development from one global concept does occur, it will be finished around age 6. From this age onward, clear differentiation between most of the self-concepts is evident.

Distinction between Differentiation
of Real and Ideal Self-Concepts
and Own and Perceived Self-Concepts (Distinctness)

Though the data are not decisive with regard to the early development of self-concept differentiation, they are with regard to the distinction between clearness between the real and ideal self-concepts, and clearness between one's own and perceived self-concepts. It was argued on the basis of the literature that these types of differentiation were conceptually different (chapter 1). The ideal self-concept, as a possible self, was considered to reflect a personal striving. People were thought to be motivated to reach this concept, that is, to decrease the distance between their real and ideal self-concepts. In contrast, the distance between one's own and perceived self-concept was thought to represent distinctness. Because a certain degree of distinctness has been found to be desirable, people were thought to strive to maintain a certain distance between their own and perceived self-concepts.

The data empirically support the distinction between real versus ideal self-concept differentiation and own versus perceived self-concept differentiation. This distinction was present in almost all results. To start with, not only did clear differentiation between one's own and perceived *real* self-concepts occur later than between the other self-concepts, the degree of differentiation between the former self-concepts also remained smaller. A somewhat larger degree of differentiation between the *ideal* own and perceived self-concepts than between the *real* own and perceived self-concepts was evident. However, this type of differentiation was also less, or at the utmost equally, differentiated as compared to the differentiation between the real and ideal self-concepts. Thus, less distinctness was present than real–ideal differentiation (chapters 4 and 5). In addition, few age-related effects for the differentiation between own and perceived self-concepts were found. Cohort effects indicated that differentiation between one's own and perceived opinion is a personalized process. In contrast, reliable age-related effects were found for the differentiation between real and ideal self-concepts, especially as far as the perceived concepts of the parents were concerned (Chapter 4). Besides, only a few children showed discrepancies between one's own and perceived self-concepts, and those who did so only showed a small number of such discrepancies. Again, this finding was in contrast to the findings for discrepancies between the real and ideal self-concepts, which were reported more often (chapters 6 and 7).

Although no age-related changes were evident for the degree of differentiation between own and perceived self-concepts, this does not mean that this type of differentiation should be omitted from study as Zigler and his colleagues did (Katz & Zigler, 1967). The sense of distinctness is a meaningful psychological construct that may even represent a core construct within the self-concept (e.g., Broughton, 1981; Markus & Kunda, 1986; Snyder & Fromkin, 1980; see also chapter 1). Also the fact that hardly any age-related effects were found on this construct is psychologically interesting. Moreover, there were other interesting effects, besides age, that were found in the present study. For example, the effect for the person whose perspective was considered. This effect was also apparent for the differentiation between real and ideal self-concepts. The general conclusion from these effects is that both distinctness and real–ideal differentiation should be differentiated further. This further differentiation of distinctness and real–ideal differentiation will now be considered separately.

Distinctness. It was expected that the sense of distinctness reflected in the differentiation between own and perceived self-concepts would increase with age (chapter 1, see also under The Onset of Clearness Between Self-Concepts). Consistent with the findings of Katz and Zigler (1967), these expectations were not confirmed by the present data (chapter 4). Indeed, the data showed that differentiation between one's own and perceived real self-concepts does not stabilize as compared to the test-retest scores until age 9. However, this finding was not replicated by direct tests for age-relatedness. In contrast to expectations, the distinctness between one's own ideal self-concept and the perceived ideal self-concept of the opposite-gender peer even decreased. That is, from childhood to early adolescence increasingly less difference was experienced between one's own expectancies for the self and the expectancies of the opposite peer. Consequently, the data indicate that the sense of distinctness does not increase in degree but that the degree of distinctness that is present becomes less ad hoc. Children do not feel that their ideas become increasingly different from the ideas of others, but they do become more certain about the eventual differences and more consistent in their answers (cf. Clearness of Self-Descriptions, chapter 3).

As was previously mentioned, there were other interesting effects on distinctness, among them the finding that more distinctness was reported between the ideal than between the real self-concepts. Children at all ages experienced their own opinions of what they would like to become relative to the opinions of others, as more different than their opinions about how they were at the moment relative to these opinions of others (chapter 4). In addition, the validity of one's own ideal self-concept as compared to the actual ideals of the parents about their children was found to be less than the validity of the remaining self-concepts (chapter 5). In chapter 1, it was suggested that possible

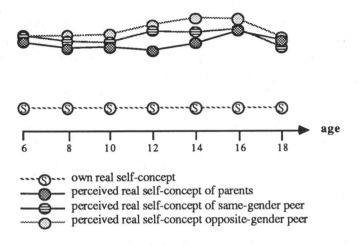

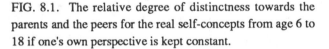

---〇--- own real self-concept
———●— perceived real self-concept of parents
———⊜— perceived real self-concept of same-gender peer
～～●～ perceived real self-concept opposite-gender peer

FIG. 8.1. The relative degree of distinctness towards the parents and the peers for the real self-concepts from age 6 to 18 if one's own perspective is kept constant.

selves, such as the ideal self-concept, might be more private and less anchored in social experiences than the real self-concept. The greater opacity of possible selves to the environment was thought to account for the lack of agreement that is often found between the individual's self-evaluation and the evaluation by others. The present findings corroborate these ideas. The larger distinctness between one's own and perceived ideal self-concepts as compared to the real self-concepts indicate indeed, that the ideal own self-concept is experienced as more private than the real own self-concept. In addition, it is precisely for this concept (i.e., one's own ideal self-concept) that the lower congruence with the ideas of others was evident. The own ideal self-concept is less influenced by the opinions of others than one's own real self-concept.

Besides the effect for real versus ideal self-concepts, effects for the perspective from which the self was considered were evident as well (see Fig. 8.1 and 8.2). In the present study besides one's own perspective, the perspectives of several significant others were included. These others were the parents and best male and female friend of the children. In chapter 1, differences in significance between the parents and the peers as well as between the parents themselves were noted. For instance, Rosenberg (1979) considered the role of the mothers to be more significant than the role of the fathers, and the role of parents as such to be more significant than the role of friends. McGuire and McGuire (1982) reported that children referred more to their same-gender parent than to the opposite-gender parent. The data from the present findings for

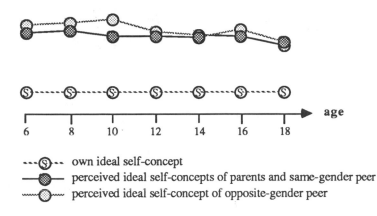

FIG. 8.2. The relative degree of distinctness towards the
parents and the peers for the ideal self-concepts from age 6 to
18 if one's own perspective is kept constant.

distinctness do not show such a distinction between the parents. However, a
distinction was found between the degree of distinctness that was reported
regarding the parents and the degree of distinctness that was reported regarding
the peers. Children of all ages differentiated less between their own real
self-concepts and the perceived real self-concepts of their parents than they
differentiated between themselves and their peers.

In addition, the data indicate that children differentiated between their
same-gender and opposite-gender peer. For the opposite-gender peer there was
more distinctness between the real self-concepts reported than for the
same-gender peer. Besides, the reported degree of distinctness between one's
own and perceived ideal self-concepts was larger if the perspective of the
opposite-gender peer was considered, than if the perspective of either one of the
parents or the same-gender peer was considered. Though the children identified
themselves mostly with their parents' opinion about them (at least as the children
perceived this opinion), they distanced themselves, however, relatively
speaking, from the perceived real opinion as well as expectancies of their
opposite-gender friend. As was described before, this distancing decreased
somewhat when the children became adolescents. Because of similar effects for
perspective with the remaining structural characteristics, and because of the
implications of these findings for the understanding of the dynamics of the
self-system, the conclusions that result from this effect will be considered
separately below.

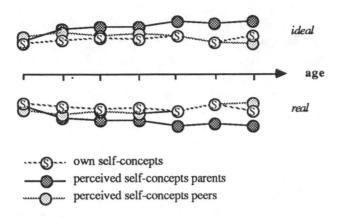

FIG. 8.3. The relative distance between the real and ideal self-concepts from one's own perspective and the perceived perspective of the parents and peers.

Differentiation Between Real and Ideal Self-Concepts. Similar to the findings that were discussed above, a distinction as to perspective is also required for the differentiation between real and ideal self-concepts (see Fig. 8.3). This type of differentiation was different for the perspective of the parents, the peers, and the self. First, the differentiation between one's own real and ideal self-concepts was smaller than the differentiation between the perceived real and ideal self-concepts of the peers, which, in turn, was smaller than the differentiation between the perceived real and ideal self-concepts of the parents. That is, the children felt more ideal in their own eyes than in the eyes of their parents and peers, but believed that their peers found them closer to their ideal than did their parents. Second, in adolescence the age-related effect for this type of differentiation was different for the perspective of the parents as compared to one's own perspective and the perspective of the peers. During childhood an increase was found for each type of differentiation. During adolescence, though, the differentiation between the real and ideal self-concepts remained stable at the higher level if the perspective of the parents was assessed, but decreased again if one's own perspective or the perspective of the peers was considered. Explanations for the different results for the several perspectives will be discussed below.

The Complicated Nature of Internal Consistency

In chapter 1, it was argued that lack of internal consistency of the self-system would be related to negative affect. In chapters 6 and 7, this assumption was taken up, with the provision that this relationship would occur only if the individual were able to integrate such contradictory information, an ability that was not expected to be present before adolescence. Neither in chapter 1 nor in chapters 6 and 7 was any distinction made in this regard between the discrepancies between self-concepts or within self-concepts; that is, between self-descriptions within one self-concept. The findings warrant several revisions to these original ideas.

To start with, discrepancies between and within self-concepts were found to represent distinct constructs. Not only were the correlations between both types of discrepancies lower than within each type of discrepancy, but also the number of discrepancies between self-concepts – at least as far as the perceived real and ideal discrepancies of the parents were concerned – increased developmentally earlier than discrepancies within self-concepts. Though this difference might be due to the present method, it was also found to be consistent with the theoretical developmental model of Higgins (1989). In addition, opposite effects on emotional functioning for both types of discrepancies were found. In accordance with the expectations, the effects for discrepancies between self-concepts were negative. The effects for discrepancies within self-concepts, however, were positive. As was argued in chapter 7, the latter effect may be due to the facilitating opportunities for self-enhancement that accompany such inconsistencies. If negative affect towards one pole of the discrepancy is experienced, the attention can be shifted towards the opposite pole.

Second, as far as relationships with emotional functioning are concerned, these relationships appeared whenever discrepancies were apparent. On the basis of the present data, no indications for a significant role of the ability to integrate contradictory information were evident.

Third, in contrast to other types of discrepancies, hardly any discrepancies for distinctness, that is, between own and perceived self-concepts, were found. Children experience few discrepancies between their own self-concepts and what they believe is the opinion of others.

Besides these necessary revisions in the understanding of internal consistency, the original perspective that drove these expectations ought to be reconsidered. The negative effect on emotional functioning was only apparent for discrepancies between the perceived real and ideal self-concepts of the parents and to some extent for discrepancies between one's own real and ideal self-concepts. The opposite effect occurred only for discrepancies within one's own self-concepts and the perceived self-concepts of the parents. For discrepancies between and within the perceived real and ideal self-concepts of the peers, no effect at all was found. Consequently, children and adolescents are only bothered by an inconsistent self-system in so far as such inconsistencies between the perceived real and ideal self-concepts of their parents or between their own real and ideal self-concepts are concerned. Similarly, they only profit from inconsistencies within either their own or the perceived self-concepts of their parents. The emotional functioning of children seems to flourish in the face of the perception of inconsistent ideas of their parents about them. By contrast, they do not seem to care about, nor profit from, inconsistencies in their peers' opinions about them.

In summary, although it has been shown that internal consistency is a psychologically meaningful construct, it must be concluded that its dynamics are more complicated than expected. As a consequence, distinctions have to be made between discrepancies between and within self-concepts, between discrepancies between self-concepts that reflect distinctness and real–ideal comparisons, and between the persons from whose perspective the self is considered.

The Fit of the Self-System:
Real Versus Ideal Self-Concepts

Only the actual concepts of the parents about their children, and not the actual concepts of the peers, were assessed. Therefore, no conclusions can be drawn for the fit of the self-concepts in relation to the actual concepts of the parents as compared to the actual concepts of different others. Other conclusions are possible, though. It was expected that due to increasing perspective taking skills, the fit between the intra and interpersonal self-concepts would increase during childhood. In addition, it was expected that this fit would remain stable or even decrease a little in adolescence because of the complexity of new situations – such as a new school, or because of preoccupation with newly acquired cognitive insights. Furthermore, it was argued that even under optimal conditions the fit between one's own and perceived (i.e., intraindividual) self-concepts and the actual concepts (i.e., the interindividual self-concepts) would not be complete, because of the children's motives for self-enhancement and self-consistency.

The findings were consistent with these expectations (chapter 5). At the same time, though, they suggest that some refinements in the original set of expectations need to be made. Despite the more limited approach with regard to the perspectives of others, further differentiation of the construct of fit is also possible. Firstly, the fit of one's own self-concepts was less than the fit of the perceived self-concepts. Though the perceived self-concepts were related more to the other intrapersonal self-concepts than to the interpersonal (actual) concepts, they nevertheless were clearly related to the actual concepts from

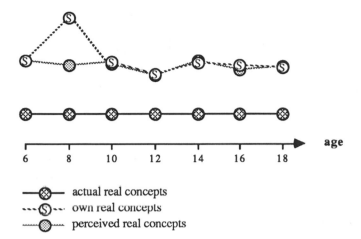

FIG. 8.4. The relative degree of fit between one's own and the perceived real self-concepts of the parents as compared to the actual concepts of the parents if the latter is kept constant.

which they were derived. Implications from this result will follow later, together with the discussion of the active role of the child.

Secondly, a distinction between the real and ideal self-concepts is suggested. The present data show a smoother developmental course for the fit between the ideal concepts than between the real concepts. With regard to the fit between the latter, irregularities were evident around age 8 to 10. In the first wave, a large variation in degree of fit was found for one's own real self-concept as compared to the actual real concept of the opposite-gender parent. In the third wave, a temporary decrease of fit for the real self-concepts between age 8 and 10 was noted. Although taken separately both findings could be regarded as artifacts of the data, together they suggest that in childhood the fit of the real self-concepts is less consistent than the fit of the ideal self-concepts. Earlier, it was concluded that the findings for distinctness in the self-system corroborate the suggestion in chapter 1 that the ideal self-concepts are more private and less influenced by the social environment than the real self-concepts. The present findings for the development of fit between the self-concepts are congruent with this conclusion. The fit of the ideal self-concepts develops smoothly in accordance with expectations that were derived from the literature on the development of perspective-taking skills. The irregularities in the fit of the real self-concepts, though, suggest that other influences are working here. Therefore, it is argued that the fit of the ideal self-concepts is primarily a function of social cognitive

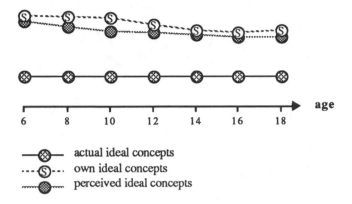

FIG. 8.5. The relative degree of fit between one's own and the perceived ideal self-concepts of the parents as compared to the actual concepts of the parents if the latter is kept constant.

development, whereas the fit of the real self-concepts is also influenced by affective factors in the social environment. Figures 8.4 and 8.5 depict the fit between the several self-concepts.

Characteristics of Self-Descriptions Within the Self-Concepts

It was argued in chapter 1 that the characteristics of the self-descriptions within the self-concepts might influence the relationships between the self-concepts and the degree to which these relationships would be related to affect. In the present study, the self-descriptions within the self-concepts were controlled for one of these characteristics, that is, personal relevance, and examined with regard to abstractness and clearness.

The self-descriptions were categorized for abstractness according to the model of Damon and Hart (1982, 1988), as modified by Oppenheimer et al. (1990). As was expected (chapters 1 and 3), the self-descriptions that were used became more abstract with age. Though the former categories remained in use, the emphasis shifted from self-descriptions in terms of physical characteristics, activities, psychological characteristics, and finally social relationships. Because of this age-related effect, the influence of abstractness on the relationships between the self-concepts was examined. As was described in chapter 3, it was concluded that the categories being used did indeed affect the relationships between the self-concepts. However, this influence was not due to the level of abstractness of the self-descriptions, but rather to their actual *content* and the perspective from which this content was considered. Thus, the degree of differentiation in the self-system depends on how the individual describes the self and from which perspective the self is considered.

Although the above finding seems self-evident, it is nevertheless an important one. First, it suggests that, besides cognitive processes, social affective processes are also involved in the differentiation between a pair of self-concepts. This suggestion will be discussed later on. Second, this finding implies that methods for self-assessment that differ in content (i.e., which context is choosen and which context-related self-descriptive items are used) and perspective (i.e., for instance, if only one's own perspective, or the generalized perspective of others, or which of a series of specific others is considered) may also produce different results. That is, decisions on such choices should be taken carefully, and comparisons of results from methods that differ on these aspects should take these differences into consideration.

In the present data no important age-related effects for clearness were found. Children of all ages were about equally clear about their own self-descriptions. This finding is not surprising if it is recognized that the self-descriptions that were used in the present study generally were age-appropriate and of high personal relevance. That is, only those self-descriptions were asked for that were well known and important to the child. It can be assumed that because the children were familiar with these self-descriptions and considered these self-descriptions important, they had also spent some time thinking about them in a way that would increase their clearness. In addition, some minor effects for clearness on self-descriptions that resulted from a difference between the child and the same-gender parent and from a similarity between the child and the same-gender peer were evident (chapter 3). Consequently, although not decisive in the present analyses, the clearness of self-descriptions might be a factor in studies on self-descriptions that are less homogeneous with regard to age-appropriateness, personal relevance, or clearness itself.

The Dynamics Within the Self-System

The dynamic of the self-system was described as an ongoing process of differentiation and integration of the self-concepts within the self-system. Following the differentiation of the several self-concepts from one global concept, the self-concepts were thought to relate in more or less balanced configurations. This process was thought to be reflected in changes in the relationships between the self-concepts, resulting in the alternate overlap and distance between the self-concepts.

As was described in chapter 4, the data from the present study were not so much confirming as congruent with the proposed dynamics of the self-system. This was especially true for the relationship between the real and ideal self-concepts. Here the expected increasing and decreasing distance was observed for the sample as a whole and as a function of age. Although only partly significant, the mean distance between one's own real and ideal self-concept, as well as the perceived real and ideal self-concepts of the best male and female friend increased during childhood and decreased again in adolescence. With the perceived real and ideal concepts of the parents, only an increase was observed. It remains unclear from the present data, whether the increase between the perceived real and ideal self-concepts of the parents would also have been followed by a decrease at later ages. (Unpublished, preliminary findings with college students, though, not reported in the present study, suggest that around age 20 decreases in the distance between the perceived real and ideal concepts of the parents may also occur.) Consequently, it can be expected that for the perceived self-concepts of the parents, the expected process occurs as an age-related phenomenon, although at a slower rate than for one's own self-concepts or the perceived concepts of the peers.

No such common trend was found for the relationships between one's own and perceived self-concepts. If increases and decreases of differentiation between these concepts are present, this is on a more personalized basis.

The Influence of the Social Environment

In chapter 1, the hypothesized influence of the environment on the children's own self-concepts was described. It was noted at that point that the perceived attitudes of significant others had been shown to be related more strongly to one's own self-concepts than the perceived attitude of the generalized other (Rosenberg, 1979; see chapter 1). Consistent with this idea, the findings of the present study indicate the importance of the study of individual perspectives, that is, the perspectives of several, specific, significant others beside one's own perspective. By attending to these perspectives, the mechanisms by which the environment influences the self-system will become more clear.

For each of the structural characteristics (i.e., distinctness, real–ideal differentiation, discrepancies between as well as within real and ideal self-concepts), effects for perspective were evident. In all cases, different results were found for the perspective of the parents versus the perspective of the peers. Further, the results for one's own perspective formed a special category. That is, differentiation between real and ideal self-concepts was less from one's own perspective than from the perspective of others. Also, more discrepancies were reported within one's own self-concepts than within the perceived self-concepts. The results for one's own perspective were alternately more in congruence with the results for the perspective of the parents or with the perspective of the peers. That is, for differentiation between real and ideal self-concepts one's own perspective was similar to the perspective of the peers. Although different in degree of differentiation, the age-related pattern for both measures was similar, and different from the pattern for the parents. However, as far as the actual similarity of the self-concepts or the affect related to the relationships were considered, children directed themselves towards their parents. Their own self-concepts were more similar to the perceived self-concepts of the parents than of the peers. The affect that went with discrepancies between and within the real and ideal self-concepts was similar for one's own perspective and for the perceived perspective of the parents, but absent for the peers.

The above findings suggest that the addition of several specific perceived perspectives contributes to the understanding of the dynamics of the self-system. Further, the addition of the present perspectives revealed that the strongest (i.e., significant) effects did not occur between one's own self-concepts but between those for the parents. That is, in some sense (i.e., with regard to the evaluation of the real self-concept as compared to the ideal self-concept) the ideas of the parents are of more significance to the children than their own ideas about themselves. For children and adolescents, the perceived ideas of their parents about them may influence their actions and feelings more than their own self-concepts. Together, these results, based on several specific perspectives, provide a differentiated understanding of the dynamics of the self-system as a clearly social process. This understanding would not have emerged if only one's own self-concepts had been assessed, or even if only the generalized other had been included. Consequently, it is argued that the self-system should be studied in interaction with the environment, represented by specific, concrete others. By doing so, the personal world of the children, and, as a consequence, their motives and reactions, will become better understood.

The Active Person

Earlier, it was argued that inputs from the environment, in particular the views of the parents, play an important role in the children's self-system. However, the development of the self-system was described in chapter 1 as the result of the reciprocal interaction between the individual and the environment. That is, the children themselves were also assumed to play an important role in the organizing dynamics of their own self-system. Support for this mutual influence of the environment and the individual on the individual's self-system was apparent particularly in the findings for fit (chapter 5). According to these findings, the intraindividual self-concepts of the children became increasingly more similar to the concepts of their parents throughout childhood. This development was ascribed to the increasing ability of the children to consider the perspective of their parents and can be interpreted as a result of the influence of the parents on the self-concepts of their children. The self-concepts of the children, though, did not become *completely* identical to the concepts of their parents. Despite the closer resemblance, some distance between these interpersonal concepts remained. In chapter 1, it was argued that such a distance might result in part from self-regulative biases in the perception of the individual, due to self-enhancing and consistency-related activities. In the present findings, the several biases were evident. To start with, the children overestimated the distance between the real and ideal concepts of the parents. They did not just mirror this distance in the organization of their own self-concepts. They differentiated clearly between one's own and perceived self-concepts and reported less differentiation between one's own real and ideal self-concepts than between either the perceived or the actual concepts of the parents. Furthermore, the concepts were organized more according to who was perceiving than to whose concepts were perceived. The concepts of the parents as perceived by the children were closer to one's own self-concepts of the children than to the actual concepts of the parents. Finally, although the children became better able to infer the perspective of their parents, they showed age-related changes in the distance between the real and ideal concepts of the parents that were not actually reported by the parents.

Several explanations have been given for the latter finding (chapter 5). Most of these explanations questioned not only the perception of the children, but also what was reported by the parents. Taking all findings together, though, it can be argued that the perceptive process of the children must be included in the explanation. If the self-concepts of the children would have been entirely determined by their environment, fewer differences between their self-concepts and the concepts of their parents should have occured. Consequently, it is argued here that beside the influence of the others, a personal influence of the children is also apparent. Though the opinion that certain specific others (in this case, the parents) hold of them may be even more important to the children than their own opinions, these personal opinions still play an important role. This role is evident in the organization of the self-system as one in which distinctness between one's own opinions and those of others is present, as well as in the interpretation of the opinion of others. It is not the actual opinions of others but how these opinions are perceived that influences children's self-concepts. In other words, the influence of the environment is filtered by the cognitions of the child.

COGNITIVE VERSUS SOCIAL
EXPLANATIONS OF THE FINDINGS

Previously, the mechanisms in the organization of children's and adolescents' self-system were described. The question remains, however, as to why these mechanisms appear in their present form. Thus far, little attention was paid to the explanations for the findings. As far as interpretations of the data were given, the emphasis was on the cognitive development of children. This emphasis results from the cognitive nature of the self-system. Because of its cognitive nature, certain cognitive abilities that develop in childhood and adolescence, such as differentiation, integration, and perspective taking, are assumed to be prerequisite to the organization of the self-system. The associated function in the organization of the self-system is not to be expected before the development of these cognitive abilities. Earlier studies, such as those of Zigler and colleagues (Glick & Zigler, 1985) and Harter (e.g., 1983, 1986) confirm this assumption. Consequently, the expectations in this study, as well as explanations for the findings, were accordant.

However, the findings, based on personalized, age-appropriate self-descriptions, confirm only part of these expectations. Though the explanations for age-related changes based on cognitive development were more or less confirmed for the development of real–ideal differentiation, this was not true for distinctness. Further, the developmental course for discrepancies within self-concepts was found to be congruent with the expectations. Additional analyses also indicated that the cognitive development of children is involved in this process. Discrepancies between self-concepts, however, developed earlier than was expected. By contrast, although the more specific findings for fit indicated that some qualification is necessary with regard to the cognitive nature of fit for real self-concepts, the general findings for this characteristic were consistent with the expectations.

Hence, although the emphasis on the cognitive level of children was corroborated for the development of interindividual and intraconceptual characteristics, some reservation with regard to the intraindividual interconceptual characteristics is required. Thus, it is argued here that for the development of the relationships *between* the *intra*individual self-concepts the social experiences of the children may be at least as important as their level of cognitive development. This argument will be sustained below by a consideration of the findings for the characteristics that reflect these relationships, that is, distinctness and real–ideal differentiation, in the framework of cognitive complexity. These considerations will also hold for discrepancies in these relationships. Following this argument, the consequences of a primarily social explanation for the generalization of the dynamics of the organization of the self-system according to these characteristics over older ages will be considered.

Cognitive Abilities Versus Social Experiences

The importance of including the perspectives of specific others in the self-system was already pointed out. The other persons in the present study were chosen because of their assumed significance to the children and greater variation in cognitive complexity. The cognitive complexity of target persons can be considered to hinder the cognitions about them. For instance, it is more difficult, on the average, to take the perspective of a person who is high in cognitive complexity than to take the perspective of a person who is low in cognitive complexity. The higher the cognitive complexity, the more complicated the cognitions concerning that person must be. In the present study, the parents of the children were assumed to be higher in cognitive complexity than the peers: first, because it can be assumed that they have acquired the full potential of their cognitive abilities, and second, because of their greater experience. That is, it could be expected that the organization of the self-system from the perspective of the peers would be advanced as compared to the organization from the perspective of the parents.

It was reported that the children experienced less distinctness in relation to their parents than in relation to their peers. If these findings are considered in the light of the complexity of the other in question, it could be argued that the children differentiated less between one's own self-concepts and the perceived self-concepts of their parents than between one's own self-concepts and the perceived self-concepts of their friends because the higher cognitive complexity of the parents made it more difficult for the children to differentiate between these concepts. This explanation does not, however, explain why more differentiation is found for the opposite-gender peer than to the same-gender peer. It is generally assumed that children – at least until early adolescence – do not tend to interact with peers of the opposite gender very frequently (Hartup, 1983). Consistent with this assumption, it was found in the present study that the children tended to know and like their opposite-gender peer less than the same-gender peer or the parents (chapter 3). These factors (familiarity and likeability) are assumed to facilitate cognitive tasks. An explanation of the present findings in the framework of cognitive complexity would imply that children find it easier to differentiate between their own self-concepts and the perceived self-concepts of the person with whom they interact and whom they like least (i.e., the opposite-gender peer) than between their own self-concepts and the perceived self-concepts of a person who is of the same level of cognitive complexity, and with whom they interact and whom they like more (i.e., the same-gender peer). What is more, if distinctness were to be a function of difficulty arising from cognitive complexity, an explanation in terms of cognitive complexity would suggest that the distinctness between one's own and perceived self-concepts would increase with age. The lack of age-related changes and the negative direction of the only age-related effect that was found (a decrease in distinctness with regard to the opposite-gender peer) contradicts this explanation. A more likely explanation is one based on affect and interaction. It is understandable at face value that it is more difficult to react against the opinion of people with whom frequent interaction as well as a close bond exist than against the opinion of people with whom interaction is less frequent and whose opinion is less cared about. This seems especially true if the close other is a parent, with whom an unequal power relation is experienced and on whose approval the children feel dependent (Hartup, 1983; Maccoby & Martin, 1983; Youniss & Smollar, 1985). Thus, for the degree of distinctness, a more social affective explanation is favored over a strict cognitive one. From such a perspective, the parents emerge as the major socializing agents who serve an important function in the development of the self-concepts. This is true for the period of childhood as well as adolescence. In this relationship, the close bond and familiarity of children with their parents seem to interfere with distinctness more than to facilitate it by decreasing the difficulty of the cognitive system of the other person.

Similar to the explanations for the effects on distinctness, a more social affective explanation of the findings for real–ideal differentiation is favored over a cognitive one. The developmental course of differentiation between real and ideal self-concepts has already been extensively described. It could be argued that the differentiation between the perceived real and ideal concepts of the parents remains high in adolescence because integration between these concepts might be more difficult for the children than integration between the perceived self-concepts of peers. The higher cognitive complexity of the parents' perspective could account for a higher degree of difficulty in a new acquired task, that is, integration. However, the cognitive complexity of the person does not explain why the children differentiated more between the perceived self-concepts of their parents than between those of their peers and the self. On the contrary, if based strictly on their cognitive complexity, it would be expected that these findings would be in the reverse direction. That is, because it is assumed that the parents are of a higher cognitive complexity than the peers, differentiation between the self-concepts of the former should be more difficult and, consequently, occur to a lesser degree than between the self-concepts of the peers. Consequently, the cognitive complexity explanation accounts for only half of the findings.

In contrast, all findings can be easily understood if, in addition to a cognitive factor, the social affective development of children is also considered. The period of childhood that was examined in the present study coincides with the entrance to and passing through elementary school. Attending elementary school makes increasing cognitive and social demands on children. They have to compete as well as cooperate with their classmates. Moreover, the emphasis shifts increasingly from play to learning, and from effort to achievement. Indeed, parental emphasis on their children's achievement has been found to increase during childhood – especially as far as the children's performance in school is concerned (Maccoby, 1984). Moreover, it has been found that during this same period, the way in which parental warmth is shown also changed. That is, although the parents report no differences in the positive attitude towards their children (see also the findings in the present study; chapter 5), they expressed this attitude less through physical affections (Maccoby). Besides the eventual increasing of differentiation skills, these social experiences may also account for the increasing differentiation between the real and ideal self-concepts. In fact, both the increasing cognitive skills and the social experiences will reciprocally intensify the process of increasing differentiation.

With the entrance into adolescence, a further differentiation in the social world of the child becomes evident (Hartup, 1983), and children become more genuinely autonomous (Maccoby, 1984). Children begin to spend more time with peers than with parents, and conformity to parental expectations decreases as compared to conformity to expectations of peers (Hartup, 1983; Maccoby & Martin, 1983). Peer norms do not necessarily conflict with parental norms, and considerable continuity in the relationship with the parents remains (Maccoby & Martin, 1983; Youniss & Smollar, 1985). However, peer relationships differ from parent relationships in several aspects, generally translated in terms of power exertion. The parents–child relationship is constrained by social obligations. The parental role requires educational and socializing demands from the parents towards their children (Maccoby & Martin). Because of this parental role, the relationship between adolescents and their parents is not completely open. Both hide an increasing number of personal experiences from each other. Adolescents do this because they perceive their parents to hold standards as criteria for approval, and because they seek this approval. Because they do not talk openly, adolescents learn to differentiate between the parental role and the individual personality of their parents only slowly, that is, to perceive their parents as persons (Youniss & Smollar). In contrast, peer relationships are not bothered by the constraints of the parental role and the resulting power functions (Hartup, 1983). Youniss and Smollar (1985) described how, as a consequence, the relationship of adolescents with peers is perceived as more accepting, intimate, and open than the relationship with parents. Peers are perceived as individuals from the start (Youniss & Smollar), and peer relationships are characterized by mutual empathic understanding and self-disclosure (e.g., Hartup, 1983; Youniss & Smollar, 1985). In addition, peer relationships are largely voluntary (Maccoby & Martin, 1983) and are ended more easily (than relationships with parents) if continuous confirmation is not provided (Hartup, 1983).

Thus, the findings for the adolescent period can also be explained by both the role of complexity in increasing integrating skills and by different social relationships with parents and peers. Although the parents are perceived in their role of setting standards that have to be met, the peers are sought for empathic understanding. That is, the mutual self-disclosure with their friends helps the adolescents to feel accepted and to accept themselves. The nature of their relationships makes the adolescents feel increasingly that they meet their own expectations as well as the expectations of their friends, although they continue to believe that their parents are not completely approving. That this parental approval remains nevertheless important was already discussed in relation to the emotional effects that result from inconsistencies between and within the perceived self-concepts of the parents. Although the peers are perceived as more accepting and understanding of the self, the children are not really bothered if they sense that their peers do not approve of them (they probably just end the relationship as discussed earlier). In contrast, parental disapproval influences emotional well-being even more than disapproval of oneself. Thus, children as well as adolescents depend emotionally on what they believe that their parents think about them and what they expect from them.

Consequences of the Social Explanation
for the Dynamics of the Self-System

The understanding of the intraindividual, interconceptual organization of the self-system as a process in which cognitive abilities are prerequisite but social experiences may be decisive has some important implications. This is true not only for the variables that should be considered in future research, but also for the expectations about the dynamics at older ages than the ones studied here.

With regard to the former, it is clear by now that predictions on the development of the self-system of children and adolescents should not only include considerations of their level of cognitive development, but also of their personal history and social environment. That is, children's affective relationships and perception of their personal circumstances should be considered. In predicting their behavior and emotions not only their own self-concepts but also those of significant others – in particular the parents or caretakers – should be addressed.

With regard to the latter, the social factor in the organization of the self-system suggests that the proposed dynamics may apply not only to children and adolescents, but also to adults. That is, that the initial increase and decrease of the distance between the real and ideal self-concepts as far as they were present might be followed by subsequent increases and decreases. This was suggested in chapter 1. Indeed, it was argued that such changes would become apparent due to changes in the self-concepts because of personal experiences and changes in the environment – for instance, as a consequence of a life-event. However, had the social affective factor that was apparent not been found, those increases and decreases that were evident should have been ascribed to the necessary prerequisites for such changes in the configuration of the self-system – the ability to differentiate and integrate the self-concepts as well as the self-descriptions within them – developing in the period under study. In this case, no generalizations for subsequent increases and decreases would have been possible. Beyond adolescence a stable relationship between the self-concepts would also have been possible. Even under the present circumstances this might be so. It is possible that because of the developing cognitive prerequisites the increases and decreases that were evident in childhood and adolescence are more significant and stronger than eventual subsequent ones. The dominance of the social affective factor suggests, however, that the general dynamics described for the self-system of children and adolescence will also apply to later ages. Though the significance of specific others may change, as well as the degree of their influence, changes are also expected in the relationships between self-concepts in adulthood.

INDICATIONS FOR FUTURE RESEARCH
FROM THE PRESENT DATA

It is clear from the above discussion that, as a result of the differentiated, multidimensional approach and the broad age-range of subjects under study, the findings from the present research throw considerable light on the dynamics of the self-system. Nevertheless, some questions remain, and new ones appeared.

Some of those are considered here. That is, questions regarding the sample, the method, and the data will now be discussed.

Generalization From the Sample

As was described in chapter 2, the children and parents who participated in the present study came from middle to high SES neighborhoods. In addition, the study concerned a somewhat personal subject (self-concepts and parental opinions of the children), required considerable investment of time, and was dependent on voluntary participation. Because of the latter, it can be expected that those children who participated in the study came from a selective population. That is, it is likely that the children who were allowed to participate were considered robust for the assessment situation and came from family situations in which there was little to hide. Consequently, although the sample was already limited with regard to the SES of the families, it was probably also a relatively "healthy" sample.

This bias of the sample was intensified by the subsequent drop-outs from the first to the second and from the second to the third wave. It was reported that those children who dropped out of the study (a) were more certain about their answers (chapter 3), (b) perceived a larger distance between their own as well as perceived real and ideal self-concepts, especially as far as the parents were concerned (chapter 4), (c) had self-concepts that were more in agreement with the actual concepts of their parents about them (chapter 5), and (d) reported more discrepancies between their perceived real and ideal self-concepts for their parents as well as for their peers (chapter 6) than children who remained in the study. That is, although these children were, with good reason, more certain about their perceptions (i.e., their self-concepts were relatively reliable and valid as compared to the retest measures and the actual opinion of their parents), they experienced relatively little approval and acceptance, not only from their parents, but often also from their peers and themselves. The findings above showed that the children who participated throughout the whole study became also more thoughtful and certain about their self-concepts. On the whole, though, they must be characterized as relatively cheerful, happy-go-lucky children as far as their self-concepts are concerned, who were not overly aware of themselves or how they come across to others, and who were not bothered too much by disapproval or unreachable goals as compared to their peers. Although the scores for neuroticism on the ABV-K (chapter 7) show that these children are no less free of emotional problems than a cross-section of their age mates, and that they are no less self-critical than their peers, the high scores for extraversion corroborate the above suggestion of a relatively easygoing sample.

Consequently, the present findings are limited to a somewhat élitist population of open, not too self-conscious children from middle to higher SES families who are relatively satisfied with themselves and who feel relatively accepted by their parents.

Given these limitations of the sample, the effects that were found are even more remarkable. That is, if a relatively homogeneous sample, as the present one appears to be, shows the reported effects, future studies with other groups of children are promising, and several interesting questions emerge. For instance, will more problematic children or children from less favorable backgrounds also adjust their own self-concepts primarily towards the perceived self-concepts of their parents, as the present findings suggest? Will they experience the same increasing distance between how they are and how they ideally might be during childhood? Will their own ideals become as congruent to the ideals of their parents? Will more self-conscious children experience more discrepancies between their self-concepts, or will they be bothered more by them? Will more introverted children attend more to their own opinions than to the perceived opinions of others? When these and other questions are answered, it might turn out that the present findings will function as a baseline. That is, although they indicate some problems for children in and of themselves, they may represent what is happening normally under relatively optimal circumstances in our society.

The Method

It has been shown throughout the chapters that the Repertory Grid procedure as used in the present study offers a sufficiently reliable and valid, but also especially fruitful way, to assess the organization of the self-system in children and adolescents. This is clearly the result of the fact that through this procedure it was possible to assess the self-system through age-appropriate, personally relevant self-descriptions, as well as to assess the self-system multi-dimensionally. Age-appropriate measurements are a necessary prerequisite to obtain a realistic image of the world of the child. Together with personal relevance, they provide meaningful data. The multidimensionality of the present procedure also increased this meaningfulness and confirmed the recent understanding that the self-system is more than a global construct.

Of particular use were also the test–retest scores. These scores provided direct insight into the reliability of the scores and, consequently, in the attitude of the children towards the questions. Because of the latter, the conclusion that the children who dropped out of the study were more serious and self-conscious than the children who remained could be drawn. Also, the age-related effect in the reliability of the procedure would not have been found without these test–retest scores. As was argued before, this age-relatedness also influenced the interpretation of the data. The conclusion that distinctness does not increase but becomes more certain was the consequence of this influence. In summary, the test–retest scores helped to do justice to the results.

Although interesting findings were obtained, the effects that were found generally were not very strong. Several reasons can be offered for this. First, the present study was a field study, which implies that several disruptive factors might have been at work. Because the purpose of the study was to obtain a realistic image of the changes in children's organization of the self-system, no particular actions were taken to control such factors. However, the result, of course, is noise in the data, and, consequently, a speculative character to some of the conclusions. Secondly, the present study was designed to examine general changes in the organization of the self-system. That is, the approach was also a general one. As was already indicated in the discussions of chapters 3 and 7, control for the content of self-descriptions, for instance by the selection of a particular context, might provide further insight into the functioning of the self-system as well as stronger effects for particular clusters of self-descriptions. For instance, recently, Cantor, Norem, and Brower (1987; see also chapter 7) explored the possibility of different effects for self-descriptions from different contexts with regard to discrepancies within the social and academic context. They concluded that discrepancies in the social context were experienced as a positive challenge, although discrepancies in the academic context were experienced as a threat. In addition, now that a general relationship with emotional functioning has been found, an instrument with a broader range of more specific emotions, suited to assess the emotions of children as well as adolescence, might be developed to replace the global measurement by means of the ABV-K. As far as is known, in The Netherlands such a valid instrument is not yet available. Higgins (e.g., 1987) reported very specific effects of discrepancies on emotions. A more specific instrument might be better able to tap such effects as well. Finally, the findings of the present study were better explained when, in addition to cognitive considerations, the social situation was considered as well. However, such conclusions cannot be decisive unless the actual level of social cognitive maturity of the children is tested. Subsequent research should include such a measurement.

Elaborating on the Present Analyses

Despite the restrictions mentioned above, the present approach yielded a rich data base on children's perception of themselves and the interaction between these perceptions and their environment. This data base, however, has so far been only partly used. That is, although the present analyses were done to answer the most evident questions, further inquiries are possible and interesting. The two most obvious ones are discussed here.

To begin with, until now, the organization of the self-system was considered in separate parts. That is, the several relationships between the self-concepts were examined separately. Although this approach provides a more comprehensive picture than do former studies, in which only one relationship was assessed, it raises the following question of how these relationships might be related to each other. For instance, the age-related effects for differentiation and discrepancies between real and ideal self-concepts are more or less comparable. Will children with large degrees of differentiation between these concepts also experience a larger number of discrepancies? The present findings indicate that discrepancies between the perceived real and ideal self-concepts of the parents may cause unpleasant feelings. It is expected that individuals will try to avoid such feelings. As long as these individuals do not succeed to decrease the discrepancies, will they increase the distance between themselves and the person whose self-concepts are perceived as discrepant? That is, will children with many discrepancies between the perceived real and ideal self-concepts of their parents report more distinctness between their own concepts and the perceived self-concepts of their parents than children who do not perceive such discrepancies? Will they experience less fit between their own concepts and those of their parents? Furthermore, discrepancies between and within self-concepts were found to exert an opposite effect on emotional functioning. If children experience both types of discrepancies with regard to the same self-concepts (for instance, the perceived real and ideal self-concept of their mother), what will happen to the related affects? In other words, will discrepancies between and within the self-concept neutralize each other's effect on emotional functioning? Subsequent analyses may answer these questions.

The second possibility for further inquiry within the present data set is related to the former questions. Until now, only subgroups based on age were distinguished. The earlier proposal implies that subgroups are also possible on the basis of personal functioning. For instance, it was assumed in chapter 1 that different configurations of the self-concepts (i.e., different types of temporary organization) may result in different organizing processes. In addition, children may differ in type as well as in strength of influence that they experience from their environment. For example, they may experience different parenting styles, or they may differ themselves in the degree to which they attend to their own opinions or those from their environment. In addition, children may have different personality traits that influence their reactions and how these impact on the organization of their self-system (Cantor et al., 1987; see chapter 7). Consequently, besides analyses on the group as a whole or comparable studies on varying groups of children (see earlier), cluster analyses and analyses of individual profiles may be fruitful.

ELABORATIONS FOR FUTURE RESEARCH
FROM THE RECENT LITERATURE

As was already described in chapter 1, other perspectives as well as other possible selves than those examined in the present study can be included in the present model. Since the beginning of this study when the model was constructed, several studies and arguments have been published that indicate that not only the inclusion of other possible selves but also the relationships between and differentiation of them may be useful. In addition, these publications show that the evaluation of the relationships between such self-concepts might be even more complex than was described previously. Some of them were already mentioned in chapter 7 to explain the somewhat weak effects between discrepancies between real and ideal self-concepts and emotional functioning. Some examples of combinations of possible selves and of more complex evaluations of discrepancies are considered here.

Combinations of Possible Selves

Recently Higgins (1990) studied the "can-self" in relation to the ideal self-concept. Strictly speaking, the can-self is not a possible self, because it is not a future self-concept for which to strive. Instead, the can-self refers to people's perception of their chances to reach a positive possible self (cf. Bandura's concept of self-efficacy, 1982). Higgins compared the ideal self-concept with this can-self, and reported that discrepancies between real and ideal self-concepts are only related to dejection-related emotions if the can-self equals the ideal self-concept. That is, his participants did not report being bothered by such discrepancies if they thought that they fulfilled their potential but that their ideal was beyond their potential; this happened only if they did not meet an ideal that they considered to be within their reach. Consequently, it can be concluded that people are more or less realistic in their evaluation of themselves.

Oyserman and Markus (1990) compared the expected-, hoped-for-, and feared-for-self with regard to the behavior of four groups of adolescents who differed in degree of delinquency. Though the hoped-for-self was generally similar for all groups, the content of their expected- and feared-for-self was different. In addition, future delinquency was best predicted by congruency between the possible selves, that is, when each possible self was directed towards the same context (i.e., the self-descriptions within them referred to the same subject), and the expected- and hoped-for-self were in the same direction, but the feared-for-self was in the opposite direction. In conclusion, similar to Higgins (1990), Oyserman and Markus found that the influence of ideals for the self are mediated by the individual's estimation of the realism of these ideals. Future research should include the measurement of this estimation to specify and strengthen the effects that were found in the present study.

Evaluations of Discrepancies

The studies of Higgins and Oyserman and Markus were still directed towards the direct relationships between self-concepts, that is, in the framework of *telic* theories (cf. Omodei & Wearing, 1990). However, recently, much support has been given to *autotelic* theories; that is, several models and studies have appeared that related to the process of reaching a goal, instead of the temporary distance from that goal, only. For instance, as was already described in chapter 7, Carver and Scheier (1990) argued that instead of the actual discrepancy between a real self-concept and a personal goal, it is the evaluation of the direction and speed of the discrepancy that are responsible for the affect that results from the discrepancy. They expected that a discrepancy is negatively evaluated when the discrepancy is increasing, or decreasing slower than is desired. They argued that a discrepancy is not negatively but, to the contrary, positively evaluated when it is decreasing at the desired speed. The findings of Omodei and Wearing are in accordance with this argument. Based on their study of desired end-states, involvement, and well-being, they concluded that it was probably more important to assess the expectations to reach a goal, than the actual discrepancy. From the model of Dweck and Leggett (1988), it can be concluded that it is not only the discrepancy or the evaluation of the process of such a discrepancy that is related to the resulting affect, but also the attitude that goes with it. That is, Dweck and Leggett argued that it is also the individual's implicit theory concerning the ideal pole of a discrepancy that influences the individual's functioning. They reported that when a goal is perceived as an entity that has to be proven, this perception will negatively influence the individual's cognitions, affect, and behavior. In contrast, if a goal is perceived as incremental, that is, as an opportunity to learn, the influence will be positive (cf. telic vs. autotelic theories). Similar findings were reported by Emmons (1986), Emmons and King (1988), and Ruehlman and Wolchik (1988).

Consequently, two conclusions can be drawn. Firstly, besides the actual discrepancy, the former state of the discrepancy (if the discrepancy was larger or smaller before) and the desired speed to decrease the discrepancy should also be measured in order to obtain a fairer indication of the resulting affect. Secondly, discrepancies as such and the expectation of not reaching a goal seem to be related to negative affect (i.e., at least as long as they are perceived to be within the individual's potential; cf. Higgins, 1990; Oyserman & Markus, 1990). A positive and active attitude towards the *process to solve* the discrepancy, such as involvement and actions for mastery, however, is related to positive affect. Although not mentioned in the literature cited here, and beyond the scope of the present study, these conclusions are surprisingly similar to what is known with regard to *coping skills*. Here also, the active approach of a problem has been found to be more effective and to result in more positive affect than avoidance tactics. Research with children on discrepancies from a process-oriented approach should include such propositions.

CONCLUSION

Thus, based on the above findings and considerations, the dynamics of the self-system can be concluded to function as follows. The self-system develops in reciprocal interaction between the child and the social environment. In this process, the environment as well as the child play an active role. That is, although the environment provides information about the child, this information is perceived through the glasses of the child's individual world. The cognitive skills of the child, such as those related to the abilities to perform various forms of differentiation and integration, are important prerequisites for this process. In addition, the environment can be considered to facilitate the development of these skills. However, as soon as a required cognitive skill is present, the social processes take over. That is, the subsequent organizations of the self-system are largely explained by children's perception of their social experiences. Though this shift does not occur before adolescence for the interindividual and intraconceptual processes, it is already present in childhood for the intraindividual, interconceptual processes.

The organization of the self-system is based on several real and possible self-concepts within the self-system. Among the self-concepts that are known to exist from age 6 onward (i.e., one's own and perceived real and ideal self-concepts), several distinct roles can be distinguished. Firstly, the ideal self-concepts function as standards for the real self-concepts. Children are thought to strive to reach these ideal self-concepts because of motives for self-enhancement. Secondly, the relationships between one's own and perceived self-concepts reflect the children's sense of distinctness, indicating the degree to which their own self-concepts are influenced by the environment. Thirdly, one's own ideal self-concept occupies a special place in that it is more private and less influenced by the environment than the other self-concepts. In addition, the perceived perception of others about the child is better understood if specific, individual perspectives are distinguished within the self-concepts than if a generalized other is considered. Parents, in particular, can be considered to be important social agents in the mechanisms of the self-system of children.

It is possible that the self-concepts develop from one global concept. However, by 6 years of age, children are already able to clearly differentiate at least the ideal self-concept from the real self-concept and their own ideal perspective from the ideal perspective of others, on the condition that their own, concrete self-descriptions are used. In addition, by about age 9, they also become certain of the distinctions between their own real self-concept and the real self-concepts that others hold for them. It is possible that around this time other possible selves also emerge. No empirical findings in this respect are available, however.

Although somewhat ad hoc until age 9 for the real self-concepts, the degree of distinctness between one's own and perceived self-concepts remains stable from 6 years old onwards. Age-related changes in distinctness are considered to be idiosyncratic. The sense of distinctness is hindered by the familiarity of the social environment. That is, less distinctness is expected if a close relationship exists between the child and the other whose perspective is considered. Children experience less distinctness in relation to their parents than in relation to their friends, especially if the friend is of the opposite gender. The general level of distinctness is low as compared to distances between real and ideal self-concepts, and little real inconsistencies between one's own and perceived self-concepts are evident.

From age 6 until about age 12, the distance between real and ideal self-concepts increases, especially if the perspectives of the parents are considered. Probably as a result of improving differentiating skills and social standards, children feel more and more that they do not meet the expectations. Following age 12, in adolescence, they still believe that their parents do not approve of them. However, differentiation of their social world, integrating skills, and self-disclosure with their friends creates a situation in which they feel increasingly accepted by themselves and their peers. It might be that after adolescence the same will be experienced with the parents. It is also possible that later other increases and decreases in distance between the real and ideal self-concepts will become evident. Such changes may be less pronounced because, at that time, the influence of the recently acquired skills of differentiation and integration will be absent. However, no data are currently available regarding these matters.

When differentiation between the real and ideal self-concepts is apparent, at age 6, inconsistencies or discrepancies between these concepts also appear. That is, the self-system not only becomes more differentiated but also less consistent. However, the number of discrepancies increases only when the perspective of the parents is considered, and only during childhood. Once such discrepancies are experienced, they are, in general, related to negative affect. This affect, though, may be mediated by the evaluation of the direction of the discrepancy (i.e., if the discrepancy increases or decreases) and the speed with which the discrepancy moves in that direction, the presence of other possible selves, and the attitude towards the discrepancy. That is, discrepancies between real and ideal self-concepts may only be related to negative affect if the ideal self is accompanied by a feared-for-self in the opposite direction, if the ideal self-concept matches realistic expectancies within the potential of the self, and if the discrepancy is perceived as a challenge or a threat. In addition, the affect that is related to such discrepancies is dependent on the perspective from which the discrepancy is perceived. Children and adolescents are not bothered by discrepancies between the perceived real and ideal self-concepts of their peers, but they are bothered by discrepancies between their own real and ideal self-concepts, and especially by discrepancies between the perceived real and ideal self-concepts of their parents.

Following the emergence of inconsistencies between self-concepts, inconsistencies within the self-concepts become really evident only in adolescence, especially between age 12 and 14. Similar to discrepancies between real and ideal self-concepts, the inconsistencies within self-concepts are perspective related. More discrepancies are evident within the real self-concepts than within the ideal self-concepts, and more are evident within one's own self-concepts than within the perceived self-concepts of others. In addition, here also, only those discrepancies in which the self or the parents are involved are related to affect. However, in contrast to the effect for discrepancies between self-concepts, the effect for discrepancies within self-concepts is positive. It is expected that this positive effect is caused by the increased possibilities for self-enhancement that result from such inconsistencies.

Although the children's real and ideal self-concepts grow apart, they become increasingly valid when measured relative to the actual ideas of the parents about their children. This process develops more smoothly for the ideal self-concepts, which may be primarily influenced by the development of perspective taking abilities, than for the real self-concepts, which may be codetermined by social affective experiences. Probably as a result of self-serving biases, that is, of the active role of the individual, the self-concepts do not become identical to the concepts of the parents, but remain stable at a slight distance in adolescence.

During the past years, theories on the self-system developed from theories on one global self-concept through differentiation into theories on several self-concepts. It was shown by means of the present study that the understanding of the self-system as a multidimensional system offers improvements in the understanding of its dynamics. Based on these findings, though, it must also be concluded that, although the stage at which psychology regarded the self-concept as one global concept is passed, we are still in the process of differentiation. It will take some time and many studies before the self-system will be understood beyond that stage. Attention to the social world around will help to reach this point.

References

Adams-Webber, J. R. (1970). Actual structure and potential chaos: Relational aspects of progressive variations within a personal construct system. In D. Bannister (Ed.), *Perspectives in personal construct theory* (pp. 31-46). London: Academic Press.

Backman, C. W. (1988). The self: A dialectical approach. In L. Berkowitz (Ed.), *Advances in experimental social psychology* (Vol. 21, pp. 229-260). New York: Academic Press.

Bailey, S. T. (1970). Independence and factor structure of self-concept metadimensions. *Journal of Counseling Psychology, 17,* 425-430.

Baldwin, J. M. (1973). *Social and ethical interpretations in mental development.* New York: Arno Press. (Original work published 1897).

Ball, L., & Chandler, M. (1989). Identity formation in suicidal and nonsuicidal youth: The role of self-continuity. *Development and Psychopathology, 1,* 257-275.

Baltes, P. B., Reese, H. W., & Nesselroade, J. R. (1977). *Life-span developmental psychology: Introduction to research methods.* Monterey, California: Brooks/Cole.

Bandura, A. (1982). The self and mechanisms of agency. In J. Suls (Ed.), *Psychological perspectives on the self* (Vol. 1, pp. 3-39). Hillsdale, NJ: Lawrence Erlbaum Associates.

Bannister, D., & Agnew, J. (1977). The child's construing of self. In J. K. Cole & A. W. Landfield (Eds.), *Nebraska symposium on motivation, 1976* (Vol. 24, pp. 99-125). Lincoln, London: University of Nebraska Press.

Barenboim, C. (1977). Developmental changes in the interpersonal cognitive system from middle childhood to adolescence. *Child Development, 48,* 1467-1474.

Barnes, B. D., Mason, E., Leary, M. R., Laurent, J., Griebel, C., & Bergman, A. (1988). Reactions to social vs self-evaluation: Moderating effects of personal and social identity orientations. *Journal of Research in Personality, 22,* 513-524.

Baumeister, R. F. (1982). A self-presentational view of social phenomena. *Psychological Bulletin, 91,* 3-26.

Baumgardner, A. H. (1990). To know oneself is to like oneself: Self-certainty and self-affect. *Journal of Personality and Social Psychology, 58,* 1062-1072.

Benenson, J. F., & Dweck, C. S. (1986). The development of trait explanations and self-evaluations in the academic and social domains. *Child Development, 57,* 1179-1187.

Benesch, K. F., & Page, M. M. (1989). Self-construct systems and interpersonal congruence. *Journal of Personality, 57,* 139-173.

Bernstein, R. M. (1980). The development of the self-system during adolescence. *Journal of Genetic Psychology, 136,* 231-245.

Bieri, J. (1975). *Clinical and social judgement: The discrimination of behavioral information.* New York: R.E. Krieger. (Original work published 1966)

Block, J. H., & Block, J. (1980). The role of ego-control and ego-resiliency in the organization of behavior. In W. A. Collins (Ed.), *Development of cognition, affect, and social relations. The Minnesota Symposia on Child Psychology* (Vol. 13, pp. 39-101). Hillsdale, NJ: Lawrence Erlbaum Associates.

Broughton, J. M. (1981). The divided self in adolescence. *Human Development, 24,* 13-32.

Brown, J. D., Collins, R. L., & Schmidt, G. W. (1988). Self-esteem and direct versus indirect forms of self-enhancement. *Journal of Personality and Social Psychology, 55,* 445-453.

Burns, R. B. (1979). *The self-concept in theory, measurement, development, and behaviour.* New York: Longman.

Butler, R. (1990). The effects of mastery and competitive conditions on self-assessment at different ages. *Child Development, 61,* 201-210.

Campbell, J. D. (1990). Self-esteem and clarity of the self-concept. *Journal of Personality and Social Psychology, 59,* 538-549.

Campbell, J. D., & Fehr, B. (1990). Self-esteem and perceptions of conveyed impressions: Is a negative affectivity associated with greater realism? *Journal of Personality and Social Psychology, 58,* 122-133.

Cantor, N., Norem, J. K., & Brower, A. M. (1987). Life-tasks, self-concept ideals, and cognitive strategies in a life transition. *Journal of Personality and Social Psychology, 53,* 1178-1191.

Carver, C. S., & Scheier, M. F. (1990). Origins and functions of positive and negative affect: A control-process view. *Psychological Review, 97,* 19-35.

Caspi, A., Bem, D. J., & Elder, G. H. (1989). Continuities and consequences of interactional styles across the life course. *Journal of Personality, 47,* 375-406.

Chaiken, S., & Baldwin, M. W. (1981). Affective-cognitive consistency and the effect of salient behavioral information on the self-perception of attitudes. *Journal of Personality and Social Psychology, 41,* 1-12.

Chandler, M. J. (1973). Egocentrism and antisocial behavior: The assessment and training of social perspective-taking skills. *Developmental Psychology, 9,* 326-332.

Chandler, M., & Boyes, M. (1982). *Social-cognitive development.* Unpublished manuscript, University of Amsterdam.

Chandler, M., Boyes, M., & Oppenheimer, L. (1983). *A Developmental Analysis of Children's Changing Conceptions of Selfhood.* Unpublished Manuscript, University of Amsterdam.

Cohen, J. (1960). A coefficient of agreement for nominal scales. *Educational and Psychological Measurement, 20,* 37-46.

Conway, M., & Ross, M. (1984). Getting what you want by revising what you had. *Journal of Personality and Social Psychology, 47,* 738-748.

Cooley, C. H. (1968). The social self: On the meanings of "I." In C. Gordon & K. J. Gergen (Eds.), *The self in social interaction: Vol. 1. Classic and contemporary perspectives* (pp. 87-91). New York: Wiley. (Original work published 1902)

Damon, W. (1983). *Social and personality development: Infancy through adolescence.* New York, London: Norton.

Damon, W., & Hart, D. (1982). The development of self-understanding from infancy through adolescence. *Child Development, 53,* 841-864.

Damon, W., & Hart, D. (1986). Stability and change in children's self-understanding. *Social Cognition, 4,* 102-118.

Damon, W., & Hart, D. (1988). *Self-understanding in childhood and adolescence.* Cambridge: Cambridge University Press.

DeChenne, T. K. (1980). Affective-cognitive consistency and self-conceptual structure. *Psychological Reports, 46*, 163-170.

Dusek, J. B., & Flaherty, J. F. (1981). The development of the self-concept during the adolescent years. *Monographs of the Society for Research in Child Development, 46*, 1-60.

Dweck, C. S., & Legget, E. L. (1988). A social-cognitive approach to motivation and personality. *Psychological Review, 95*, 256-273.

Easterby-Smith, M. (1981). The design, analysis and interpretation of repertory grids. In M. L. G. Shaw (Ed.), *Recent advances in personal construct theory* (pp. 9-30). New York: Academic press.

Edwards, A. L., & Klockars, A. J. (1981). Significant others and self-evaluation: Relationships between perceived and actual evaluations. *Personality and Social Psychology Bulletin, 7*, 244-251.

Elkind, D. (1967). Egocentrism in adolescence. *Child Development, 38*, 1025-1034.

Emmons, R. A. (1986). Personal strivings: An approach to personality and subjective well-being. *Journal of Personality and Social Psychology, 51*, 1058-1068.

Emmons, R. A., & King, L. A. (1988). Conflict among personal strivings: Immediate and long-term implications for psychological and physical well-being. *Journal of Personality and Social Psychology, 54*, 1040-1048.

Epstein, S. (1973). The self-concept revised: Or a theory of a theory. *American Psychologist, 28*, 404-416.

Erikson, E. H. (1969). *Childhood and society.* New York: Norton. (Original work published 1950)

Erikson, E. H. (1971). *Identity, youth and crisis.* London: Faber & Faber. (Original work published 1968).

Eshel, Y., & Klein, Z. (1981). Development of academic self-concept of lower-class and middle-class primary school children. *Journal of Educational Psychology, 73*, 287-293.

Feldman, N. S., & Ruble, D. N. (1988). The effect of personal relevance on psychological inference: A developmental analysis. *Child Development, 59*, 1339-1352.

Fitts, W. H. (1981). Issues regarding self-concept change. In M. D. Lynch, A. A. Norem-Hebeisen, & K. J. Gergen (Eds.), *Self-concept: Advances in theory and research* (pp. 261-272). Cambridge, Massachusetts: Ballinger.

Flett, G. L., Hewitt, P. L., & Dyck, D. G. (1989). Self-oriented perfectionism, neuroticism and anxiety. *Journal of Personality and Individual Differences, 10*, 731-735.

Fransella, F. & Bannister, D. (1977). *A manual for repertory grid technique.* London: Academic Press.

Fromkin, H. L. (1970). Effects of experimentally aroused feelings of undistinctiveness upon valuation of scarce and novel experiences. *Journal of Personality and Social Psychology, 16*, 521-529.

Gecas, V., & Schwalbe, M. L. (1983). Beyond the looking-glass self: Social structure and efficacy-based self-esteem. *Social Psychology Quarterly, 46*, 77-88.

Glick, M., & Zigler, E. (1985). Self-image: A cognitive-developmental approach. In R. L. Leahy (Ed.), *The Development of the Self* (pp. 1-53). London: Academic Press.

Gollwitzer, P. M., & Wicklund, R. A. (1985). Self-symbolizing and the neglect of other's perspectives. *Journal of Personality and Social Psychology, 48*, 702-715.

Gordon, C., & Gergen, K. J. (Eds.). (1968). *The self in social interaction: Vol. 1. Classic and contemporary perspectives.* New York: Wiley.

Green, J. A. (1988). Loglinear analysis of cross-classified ordinal data: Applications in developmental research. *Child Development, 59*, 1-25.

Greenwald, A. G. (1980). The totalitarian ego: Fabrication and revision of personal history. *American Psychologist, 35*, 603-618.

Greenwald, A. G., Bellezza, F. S., & Banaij, M. R. (1988). Is self-esteem a central ingredient of the self-concept? *Personality and Social Psychology Bulletin, 14*, 34-45.

Harter, S. (1982). The perceived competence scale for children. *Child Development, 53*, 87-97.

Harter, S. (1983). Developmental perspectives in the self-system. In P. H. Mussen (Ed.), *Handbook of child psychology. Vol. 4: Socialization, personality, and social development* (pp. 275-385). New York: Wiley.

Harter, S. (1985). Competence as a dimension of self-evaluation: Toward a comprehensive model of self-worth. In R. L. Leahy (Ed.), *The Development of the Self* (pp. 55-121). London: Academic Press.

Harter, S. (1986). Cognitive-developmental processes in the integration of concepts about emotions and the self. *Social Cognition, 4*, 119-151.

Hartup, W. W. (1983). Peer relations. In P. H. Mussen (Ed.), *Handbook of Child Psychology. Vol. 4: Socialization, Personality, and Social Development* (pp. 103-196). New York: Wiley.

Hauser, S. T. (1972). Adolescent self-image development: Longitudinal studies of black and white boys. *Journal of Genetic Psychiatry, 27*, 537-541.

Hauser, S. T. (1976). Self-image complexity and identity formation in adolescence: Longitudinal studies. *Journal of Youth and Adolescence, 5*, 161-177.

Hauser, S. T., & Shapiro, R. L. (1973). Differentiation of adolescent self-images. *Genetic Psychiatry, 29*, 63-68.

Heaven, P. C. L. (1989). Extraversion, neuroticism and satisfaction with life among adolescents. *Journal of Personality and Individual Differences, 10*, 489-492.

Hewitt, P. L., & Genest, M. (1990). The ideal self: Schematic processing of perfectionistic content in dysphoric university students. *Journal of Personality and Social Psychology, 59*, 802-808.

Higgins, E. T. (1987). Self-discrepancy: A theory relating self and affect. *Psychological Review, 94*, 319-340.

Higgins, E. T. (1989). Continuities and discontinuities in self-regulatory and self-evaluative processes: A developmental theory relating self and affect. *Journal of Personality, 57*, 407-444.

Higgins, E. T. (1990). Self-state representations: Patterns of interconnected beliefs with specific holistic meanings and importance. *Bulletin of the Psychonomic Society, 28*, 248-253.

Higgins, E. T., Bond, R. N., Klein, R., & Strauman, T. (1986). Self-discrepancies and emotional vulnerability: How magnitude, accessibility, and type of discrepancy influence affect. *Journal of Personality and Social Psychology, 51*, 5-15.

Higgins, E. T., Klein, R., & Strauman, T. (1985). Self-concept discrepancy theory: A psychological model for distinguishing among different aspects of depression and anxiety. *Social Cognition, 3*, 51-76.

Jackson, A. E. (1987). *Perceptions of a new acquaintance in adolescence.* Groningen: Stichting Kinderstudies & A. E.Jackson.

James, W. (1950). *The Principles of psychology* (pp. 291-401). New York: Dover. (Original work published 1890)

James, W. (1968). Psychology: The briefer course; The self. In C. Gordon, & K. J. Gergen (Eds.), *The self in social interaction. Vol. 1: Classic and contemporary perspectives* (pp. 41-49). New York: Wiley. (Original work published 1910)

Katz, P., & Zigler, E. (1967). Self-image disparity: A developmental approach. *Journal of Personality and Social Psychology, 5*, 186-195.

Katz, P. A., Zigler, E., & Zalk, S. R. (1975). Children's self-image disparity: Effects of age, maladjustment, and action-thought orientation. *Developmental Psychology, 11*, 546-550.

Keen, T. R., & Bell, R. C. (1981). One thing leads to anaother: A new approach to elicitation in the Repertory Grid Technique. In M. L. G. Shaw (Ed.), *Recent advances in personal construct theory* (pp. 81-94). New York: Academic press.

Keeton, W. P., Cash, T. F., & Brown, T. A. (1990). Body image or body images? Comparative, multidimensional assessment among college students. *Journal of Personality Assessment, 54*, 213-230.

Kelly, G. A. (1963). *A theory of personality: The psychology of personal constructs.* New York: Norton. (Original work published 1955)

Koestner, R., Bernieri, F., & Zuckerman, M. (1989). Trait-specific versus person-specific moderators of cross-situational consistency. *Journal of Personality, 57*, 1-16.

Krosnick, J. A., & Sedikides, C. (1990). Self-monitoring and self-protective biases in use of consensus information to predict one's own behavior. *Journal of Personality and Social Psychology, 58*, 718-728.

Kuiper, N. A., & Rogers, T. B. (1979). Encoding of personal information: Self-other differences. *Journal of Personality and Social Psychology, 37*, 499-514.

Kulik, J. A., Sledge, P., & Mahler, H. I. M. (1986). Self-confirmatory attribution, egocentrism, and the perpetuation of self-beliefs. *Journal of Personality and Social Psychology, 50*, 587-594.

Kwiatkowska, A. (1990). Sense of personal continuity and distinctiveness from others in childhood. In L. Oppenheimer (Ed.), *The self-concept: European perspectives on its development, aspects, and applications* (pp. 63-74). Berlin, Heidelberg: Springer.

Lane, R. D., Merikangas, K. R., Schwartz, G. E., Huang, S. S., & Prusoff, B. A. (1990). Inverse relationship between defensiveness and lifetime prevalence of psychiatric disorder. *American Journal of Psychiatry, 147*, 573-578.

Lapsley, D. K., & Quintana, S. M. (1985). Integrative themes in social and developmental theories of self. In J. B. Pryor & J. D. Day (Eds.), *The development of social cognition* (pp. 153-176). New York: Springer.

Leahy, R. L., & Huard, C. (1976). Role taking and self-image disparity in children. *Developmental Psychology, 12*, 504-508.

Leahy, R. L., & Shirk, S. R. (1985). Social cognition and the development of the self. In R. L. Leahy (Ed.), *The development of the self* (pp. 123-150). London: Academic Press.

Lerner, R. M., & Tubman, J. G. (1989) Conceptual issues in studying continuity and discontinuity in personality development across life. *Journal of Personality, 57*, 343-373.

Lewicki, P. (1984). Self-schemata and social information processing. *Journal of Personality and Social Psychology, 47*, 1177-1190.

Linville, P. W. (1985). Self-complexity and affective extremity: Don't put all of your eggs in one cognitive basket. *Social Cognition, 3*, 94-120.

Linville, P. W. (1987). Self-complexity as a cognitive buffer against stress-related illness and depression. *Journal of Personality and Social Psychology, 52*, 663-676.

Livesley, W. J., & Bromley, D. B. (1973). *Person perception in childhood and adolescence.* London, New York: Wiley.

Luhmann, N. (1986). The individuality of the individual: Historical meanings and contemporary problems. In T. C. Heller, M. Sosna, & D. E. Wellbery (Eds.), *Reconstructing individualism: Autonomy, individuality, and the self in western thought* (pp. 313-325). Stanford, CA: Stanford University Press.

Lyon, M. A., & MacDonald, N. T. (1990). Academic self-concept as a predictor of achievement for a sample of elementary school students. *Psychological Reports, 66*, 1135-1142.

Maccoby, E. E. (1984). Middle childhood in the context of the family. In W. A. C. Collins (Ed.), *Development during middle childhood* (pp. 184-239). Washington: National Academy press.

Maccoby, E. E., & Martin, J. A. (1983). Socialization in the context of the family: Parent-child interaction. In P. H. Mussen (Ed.), *Handbook of child psychology. Vol. 4: Socialization, personality, and social development* (pp. 1-101). New York: Wiley.

Markus, H. (1977). Self-schemata and processing information about the self. *Journal of Personality and Social Psychology, 35*, 63-78.

Markus, H., & Kunda, Z. (1986). Stability and malleability of the self-concept. *Journal of Personality and Social Psychology, 51*, 858-866.

Markus, H., & Nurius, P. (1984). Self-understanding and self-regulation in middle childhood. In W. A. C. Collins (Ed.), *Development during middle childhood* (pp. 147-183). Washington: National Academy press.

Markus, H., & Nurius, P. (1986). Possible selves. *American Psychologist, 41,* 954-969.

Markus, H., & Sentis, K. (1982). The self in social information processing. In J. Suls (Ed.), *Psychological perspectives on the self* (Vol. 1, pp. 41-70). Hillsdale, NJ: Lawrence Erlbaum Associates.

Markus, H., & Wurf, E. (1987). The dynamic self-concept: A social psychological perspective. *Annual Review of Psychology, 38*, 299-337.

Marsh, H. W. (1989). Age and sex effects in multiple dimensions of self-concept: Preadolescent to early adulthood. *Journal of Educational Psychology, 81*, 417-430.

McCrae, R. R. (1987). Creativity, divergent thinking, and openness to experience. *Journal of Personality and Social Psychology, 52*, 1258-1265.

McGuire, W. J., & McGuire, C. V. (1982). Significant others in self-space: Sex differences and developmental trends in the self. In J. Suls (Ed.), *Social psychological perspectives on the self* (Vol. 1, pp. 71-96). Hillsdale, NJ: Lawrence Erlbaum Associates.

McGuire, W. J., & McGuire, C. V. (1988) Content and process in the experience of self. In L. Berkowitz (Ed.), *Advances in experimental social psychology* (Vol. 21, pp. 97-144). New York: Academic Press.

McGuire, W. J., McGuire, C. V., & Cheever, J. (1986). The self in society: Effects of social contexts on the sense of self. *British Journal of Social Psychology, 25,* 259-270.

Mead, G. H. (1972). *Mind, self, and society: From the standpoint of a social behaviorist.* Chicago: The University of Chicago Press. (Original work published 1934)

Meyer, J. W. (1986). Myths of socialization and of personality. In T. C. Heller, M. Sosna, & D. E. Wellbery (Eds.), *Reconstructing individualism: Autonomy, individuality, and the self in Western thought* (pp. 208-221). Stanford, CA: Stanford University Press.

Millar, M. G., & Tesser, A. (1986). Thought-induced attitude change: The effects of a schema structure and commitment. *Journal of Personality and Social Psychology, 51,* 259-269.

Montemayor, R., & Eisen, M. (1977). The development of self-conceptions from childhood to adolescence. *Developmental Psychology, 13,* 314-319.

Moretti, M. M., & Higgins, E. T. (1990). Relating self-discrepancies to self-esteem: The contribution of discrepancy beyond actual-self ratings. *Journal of Experimental Social Psychology, 26,* 108-123.

Moskowitz, D. S. (1990). Convergence of self-reports and independent observers: Dominance and friendliness. *Journal of Personality and Social Psychology, 58,* 1096-1106.

Murray, N., Sujan, H., Hirt, E. R., & Sujan, M. (1990). The influence of mood on categorization: A cognitive flexibility interpretation. *Journal of Personality and Social Psychology, 59,* 411-425.

Neimeyer, R. A., Neimeyer, G. J., & Landfield, A. W. (1983). Conceptual differentiation, integration, and empathic prediction. *Journal of Personality, 51,* 185-191.

Noom, M. (1989). *The development of the self-concept.* Unpublished master's thesis, University of Amsterdam.

Nurius, P. S., & Majerus, D. (1988). Rethinking the self in self-talk: A theoretical note and case example. *Journal of Social and Clinical Psychology, 6*(3/4), 335-345.

Ogilvie, D. M. (1987). The undesired self: A neglected variable in personality research. *Journal of Personality and Social Psychology, 52,* 379-385.

Omodei, M. M., & Wearing, A. J. (1990). Need satisfaction and involvement in personal projects: Toward an integrative model of subjective well-being. *Journal of Personality and Social Psychology, 59,* 762-769..

Oosterwegel, A. (1992). *The organization of the self-system: Developmental changes in childhood and adolescence.* Unpublished doctoral thesis. University of Amsterdam.

Oosterwegel, A., & Oppenheimer, L. (1990). Concepts within the self-concept: A developmental study on differentiation. In L. Oppemheimer (Ed.), *The self-concept: European perspectives on its development, aspects, and applications* (pp. 9-21). Berlin, Heidelberg: Springer.

Oppenheimer, L., & De Groot, W. (1981). Development of concepts about people in interpersonal situations. *European Journal of Social Psychology, 11*, 209-225.

Oppenheimer, L., Mur, Y., Koeman, H., & Chandler, M. J. (1983). *Children's conceptions of selfhood.* Unpublished manuscript, University of Amsterdam.

Oppenheimer, L., & Oosterwegel, A. (in press). The pure ego: An empirical approach to the subjective self. In R. Duba & L. Derks (Eds.), *Proceedings of the 1990 Principles Congress.*

Oppenheimer, L., Warnars-Kleverlaan, N., & Molenaar, P. C. M. (1990). Children's conceptions of selfhood and others: Self – other differentiation. In L.Oppenheimer (Ed.), *The self-concept: European perspectives on its development, aspects, and applications* (pp. 45-61). Berlin, Heidelberg: Springer.

Osberg, T. M., & Shrauger, J. S. (1986). Self-prediction: Exploring the parameters of accuracy. *Journal of Personality and Social Psychology, 51*, 1044-1057.

Oyserman, D., & Markus, H. R. (1990). Possible selves and delinquency. *Journal of Personality and Social Psychology, 59*, 112-125.

Peevers, B. H. (1984, July). *The self as observer of the self: A developmental analysis of the subjective self.* Paper presented at the Conference on Self and Identity, Cardiff, Wales.

Peevers, B. H., & Secord, P. F. (1973). Developmental changes in attribution of descriptive concepts to persons. *Journal of Personality and Social Psychology, 27*, 120-128.

Pekrun, R. (1990). Social support, achievement evaluations, and self-concepts in adolescence. In L. Oppenheimer (Ed.), *The self-concept: European perspectives on its development, aspects, and applications* (pp. 107-119). Berlin, Heidelberg: Springer.

Phillips, D. A., & Zigler, E. (1980). Children's self-image disparity: Effects of age, socioeconomic status, ethnicity, and gender. *Journal of Personality and Social Psychology, 39*, 689-700.

Pintrich, P. R., & Blumenfeld, P. C. (1985). Classroom experience and children's self-perceptions of ability, effort, and conduct. *Journal of Educational Psychology, 77*, 646-657.

Pratt, M. W., Pancer, M., Hunsberger, B., & Manchester, J. (1990). Reasoning about the self and relationships in maturity: An integrative complexity analysis of individual differences. *Journal of Personality and Social Psychology, 59*, 575-581.

Prentice, D. A. (1990). Familiarity and differences in self- and other-representations. *Journal of Personality and Social Psychology, 59*, 369-383.

Rogers, C. R. (1951). *Client-centered therapy: Its current practice, implications, and theory.* Boston: Houghton Mifflin.

Rosales, I., & Zigler, E. (1989). Role taking and self-image disparity: A further test of cognitive-developmental thought. *Psychological Reports, 64*, 41-42.

Rosenberg, M. (1979). *Conceiving the self.* New York: Basic Books.

Rosenholtz, S. J., & Simpson, C. (1984). The formation of ability conceptions: Developmental trend or social construction? *Review of Educational Research, 54*, 31-63.

Ruble, D. N., & Flett, G. L. (1988). Conflicting goals in self-evaluative information seeking: Developmental and ability level analyses. *Child Development, 59*, 97-106.

Ruehlman, L. S., & Wolchik, S. A. (1988). Personal goals and interpersonal support and hindrance as factors in psychological distress and well-being. *Journal of Personality and Social Psychology, 55*, 293-301.

Salmon, P. (1976). Grid measures with child subjects. In P. Slater (Ed.), *The measurement of intrapersonal space by Grid Technique: Vol. I: Explorations of intrapersonal space* (pp. 15-46). London: Wiley.

Sande, G. N., Goethals, G. R., & Radloff, C. E. (1988). Perceiving one's own traits and others': The multifaceted self. *Journal of Personality and Social Psychology, 54*, 13-20.

Scarlett, H. H., Press, A. N., & Crockett, W. H. (1971). Children's descriptions of peers: A Wernerian developmental analysis. *Child Development, 42*, 439-453.

Schaie, K. W. (1965). A general model for the study of developmental problems. *Psychological Bulletin, 64*, 92-107.

Scheier, M. F., & Carver, C. S. (1983). Two sides of the self: One for you and one for me. In J.Suls & A. G. Greenwald (Eds.), *Psychological perspectives on the self* (Vol. 2, pp. 123-157). Hillsdale, NJ: Lawrence Erlbaum Associates.

Schlenker, B. R., & Weigold, M. F. (1990). Self-consciousness and self-presentation: Being autonomous versus appearing autonomous. *Journal of Personality and Social Psychology, 59*, 820-828.

Schlenker, B. R., Weigold, M. F., & Hallam, J. R. (1990). Self-serving attributions in social context: Effects of self-esteem and social pressure. *Journal of Personality and Social Psychology, 58*, 855-863.

Selman, R. L. (1980). *The growth of interpersonal understanding: Developmental and cinical analyses.* New York: Academic Press.

Shantz, C. U. (1983). Social cognition. In P. H. Mussen (Ed.), *Handbook of child psychology: Vol. 3. Cognitive development* (pp. 495-555). New York: Wiley.

Shavelson, R. J., Hubner, J. J., & Stanton, G. C. (1976). Self-concept: Validation of construct interpretations. *Review of Educational Research, 46*, 407-441.

Shoda, Y., Mischel, W., & Peake, P. K. (1990). Predicting adolescent cognitive and self-regulatory competencies from preschool delay of gratification: Identifying diagnostic conditions. *Developmental Psychology, 26*, 978-986.

Shrauger, J. S., & Schoeneman, T. J. (1979). Symbolic interactionist view of self-concept: Through the looking glass darkly. *Psychological Bulletin, 86*, 549-573.

Siegal, M. (1987). Are sons and daughters treated more differently by fathers than by mothers? *Developmental Review, 7*, 183-209.

Slater, P. (Ed.). (1977). *The measurement of intrapersonal space by Grid Technique: Vol. 2. Dimensions of intrapersonal space.* London: Wiley.

Smith, R. E., & Smoll, F. L. (1990). Self-esteem and children's reactions to youth sport coaching behaviors: A field study of self-enhancement processes. *Developmental Psychology, 26*, 987-993.

Smollar, J., & Youniss, J. (1985). Adolescent self-concept development. In R. L. Leahy (Ed.), *The development of the self* (pp. 247-265). London: Academic Press.

Snyder, C. R., & Fromkin, H. L. (1980). *Uniqueness: The human pursuit of differences*. New York: Plenum Press.

Snyder, M. (1979). Self-monitoring processes. In L. Berkowitz (Ed.), *Advances in experimental social psychology* (Vol. 12, pp. 85-128). New York: Academic Press.

Srull, T. K., & Gaelick, L. (1983). General principles and individual differences in the self as a habitual reference point: An examination of self--other judgements of similarity. *Social Cognition, 2*, 108-121.

Stipek, D. J., & Tannatt, L. M. (1984). Children's judgements of their own and their peers' academic competence. *Journal of Educational Psychology, 76*, 75-84.

Strachan, A., & Jones, D. (1982). Changes in identification during adolescence: A personal construct theory approach. *Journal of Personality Assessment, 46*, 529-535.

Strauman, T. J. (1989). Self-discrepancies in clinical depression and social phobia: Cognitive structures that underlie emotional disorders. *Journal of Abnormal Psychology, 98*, 14-22.

Swann, W. B., Jr. (1983). Self-verification: Bringing social reality into harmony with the self. In J.Suls & A. G. Greenwald (Eds.), *Psychological perspectives on the self* (Vol. 2, pp. 33-66). Hillsdale, NJ: Lawrence Erlbaum Associates.

Swann, W. B., Jr. (1987). Identity negotiation: Where two roads meet. *Journal of Personality and Social Psychology, 53*, 1038-1051.

Swann, W. B., Jr., Griffin, J. J., Predmore, S. C., & Gaines, B. (1987). The cognitive--affective crossfire: When self-consistency confronts self-enhancement. *Journal of Personality and Social Psychology, 52*, 881-889.

Swann, W. B., Jr., & Hill, C. A. (1982.). When our identities are mistaken: Reaffirming self-conceptions through social interaction. *Journal of Personality and Social Psychology, 43*, 59-66.

Swann, W. B., Jr., Hixon, J. G., Stein-Seroussi, A., & Gilbert, D. T. (1990). The fleeting gleam of praise: Cognitive processes underlying behavioral reactions to self-relevant feedback. *Journal of Personality and Social Psychology, 59*, 17-26.

Swann, W. B., Jr., Pelham, B. W., & Krull, D. S. (1989). Agreeable fancy or disagreeable truth? Reconciling self-enhancement and self-verification. *Journal of Personality and Social Psychology, 57*, 782-791.

Swann, W. B., Jr., & Predmore, S. C. (1985). Intimates as agents of social support: Sources of consolation or despair? *Journal of Personality and Social Psychology, 49*, 1609-1617.

Swann, W. B., Jr., & Read, S.J. (1981). Acquiring self-knowledge: The search for feedback that fits. *Journal of Personality and Social Psychology, 41*, 1119-1128.

Tesser, A., & Campbell, J. (1983). Self-definition and self-evaluation maintenance. In J.Suls & A. G. Greenwald (Eds.), *Psychological perspectives on the self* (Vol. 2, pp. 1-31). Hillsdale, NJ: Lawrence Erlbaum Associates.

Tesser, A., Millar, M., & Moore, J. (1988). Some affective consequences of social comparison and reflection processes: The pain and pleasure of being close. *Journal of Personality and Social Psychology, 54*, 49-61.

Van de Poel, S. F. P. (1990, October). *Discrepancy between the perceived real and ideal self-concepts of others*. Unpublished master's thesis, University of Amsterdam.

Van der Maas, H. L. J., & Molenaar, P. C. M. (in press). A catastrophe theoretical approach to stagewise cognitive development. *Psychological Review*.

Van der Werff, J. J. (1985). *Identiteitsproblemen: Zelfbeschouwingen in de psychologie* [Identity problems: Self-conceptions in psychology]. Muiderberg: Dick Coutinho.

Van Dijl, H., & Wilde, G. J. S. (1982). *Handleiding bij de Amsterdamse Biografische Vragenlijst voor Kinderen (ABVK) en de Korte Amsterdamse Biografische Vragenlijst voor Kinderen. (KABVK)* [A manual for the ABVK and the KABVK] (2nd ed.). Amsterdam: Van Rossen.

Van Hook, E., & Higgins, E. T. (1988). Self-related problems beyond the self-concept: Motivational consequences of discrepant self-guides. *Journal of Personality and Social Psychology, 55*, 625-633.

Van Lieshout, C. F. M. (1987). Coping door kinderen en jeugdigen en de structuur van hun zelfbeeld [Children's coping and the structure of their self-concept]. In H. J. Groenendaal, R. Meijer, J. W. Veerman, & J. de Wit (Eds.), *Protectieve factoren in de ontwikkeling van kinderen en adolescenten* (pp. 91-106) [Protective factors in the development of children and adolescents]. Lisse, Holland: Swets & Zeitlinger.

Visser, R. S. H., Van Vliet-Mulder, J. C., Evers, A., & Ter Laak, J. (1982). *Documentatie van tests en testresearch in Nederland* [Documentation of tests and test research in The Netherlands] (pp. 509-514). Nijmegen: Van Mameren.

Wagner, U., Wicklund, R. A., & Shaigan, S. (1990). Open devaluation and rejection of a fellow student: The impact of threat to a self-definition. *Basic and Applied Social Psychology, 11*, 61-76.

Werner, H. (1957). The concept of development from a comparative and organismic point of view. In B. Harris (Ed.), *The concept of development* (pp. 125-148). Minneapolis: University of Minnesota Press.

Wicklund, R. A. (1982). Self-focussed attention and the validity of self-reports. In M. P. Zanna, E. T. Higgins, & C. P. Herman (Eds.), *Consistency in social behavior. The Ontario Symposium* (Vol. 2, pp. 149-172). Hillsdale, NJ: Lawrence Erlbaum Associates.

Wicklund, R. A., & Gollwitzer, P. M. (1982). *Symbolic Self-Completion*. Hillsdale, NJ: Lawrence Erlbaum Associates.

Wicklund, R. A., & Gollwitzer, P. M. (1983). A motivational factor in self-report validity. In J. Suls & A. G. Greenwald (Eds.), *Psychological perspectives on the self* (Vol. 2, pp. 67-92). Hillsdale, NJ: Lawrence Erlbaum Associates.

Winer, B. J. (1971). *Statistical principles in experimental design*. New York: McGraw Hill.

Wohlwill, J. F. (1973). *The sudy of behavioral development*. New York: Academic Press.

Wylie, R. C. (1974). *The self-concept: Vol. 1. A review of methodological considerations and measuring instruments* (rev. ed.). Lincoln: University of Nebraska Press. (Original work published 1961).

Wylie, R. C. (1979). *The Self-Concept: Vol. 2. Theory and research on selected topics* (rev. ed.). Lincoln: University of Nebraska Press. (Original work published 1961).

Youniss, J., & Smollar, J. (1985). *Adolescent relations with mothers, fathers, and friends*. Chicago: The University of Chicago Press.

Zajonc, R. B. (1980). Feeling and thinking: Preferences need no inferences. *American Psychologist, 35*, 151-175.

Zanna, M. P., Olson, J. M., & Fazio, R. H. (1981). Self-perception and attitude-behavior consistency. *Personality and Social Psychology Bulletin, 7*, 252-256.

Zigler, E., Balla, D., & Watson, N. (1972). Developmental and experimental determinants of self-image disparity in institutionalized and noninstitutionalized retarded and normal children. *Journal of Personality and Social Psychology, 23*, 81-87.

Author Index

Adams-Webber, J. W., 19, 30
Agnew, J., 24

Backman, C. W., 14-16, 87
Bailey, S. T., 19, 20, 32, 33
Baldwin, J. M. xii, 13, 21,
Baldwin, M. W., 62
Balla, D., 7
Baltes, P. B., 46
Banaij, M. J., 32
Bandura, A., 161
Bannister, D., 24, 43-46
Barenboim, C., 8, 85, 102
Barnes, B. D., 25, 133
Baumeister, R. F., 14, 87
Baumgardner, A. H., 21
Bell, R. C., 45
Bellezza, F. S., 32
Bem, D. J., 87
Benenson, J. F., 28
Benesch, K. F., 27, 43, 52
Bergman, A., 25
Bernieri, F., 133
Bernstein, R. M., 9, 85, 103
Bieri, J., 19, 29
Block, J., 30
Block, J. H., 30
Blumenfeld, P. C., 88, 97
Bond, R. N., 23
Boyes, M., 31, 42, 88, 100
Bromley, D. B., 5, 8, 42, 58, 102
Broughton, J. M., 24, 25, 139
Brower, A. M., 133, 159
Brown, J. D., 15
Brown, T. A., 121
Burns, R. B., 43
Butler, R., 28

Campbell, J. D., 14, 21, 22, 25, 62

Cantor, N., 133, 159, 161
Carver, C. S., 25, 133, 162
Cash, W. P., 121
Caspi, A., 87
Chaiken, S., 21, 62
Chandler, M. J., 8, 31, 42, 88, 100
Cheever, J., 11
Cohen, J., 56, 59, 63
Collins, R. L., 15
Conway, M., 13
Cooley, C. H., 9, 12
Crockett, W. H., 5

Damon, W., xi, 2, 3, 5, 6, 9, 16,
    18, 24, 31, 33, 59, 67, 100,
    146
De Groot, W., 5, 100
DeChenne, T. K., 20, 29
Dusek, J. B., 31
Dweck, C. S., 28, 162
Dyck, D. G., 121

Easterby-Smith, M., 45
Edwards, A. L., 98, 133
Eisen, M., 20
Elder, G. H., 87
Elkind, D., 89
Emmons, R. A., 104, 122, 123, 162
Epstein, S., xi, 23, 29, 33
Erikson, E. H., 9, 24
Eshel, Y., 28
Evers, A., 124

Fazio, R. H., 27
Fehr, B., 25
Feldman, N. S., 18
Fitts, W. H., 18, 23, 32, 33
Flaherty, J. F., 31

Flett, G. L., 16, 17, 28, 100, 121, 123
Fransella, F., 43-46
Fromkin, H. L., 24, 25, 139

Gaelick, L., 25
Gaines, B., 16
Gecas, V., 13
Genest, M., 6
Gergen, K. J., 1
Gilbert, D. T., 16
Glick, M., 7, 20, 23, 70, 101, 102, 151
Goethals, G. R., 29
Gollwitzer, P. M., 14, 26-28, 33, 87
Gordon, C., 1
Green, J. A., 60
Greenwald, A. G., 13, 17, 29, 32, 88
Griebel, C., 25
Griffin, J. J., 16

Hallam, J. R., 15, 87
Hart, D., xi, 2, 3, 5, 6, 9, 16, 18, 24, 31, 33, 59, 67, 100, 146
Harter, S., 3, 5, 6, 9, 16-18, 23, 32, 69, 85, 88, 97, 103, 123, 131, 151
Hartup, W. W., 66, 152-155
Hauser, S. T., 21, 102
Heaven, P. C. L., 124
Hewitt, P. L., 6, 121
Higgins, E. T., 6, 23, 32, 51, 72, 101, 102, 104, 120-122, 131, 143, 161-163
Hill, C. A., 15
Hirt, E. R., 29
Hixon, J. G., 16
Huang, S. S., 88
Huard, C., 8, 71
Hubner, J. J., 3
Hunsberger, B., 19, 25

Jackson, A. E., 43, 44
James, W., xii, 1-3, 12, 13, 18, 33

Jones, D., 8

Katz, P. A., 7, 8, 70, 71, 139
Keen, T. R., 45
Keeton, W. P., 121
Kelly, G. A., 43, 44, 46
King, L. A., 104, 122, 123, 162
Klein, R., 23
Klein, Z., 28
Klockars, A. J., 98, 133
Koeman, H., 31
Koestner, R., 133
Krosnick, J. A., 87
Krull, D. S., 16
Kuiper, N. A., 13
Kulik, J. A., 14
Kunda, Z., 24, 25, 31, 139
Kwiatkowska, A., 24, 31

Landfield, A. W., 27
Lane, R. D., 88
Lapsley, D. K., 13, 16
Laurent, J., 25
Leahy, R. L., 8, 23, 70-72, 84, 102
Leary, M. R., 25
Leggett, E. L., 162
Lerner, R. M., 16
Lewicki, P., 13
Linville, P. W., 20, 22, 132
Livesley, W. J., 5, 8, 42, 58, 102
Luhmann, N., xiii
Lyon, M. A., 26, 33

Maccoby, E. E., 17, 153-155
MacDonald, N. T., 26, 33
Mahler, H. I. M., 14
Majerus, D., 104, 122
Manchester, J., 19, 25
Markus, H., xi, xiii, 1, 4-7, 11, 13, 16-19, 21, 24, 25, 31, 33, 42, 62, 87, 139, 161-163
Marsh, H. W., 3
Martin, J. A., 17, 153-155
Mason, E., 25
McCrae, R. R., 30

McGuire, W. J., 10, 11, 25, 43, 140
McGuire, C. V., 10, 11, 25, 43, 140
Mead, G. H., xii, 1, 8, 9, 12
Merikangas, K. R., 88
Meyer, J. W., xii, xiii
Millar, M. G., 14, 19, 20
Mischel, W., 17
Molenaar, P. C. M., 5, 112
Montemayor, R., 20
Moore, J., 14
Moretti, M. M., 32, 51
Moskowitz, D. S., 27
Mur, Y., 31
Murray, N., 29

Neimeyer, R. A., 27
Neimeyer, G. J., 27
Nesselroade, J. R., 46
Noom, M., 59, 60
Norem, J. K., 133, 159
Nurius, P. S., 6, 7, 16, 17, 104, 122

Ogilvie, D. M., 6, 23
Olson, J. M., 27
Omodei, M. M., 162
Oosterwegel, A., v, xii, 79
Oppenheimer, L., xii, 5, 31, 59, 67, 79, 100, 146
Osberg, T. M., 27
Oyserman, D., 161-163

Page, M. M., 27, 43, 52
Pancer, M., 19, 25
Peake, P. K., 17
Peevers, B. H., 5, 16, 31, 42
Pekrun, R., 10
Pelham, B. W., 16
Phillips, D. A., 7, 70
Pintrich, P. R., 88
Pratt, M. W., 19, 25
Predmore, S. C., 15, 16
Prentice, D. A., 19
Press, A. N., 5
Prusoff, B. A., 88

Quintana, S. M., 13, 16

Radloff, C. E., 29
Read, S. J., 15
Reese, H. W., 46
Rogers, C. R., 6, 101
Rogers, T. B., 13
Rosales, I., 7, 70, 71, 85
Rosenberg, M., 9, 10, 32, 42, 85, 87, 140, 148
Rosenholtz, S. J., 11, 12, 17, 87, 88, 97, 132
Ross, M., 13
Ruble, D. N., 16-18, 28, 100
Ruehlman, L. S., 162

Salmon, P., 43-46
Sande, G. N., 29
Scarlett, H. H., 5, 42
Schaie, K. W., 46
Scheier, M. F., 25, 133, 162
Schlenker, B. R., 15, 25, 87
Schmidt, G. W., 15
Schoeneman, T. J., 7, 9, 10, 26, 98
Schwalbe, M. L., 13
Schwartz, G. E., 88
Secord, P. F., 5, 42
Sedikides, C., 87
Selman, R. L., 8, 16, 24, 88, 102
Sentis, K., 13, 19
Shaigan, S., 14
Shantz, C. U., 42
Shapiro, R. L., 102
Shavelson, R. J., 3, 4
Shirk, S. R., 8, 23, 71, 72, 84, 102
Shoda, Y., 17
Shrauger, J. S., 7, 9, 10, 26, 27, 98
Siegal, M., 125
Simpson, C., 11, 12, 17, 87, 88, 97, 132
Slater, P., 44, 45
Sledge, P., 14
Smith, R. E., 16, 17
Smoll, F. L., 16, 17
Smollar, J., 11, 153-155

Snyder, C. R., 24, 25, 139
Snyder, M., 133
Srull, T. K., 25
Stanton, G. C., 3
Stein-Seroussi, A., 16
Stipek, D. J., 16-18, 28
Strachan, A., 8
Strauman, T. J., 23, 101, 121
Sujan, H., 29
Sujan, M., 29
Swann, W. B., 14-16, 18, 87

Tannatt, L. M., 16-18, 28
Ter Laak, J., 124
Tesser, A., 14, 19, 20
Tubman, J. G., 16

Van der Maas, H. L. J., 112
Van der Poel, S. F. P., 59, 61, 62
Van der Werff, J. J., xi, 23, 52
Van Dijl, H., 51, 123
Van Hook, E., 104, 122
Van Lieshout, C. F. M., 87
Van Vliet-Mulder, J. C., 124
Visser, R. S. H., 124

Wagner, U., 14
Warnars-Kleverlaan, N., 5
Watson, N., 7
Wearing, A. J., 162
Weigold, M. F., 15, 25, 87
Werner, H., 7, 9, 19, 36, 69, 137
Wicklund, R. A., 14, 26-28, 33, 87
Wilde, G. J. S., 51, 123
Winer, B. J., 113
Wohlwill, J. F., 60
Wolchik, S. A., 162
Wurf, E., xi, xiii, 1, 4-6, 11, 13, 18,
    24, 31, 33, 42, 87
Wylie, R. C., xiii

Youniss, J., 11, 153-155

Zajonc, R. B., 16
Zalk, S. R., 7
Zanna, M. P., 27
Zigler, E., 7, 8, 20, 23, 70-72, 84,
    85, 101, 102, 139, 151
Zuckerman, M., 133

Subject Index

Active self, *see* Self-descriptions
Affective development, 154-155
Affective functioning, 157-159
Agency, 2, *see also* "I" concept

Clearness, 21-22, 41, *see also*
    Self-concept
Cognition, *see* Intelligence
Cognitive complexity, 42, 152-154
Cognitive development, 7, 151-155
Cohort effects, 80 82, 94-95,
    115-118
Continuity, 18-19, *see also*
    "I" concept
Contradiction, *see* Discrepancy,
    Information about the self

Differentiation, 34-38, 52-53,
    137-142, *see also* Self-concept
Discrepancies, 34-38, *see also*
    Self-concept
    and affect, 102-104, 121-123,
        127-134, 160, 162-163
    and goals, 162-163
    and optimism - pessimism, 133
    as process, 133-134
    between and within self-concepts,
        103-104, 118-120, 127-134
Distance, 36-38, *see also*
    Self-concept, Differentiation
    relative, 74-77
Distinctness, 2, 18, 22-26, 139-142,
    see also Differentiation,
    "I" concept
    and affect, 25
    and self-esteem, 25
    and self-evaluation, 140
    validity of, 26-29
Drop-outs, 57, 80-82, 115-118, 157

Ego-resiliency,
    flexibility, 30
Egocentrism, 122
Emotions, *see* Affective
    development, Discrepancies and
    affects, Internal consistency
Environment, 12, 156, *see also*
    Self-concept
    characteristics of, 12
    fit between concepts of, 95
    concept of, and self-concept,
        95-100
    role-taking, 98-100

Flexibility, 29-30, *see also*
    Self-system

Gender-differences,
    self-descriptions, 63-65
    significant others, 10-11
Goals, 162-163, *see also*
    Discrepancies

"I" concept, 1-3
    characteristics, 2
    contents, 2-3
    continuity, 18-19
    organization, 3
Ideal self-concept, *see* Self-concept
Individual,
    active, 149-151
    characteristics of, 10-11
Information about the self,
    contradictory, 119
    egocentrism, 13
    organization, 1, 3
    relevance, 3
    role-taking, 88-89

self-consistency, 15-18
self-enhancement, 15-18
Intelligence, 8
Internal consistency, *see also*
Self-concept
affective functioning, 143-144

"**Me**" concept, 1-3
characteristics, 2-3
Method,
ABVK, 51-52, 123-124
self-report questionnaires, 43-44
Repertory Grid, 43-46, 49-51,
158-159
time sequential design, 46-48
Motive, 33-34, 149
self-enhancement, 34
self-consistency, 34

Objective self, *see* "Me" concept

Parent-child relations, 154-155
Person perception, 58-59, 150
Personal history, 156
Perspective-taking, *see* Role-taking
Physical self, *see* Self-descriptions
Possible self, 6-9, 22-24, 161-162,
see also Self-concept
age-related changes, 7-9
cognitive development, 7
function, 6
motivation, 6
social comparison, 7
Psychological self, *see*
Self-descriptions

Real self-concept, *see* Self-concept
Repertory Grid procedure, 43-47,
49-51, 158-159, *see also* Method
reliability, 55-56, 65-66, 158-159
Role-taking, 8-9, 71-72, *see also*
Environment, Information about
the self, Self-concept

School performance, 154
Self
and family, 11
Self-as-known, *see* "Me" concept
Self-as-knower, *see* "I" concept
Self-as-object, *see* "Me" concept
Self-as-subject, *see* "I" concept
Self-concept, 38, *see also*
Self-system
active, 4-5
actual, 38
clearness, 21-22, 41
and cognitive development, 13,
70-72, 102-103, 151-155
congruency, 15-16
with behavior, 15
with environment, 15
context-related, 4-6, 133-134
continuity, 30-31, *see also*
Stability
differentiation, 70-73, 82-86,
137-142
discrepancies, 34-37, 101-104,
127-134
distinctness, 24-26, 139-142
domain-related, 6-9
dynamic, 1
environment, 87-88, 148-149
fit, 89-94, 144-146, 150, 156
internal consistency, 22-24,
142-144
multidimensional, 1
perceived, 38
role of individual, 13-18, 149-152
development, 16-18
role-taking, 151
social constraints, 13
validity, 26-29
development, 28-29
fit, 26-28
predictability of behavior,
26-29
working, 4
Self-descriptions, 4-9, 32-33, 38
146-147
abstractness, 32-33, 59-62,
66-67, 146

stability, 33
central vs peripheral, 5
clearness, 62-65, 146-147
development, 5-6, 59-62
differentiation,
    role-taking, 8-9
integration, 8-9, 134
general vs specific, 4-5
positiveness, 32
    affect, 32
    self-esteem, 32
relevance, 5, 33, 67, 146
Self-enhancement, *see* Information
    about the self, Self-esteem
Self-esteem, 10
    self-enhancement 15-16
    affect, 16
Self-other differentiation, 24, 26,
    82-84, 95-100, 150-151, *see also*
    Distinctness
Self reflection, 2, *see also*
    "I" concept
Self-representation, *see* Self-concept
Self-regulation, 16-18
    self-esteem, 17
Self-system, 38, *see also*
    Self-concept
    complexity, 18-29, 42-43
    conflicts, 122-123
    dynamics, 34-35, 147-149
    model of, 1, 33-39, 135-136
    organization, 29-33, 35-37,
        149-151, 163-166
        flexibility, 29-30
Self-understanding, 1-3
    Damon's model, 2-3
Significant others, 10-12, 58-59,
    140-141, 148-149, 153-155, *see
    also* Parent-child relations
    dependence on, 153
    gender differences, 10-11, 141
    familiarity, 58-59, 66, 153
    fit between concepts of, 95
    likeability, 58-59, 66
Social cognition, *see* Role-taking
Social comparison, 7
Social constraints, 154-155

Social development, 154-155
Social economical status, 157-158
Social experience, 7-8, 152-155
Social self, *see* Self-descriptions
Stability, 30-31, *see also* Continuity,
    Self-concept
Subjective self, *see* "I" concept
Symbolic interactionism, 9

Test-retest reliability, 56

Uniqueness, *see* Distinctness

Validity, 26-29, 41, *see also*
    Self-concept
Volition, 2, *see also* "I" concept